MIGRATION AND ECONOMIC GROWTH IN THE UNITED STATES

National, Regional, and
Metropolitan Perspectives

STUDIES IN URBAN ECONOMICS

Under the Editorship of

Edwin S. Mills
Princeton University

MIGRATION AND ECONOMIC GROWTH IN THE UNITED STATES

National, Regional, and Metropolitan Perspectives

MICHAEL J. GREENWOOD

Department of Economics
University of Colorado
Boulder, Colorado

ACADEMIC PRESS
A Subsidiary of Harcourt Brace Jovanovich, Publishers
New York   London   Toronto   Sydney   San Francisco

ACADEMIC PRESS, INC.
111 Fifth Avenue, New York, New York 10003

United Kingdom Edition published by
ACADEMIC PRESS, INC. (LONDON) LTD.
24/28 Oval Road, London NW1   7DX

Library of Congress Cataloging in Publication Data

Greenwood, Michael J.
    Migration and economic growth in the United States.

    (Studies in urban economics)
    Includes bibliographical references and index.
    1. Migration, Internal--United States. 2. Cities
and towns--United States--Growth. 3. Industries,
Location of--United States. 4. Labor supply--United
States. I. Title. II. Series.
HB1965.G73   307.7'6'0973   80-1773
ISBN 0-12-300650-3

TO MOM AND POP
   whose love, patience, support, and
   encouragement have filled my life

Contents

Preface

My objectives in this book are threefold. They are to present a fairly detailed description of the post-World-War-II behavior of selected variables that are central to an understanding of the evolution of urban size and composition in the United States; to develop and empirically test models of both metropolitan growth and intrametropolitan location—models that are aimed at explaining the observed behavior of many of the variables described herein; and to provide, in the context of the descriptive chapters, a good deal of carefully composed data that other students of urban processes and policies might find useful in their work.

The descriptive chapters are organized on the premises that the behavior of central cities and their suburbs is best described in the context of the behavior of the entire metropolitan area of which they are part, and that the behavior of the entire metropolitan area is usefully considered in the context of the behavior of neighboring metropolitan areas in a region. Finally, the behavior over time of the nation's major regions is meaningfully described in the context of the behavior of the national economy, or at least of certain forces that are national in scope.

Thus, I begin in Chapter 1 by providing a brief historical overview of the urbanization process in the United States. In Chapter 2 I discuss certain national forces that I regard as important in shaping the spatial distribution of population and economic activity during the postwar period. Then, in Chapter 3 I consider these forces in the context of specific regions of the country (Northeast, North Central, South, and West). In Chapter 4 I describe the behavior over time of 62 major metropolitan areas, and each area is considered relative to the region in which it is located. I treat the behavior of the central cities and suburban rings of these 62 metropolitan areas in Chapter 5. In the descriptive chapters I have attempted to be as current as the data allow.

Chapter 6 describes a model of metropolitan growth, and Chapter 7 provides estimates of this model for two different time periods, 1950–1960 and 1960–1970. Chapter 8 both describes a model of intrametropolitan location of employment, housing, and labor force and provides estimates of this model, again for the 1950–1960 and 1960–1970 periods. Chapter 9 contains a discussion of the employment policy implications of population redistribution in the United States.

Migration is a recurring theme that is woven into each chapter. Migration is treated as one of the central forces that has shaped not only regional and metropolitan growth patterns, but also patterns of intrametropolitan location.

Much of the data that urban scholars and urban policymakers must use in the pursuit of their interests is not well suited to temporal applications. For example, central city boundaries change over time through annexation, and metropolitan boundaries change as new counties are added to or deleted from an area definition. Failure to take these changes into account and to control for the spatial area under consideration can have potentially serious consequences in analytical and in policy work. I have convinced myself of the justification for this statement by estimating certain of my own models with both "corrected" and "uncorrected" data, as well as by reestimating with corrected data models developed by others, where I knew with certainty that these models were not originally estimated with properly adjusted data. The types of data corrections to which I refer are very time consuming since they must typically be done by hand-picking adjustment figures from old census volumes. In every instance where the data I present in this volume have had the potential to be adjusted, I have in fact made the adjustments. I am hopeful that one of the lasting benefits of this book is that it is useful to urban scholars and policymakers as a source of data of relevance to them.

Acknowledgments

Parts of Chapters 2, 3, 5, and 9 are adapted from a paper entitled "Population Redistribution and Employment Policy," in Brian J. L. Berry and Lester P. Silverman (eds.), *Population Redistribution and Public Policy* (Washington, D.C.: National Academy of Sciences, 1980), 114–168. The section beginning on page 90 is adapted from a paper that I coauthored with James A. Chalmers,

"Thoughts on the Rural to Urban Migration Turnaround," *International Regional Science Review*, Vol. 2, No. 2 (Winter, 1977), 167–170. The section beginning on page 148 is taken from "An Econometric Model of Internal Migration and Regional Economic Growth in Mexico," published in the *Journal of Regional Science*, Vol. 18, No. 1 (April, 1978), 17–31. The section beginning on page 151 and Chapter 7 are adapted from my paper entitled "A Simultaneous-Equations Model of Urban Growth and Migration," *Journal of the American Statistical Association*, Vol. 70, No. 352 (December, 1975), 797–810. My initial research on urban growth models was supported by the Ford-Rockefeller Program in Population Policy Research. The essence of Chapter 8 is drawn from my paper entitled "Metropolitan Growth and the Intrametropolitan Location of Employment, Housing, and Labor Force," *Review of Economics and Statistics*, Vol. 62, No. 4 (November, 1980), 491–501. Bits and pieces are scattered throughout the book from my survey article on migration, "Research on Internal Migration in the United States: A Survey," *Journal of Economic Literature*, Vol. 13, No. 2 (June, 1975), 397–433. Finally, much material in Chapters 2, 3, 4, 5, and 9 has been drawn from a report I prepared under the sponsorship of the Economic Development Administration, United States Department of Commerce, entitled "Metropolitan Growth and Intrametropolitan Location of Economic Activity: Trends and Policy Implications," Contract No. 8-27507, EDA 99-7-13421. The statements, findings, conclusions, recommendations, and other data in this report are solely those of the author and do not necessarily reflect the views of the Economic Development Administration. I wish to thank the editors and publishers of these works, as well as the Economic Development Administration, for permission to adapt material presented herein.

I am very grateful to Paul DePippo and to my wife, Bonnie. Paul has capably assisted me for several years. He kept careful track of many large data files, and he did much of the programming that underlies the model estimation presented here. Everything he did for me, Paul did well. Bonnie almost flawlessly typed many drafts of the manuscript. Her patience was beyond the call. My mother and father proofread the entire manuscript, for which I am also most grateful. I dedicate this book to them for their love, patience, support, and encouragement that have filled my life.

James A. Chalmers, Shelby D. Gerking, and Herbert Kaufman provided helpful comments on certain of the initial articles that underlie chapters or sections presented herein. Edwin S. Mills read the entire manuscript and also provided a number of helpful suggestions. I am most grateful to each of them.

1

Introduction

For any given urban area, population growth must originate from one or more of the following sources:

1. Reclassification of previously nonurban population
2. Natural growth
3. Net in-migration

Historically, relatively little urban population growth has been due to spatial reclassification of existing population. Of course, as urban areas have grown and encompassed more land, substantial growth has occurred in spatial areas that during the past had been classified as nonurban. Note that the distinction here is between absorbing an existing population into an urban area through reclassification and absorbing a land area in which subsequent population growth occurs. Data are usually sufficient to distinguish reclassification as a source of urban population and employment growth. Data utilized in the present study do permit such distinctions for each of the 62 major metropolitan areas on which the analysis described in subsequent chapters focuses. Over 32 million employed persons resided in sample metropolitan areas in 1960. If the 1970 spatial area defines the metropolitan areas, total employment in 1960 is 2.2% higher than if the 1960 spatial area defines the metropolitan areas.

In a nation in which 73.5% of the 1970 population resided in areas categorized as urban, a sizeable component of absolute urban population growth must be due to natural increase.[1] Historically, however, the rate of natural increase has been higher in rural than in urban areas, though the differential has clearly narrowed during recent decades. In 1910, for example, the number of children under 5 years of age was 772 per 1000 rural white women 20 to 44 years old but was only 469 per 1000 urban white women of the same ages.[2] By 1970 the figures for white women 15 to 44 years of age had narrowed to 407 children under 5 per 1000 for rural women compared to 357 per 1000 for urban women.[3] Thus, natural increase was not a source of the higher rates of urban population growth that characterized the United States until approximately 1970.

Net in-migration from rural to urban areas, which has occurred during most decades in U.S. history, must therefore have been the primary source of differential rates of population growth that favored urban areas. The relatively low income elasticity of demand (typically less than unity) for the output of the agricultural sector in conjunction with the application of advanced technology to agricultural production has historically resulted in the "freeing" of labor in the agricultural sector and has permitted the "absorption" of this labor by the nonagricultural sector. Consequently, the developing U.S. economy was structurally transformed from one dominated by agricultural employment and production to one dominated by nonagricultural employment and production. Kuznets (1965) and others have shown that such a transformation requires the transfer of labor resources from the agricultural sector, where labor is in relatively abundant supply and where, as shown previously, the rate of natural increase of the labor force is relatively high, to the nonagricultural sector, where labor is in relatively short supply and where the rate of natural increase of the labor force is relatively low. Due both to the magnitude and rate of the impacts that economic growth has on the nonagricultural sector, population redistribution primarily through internal migration rather than through natural change must accompany economic growth.

For most workers involved in the process, the transfer from agricultural to

[1]In the 1970 Census population was categorized as urban according to the following three criteria:
  a. Persons living in places of at least 2500 inhabitants that are incorporated as cities, villages, boroughs, and towns
  b. Persons living in unincorporated places of 2500 inhabitants or more
  c. Persons living in other territory, incorporated or unincorporated, that is included in urbanized areas. An urbanized area generally consists of at least one city of 50,000 inhabitants or more and the surrounding closely settled area that meets certain criteria of population density or land use
Any population not categorized as urban is categorized as rural. The source of the 73.5% figure given above is U.S. Bureau of the Census (1973a), Table 3.
[2]U.S. Bureau of the Census (1978c), Table 4.1.
[3]Calculated from data presented in U.S. Bureau of the Census (1973a), Section 1, Table 76.

nonagricultural pursuits entailed the relocation of the worker's household and hence necessitated geographic labor mobility as well as occupational and industrial labor mobility. In most countries that have experienced successful development efforts, the decision to relocate rested with the individual. Hence, certain forces must have been at work to induce workers not only to change their occupations but also to change the location of their residences, generally from rural to urban areas. The forces that induced such moves consisted in large part of the "push" of lack of employment opportunities and relatively low incomes and/or wage levels in the agricultural sector and of the "pull" of employment opportunities and relatively high income and/or wage levels in the nonagricultural sector. In turn, migration to urban areas allowed such areas to achieve scale and agglomeration economies relatively fast and hence allowed still more efficient urban production and higher urban wages.

Kuznets stresses the idea that internal migration and hence regional population redistribution are important ways in which persons respond to changing economic opportunities that emerge in the course of economic growth. Kuznets (1964, p. xxiii) argues that migration induced by economic growth has been sufficiently massive in advanced economies to warrant the view "that the relation between population redistribution and economic development is an important and indispensable link in the mechanism of modern economic growth." Obviously, Kuznets has specified a situation in which migration is not only a consequence of economic growth but also an indispensable cause of growth.

Moreover, Myrdal (1957) recognizes the importance of the selective nature of migration in determining the impacts of geographic mobility. He argues that in-migration may induce greater income growth in receiving regions and that out-migration may induce lesser income growth in sending regions. Myrdal's argument involves the notion of "circular and cumulative causation" and runs as follows. Migration is selective of the younger, better-educated, and more highly productive workers. Such workers will be attracted away from those areas where labor demand is growing least rapidly and to those areas where labor demand is growing most rapidly. The selective character of migration will result in additional increased demand in receiving regions and decreased demand in sending regions. Further disparities in interregional wage differentials and growth will thus result, which will cause still more migration.

Since the U.S. population is already highly urbanized, in the recent context growth of one urban area, or of one group of urban areas, is more likely to be due to migration from other urban areas than to migration from rural areas. Consequently, as pointed out by Alonso (1978), while certain urban areas are growing due to migration, others will be declining due to the same migration. In this sense, urban migration is, argues Alonso, now like a zero-sum game, with some gainers and some losers within a nearly self-contained system.

In a study that treats the growth of specific urban areas, migration, whether from or to other urban areas or rural areas, must be given careful consideration. Migration is the major vehicle through which the national locus of urban growth can change over relatively short periods of time.[4] Furthermore, not only are the numbers of in- and out-migrants likely to serve as important determinants of the nature of urban growth in any given locality, but also, as suggested by Myrdal, characteristics of the migrants are likely to be of critical importance.

In this volume migration processes are viewed as central to an understanding of the phenomena of urbanization, metropolitan growth or decline, and intrametropolitan location. Hence, the discussion of various aspects of migration is given a prominent place herein.

Postwar Urban Growth in Historical Context

Since this volume focuses on the period following World War II, and especially on the period from 1950 to 1970, the postwar period might appropriately be considered in historical context. Table 1.1 reports the population of the United States as enumerated in each census from 1790 to 1970. This table also reports the regional distribution of U.S. population.

Except for the period from 1890 to 1930, the Northeast was characterized by a steadily declining share of total U.S. population. Inasmuch as the nation was settled from east to west, this declining share of population is not surprising. Since 1890 the North Central region has also experienced a steadily declining share of U.S. population. The South has, since 1870, maintained its share at slightly over 30%. (The South's share has ranged from 30.7 to 32.9% during this 100-year period.) Thus, the increasing share of population held by the West has been almost solely at the expense of the Northeast and North Central regions. In the sense that the West's share of U.S. population has apparently not peaked or stabilized, but rather continues to grow steadily, it may be concluded that the western settlement of the United States has not ended.

If a region is characterized as being urbanized when at least half of its population resides in urban areas, then clearly the Northeast became urbanized many years earlier than any other region. The 1880 Census reported 50.8% of the Northeast's population residing in urban areas. The North Central region and the

---

[4]Prior to the early 1920s migration from abroad, which was predominantly directed to urban areas, was of sufficient magnitude to have important impacts on urban population growth. Since that time immigration has been a much less important source of urban population growth, though certain cities, such as New York, still receive sizeable numbers of immigrants. North and LeBel (1978) estimate that in 1975 19.1% of U.S. immigrants (who were enumerated), or 73,630 persons, had New York City as a destination. North (1974), however, points out that after they have been in the U.S. for a short time, immigrants appear to migrate internally in roughly the same patterns as indigenous residents.

TABLE 1.1
U.S. Population, Regional Distribution of U.S. Population, and Percentage of Regional
Population Residing in Urban Areas, 1790-1970

Year	U.S. Population (millions)	Percentage of U.S. population in				Percentage of regional population residing in urban areas			
		North-east	North Central	South	West	North-east	North Central	South	West
1790	3.9	50.1		49.9		8.1		2.1	
1800	5.3	49.6	1.0	49.4		9.3		3.0	
1810	7.2	48.2	4.0	47.8		10.9	0.9	4.1	
1820	9.6	45.2	8.9	45.9		11.0	1.1	4.6	
1830	12.9	43.1	12.5	44.4		14.2	2.6	5.3	
1840	17.1	39.6	19.6	40.7		18.5	3.9	6.7	
1850	23.2	37.2	23.3	38.7	0.8	26.5	9.2	8.3	6.4
1860	31.4	33.7	28.9	35.4	2.0	35.7	13.9	9.6	16.0
1870	38.6	31.9	33.7	31.9	2.6	44.3	20.8	12.2	25.8
1880	50.2	28.9	34.6	32.9	3.6	50.8	24.2	12.2	30.2
1890	63.0	27.6	35.6	31.8	5.0	59.0	33.1	16.3	37.0
1900	76.2	27.6	34.6	32.2	5.7	66.1	38.6	18.0	39.9
1910	92.2	28.0	32.4	31.9	7.7	71.8	45.1	22.5	47.9
1920	106.0	28.0	32.1	31.2	8.7	75.5	52.3	28.1	51.8
1930	123.2	27.9	31.3	30.7	10.0	77.6	57.9	34.1	58.4
1940	132.2	27.2	30.4	31.5	10.9	76.6	58.4	36.7	58.5
1950	151.3	26.1	29.4	31.2	13.3	75.4	61.1	44.6	59.9
1960	179.3	24.9	28.8	30.7	15.6	72.8	63.9	52.7	66.1
			New Definition						
1950						79.5	64.1	48.6	69.5
1960						80.2	68.7	58.5	77.7
1970	203.2	24.1	27.8	30.9	17.1	80.4	71.6	64.6	82.9

Source: U.S. Bureau of the Census (1973a), Section 1, Tables 8 and 18.

West did not pass the 50% benchmark until 1920, and the South did not achieve this level of urbanization until 1960. The period from 1950 to 1970 is therefore one of considerable regional diversity in the urbanization process. The industrially mature Northeast maintained its fraction of urban population at roughly 80% during this 20-year period, which may suggest that the process of urbanization has ended in the Northeast. The North Central region continued to experience an increase in the fraction of its population residing in urban areas, as rural to urban migration persisted over the period.

Due in part to heavy rural out-migration from the South to both Southern and Northern urban areas, the South experienced a 16.0 percentage point increase between 1950 and 1970 in the fraction of its population residing in urban areas. The percentage point increase in the South's degree of urbanization over the 1950 to 1970 period is quite high relative to almost any 20-year period in the history of the nation's various regions. The West experienced a larger percentage point increase in its early history, namely, from 1850 to 1870, and the Northeast experienced a larger increase between 1850 and 1870 as well. But after 1940, the urbanization process in the South proceeded at an extremely high rate.

The postwar period is thus characterized by considerable regional diversity in the urbanization process. Whereas urbanization occurred at a rapid pace in the South and at only a slightly lower pace in the West, the North Central region experienced only a modest increase and the Northeast almost none.

Since roughly 1970 certain seemingly new phenomena appear to be unfolding in U.S. settlement patterns. Between 1970 and 1977 Northeastern metropolitan areas experienced an absolute decrease in population of 933,000 persons, or about 2.4%. During this same period, the central cities of Northeastern metropolitan areas suffered a population loss of 1,677,000, or 9.8% of their 1970 populations. While metropolitan population grew in each of the other regions, central city population declined absolutely in both the North Central region (1,704,000, or 10.1%) and the South (297,000, or 1.7%). In the South absolute population losses were concentrated in the largest metropolitan areas, namely those with population over 1 million, but in the Northeast and North Central regions central city population declined absolutely both in metropolitan areas with population greater than 1 million and in those with population less than 1 million.[5]

These phenomena are in part due to the observed reversal of the longstanding net flow of migrants from nonmetropolitan to metropolitan areas. They are also due in part to the low birth rates that have prevailed through the 1970s. The factors behind this so-called "rural to urban migration turnaround" are discussed in some detail in Chapter 4. Clearly, however, this turnaround has important implications for the process of urbanization and for the form and structure of U.S. metropolitan areas during the 1980s.

[5]U.S. Bureau of the Census (1978d), Table 3.

2

National Forces Affecting the Spatial Distribution of Population and Economic Activity in the Post-World-War-II Era

Employment in any given area, urban or otherwise, can change due to basically three forces. First, if the area's labor supply and demand conditions are given and if its labor market is out of equilibrium, wage changes that result from equilibrating market forces could cause employment changes. The most obvious example of such a situation is that in which excess labor supply exists in the local labor market. Downward pressure on local wages resulting from unemployment would encourage an increase in the quantity of labor demanded.

Second, if the local labor supply curve is not perfectly inelastic, a change in labor demand could cause a change in the equilibrium level of employment. Since labor force participation rates are known to be responsive to wage or earnings levels, local labor supply is unlikely to be perfectly inelastic.[1] Changes in labor demand could occur due to a number of factors, such as changes in the state of the national economy, changes in area income, population changes brought on by natural increase and/or by net migration, changes in population composition, and changes in consumer preferences. Several or all of these factors could, of course, be related.

Third, if local labor demand is not perfectly inelastic, a change in labor

---

[1]Bowen and Finegan (1969).

supply could also cause a change in the equilibrium level of employment. Perfectly inelastic labor demand is also extremely unlikely for the types of areas discussed in this study. Changes in labor supply could result from a number of factors, including changes in population of labor force age brought on by natural change and/or net migration and changes in labor force participation rates that are independent of wage levels.

While each of the three forces described above is typically operating simultaneously, in local economies that are growing at rates well above or well below the national average rate of growth, the latter two forces are likely to be predominant.[2] Each of these forces, however, unfolds in the context of the national economy. Regional changes in employment, population, and labor force are therefore not appropriately removed from their national setting. Several students of urban problems feel with some justification that many of these problems are less uniquely urban than they are regional, which suggests that neither are local changes appropriately removed from their regional setting.

The present chapter presents a description of certain economic and demographic forces operating at the national level that have particularly important spatial implications. Major emphasis is placed on the period from roughly 1965 to 1975 relative to the earlier post-World-War-II years. The analysis is not intended to be exhaustive. Rather, the presentation summarizes certain of the most significant national trends that have had an important bearing on the spatial distribution of economic activity. The emphasis of this chapter is almost solely on factors that have had their direct or primary impacts on the distribution of population. Factors affecting the distribution of employment are discussed in Chapter 3.

Although many investigators believe that employment has generally followed population, the treatment here of population before employment should not be construed as reflecting this position. By and large, the two factors are viewed in this study as being jointly determined, but it is recognized that specific instances can be found where one has followed the other as cause and effect.

---

[2]Note too that whether the analyst takes a theoretical perspective of viewing the system as being in disequilibrium as opposed to being in equilibrium has important implications. In the former case the system is seen as being initially out of equilibrium and any adjustments that occur are presumed to be equilibrating adjustments. Thus, for example, interregional wage differentials that are assumed to be the result of disequilibrium would presumably encourage migration from low- to high-wage regions. In the latter case the system is seen as being initially in equilibrium and as adjusting to a new equilibrium. Thus, interregional wage differentials that are assumed to be equilibrium (or compensated) differentials would presumably not encourage interregional migration. Rather, migration would only occur to facilitate an adjustment to a new equilibrium position. Hence, changes in wages and in the relative wage structure would encourage migration, as would changes in demand for nontraded goods, such as location-specific amenities. These latter changes in demand might result from income changes. See Graves and Linneman (1979) for a discussion of the influence of nontraded goods on migration. The migration literature is predominantly oriented toward disequilibrium models.

At the national level three factors especially stand out as distinguishing the period from roughly 1965 to 1975 from the earlier post-World-War-II years:

1. The national rate of employment growth altered sharply at about 1963, after which the rate averaged almost twice its prior average, and the rate of growth from 1963 to 1969 was particularly high relative to typical rates prevailing either before or since.
2. The aging of the so-called war baby cohort brought an extremely large number of young persons into the labor force, and young persons tend to be quite mobile geographically.
3. Substantial changes in fertility patterns and family composition, combined with a number of other factors, contributed to appreciable increases in labor force participation rates among young whites. Such increased rates, in combination with the increased size of the young population cohort, also contributed greatly to increasing the size of the labor force.

These three factors are, of course, not independent of one another or of other forces operating in the economy and in society in general. Let us next discuss each factor in turn and consider the relevance of each to changes in the spatial distribution of economic activity.

The National Rate of Employment Growth

In Table 2.1 is reported the national rate of employment growth for each year from 1947–1948 to 1976–1977. This 31-year period (30 observations) can conveniently be divided into two subperiods, one running from 1947–1948 to 1962–1963 and one running from 1963–1964 to 1976–1977. The earlier period was characterized by an average annual rate of employment growth of 1.1%, while the later period was characterized by an average annual rate of 2.1%. In only 5 of the earlier 16 years (1947–1948, 1949–1950, 1954–1955, 1955–1956, and 1958–1959) did the rate of growth rise above the average rate for the later period, whereas in only 3 of the most recent 14 years (1969–1970, 1970–1971, and 1974–1975) did the rate fall below the average rate for the earlier period.

The years since 1963–1964 can be further divided into two intervals. Between 1963–1964 and 1968–1969 the annual rate of employment growth never fell below 2.0% and averaged 2.4%. Between 1969–1970 and 1976–1977, however, the average annual rate was 1.9%. The high and sustained rate of employment growth between 1963 and 1969 was due in part to the effects of the Vietnam War and to sizeable increases in the labor force. Probably less important contributing factors were the permanent tax cut of 1964 and credit ease beginning in 1966. The more moderate rate of growth after 1970 was caused in part by dislocations and reallocations brought on by post-Vietnam adjustments, by the

TABLE 2.1
Annual National Rates of Employment Growth, 1947-1977

Period I		Period II	
Year	Growth rate (%)	Year	Growth rate (%)
1947-1948	2.29	1963-1964	2.28
1948-1949	-1.19	1964-1965	2.57
1949-1950	2.20	1965-1966	2.54
1950-1951	1.77	1966-1967	2.03
1951-1952	0.49	1967-1968	2.08
1952-1953	1.54	1968-1969	2.61
1953-1954	-1.75	1969-1970	0.93
1954-1955	3.43	1970-1971	0.63
1955-1956	2.62	1971-1972	3.26
1956-1957	0.42	1972-1973	3.31
1957-1958	-1.62	1973-1974	1.81
1958-1959	2.53	1974-1975	-1.34
1959-1960	1.78	1975-1976	3.19
1960-1961	-0.05	1976-1977	3.50
1961-1962	1.45		
1962-1963	1.59		

Source: Calculated from data presented in U.S. Department of Labor, *1978 Employment and Training Report of the President* (Washington, D.C.: U.S. Government Printing Office, 1978), Table A-1.

quadrupling of oil prices in 1973, and by deficient aggregate demand. The recession of 1974-1975 was the most serious since 1950. The national rate of unemployment averaged 8.5% during 1975, compared to 5.6% during 1974.

Many of the nation's major urban areas had 1975 unemployment rates that were two to three times higher than those prevailing in 1970. The Boston metropolitan area, for example, had a 1970 unemployment rate of 3.9% and a 1975 rate of 10.6%; New York's increase was from 4.4 to 10.2%; Detroit's, from 7.0 to 13.1%; and Phoenix's, from 4.3 to 13.1%. Western metropolitan areas, especially those on the West Coast, tended to have higher 1970 unemployment rates than those in other regions of the country, while North Central and especially Northeastern metropolitan areas tended to suffer the largest percentage point increases in their unemployment rates between 1970 and 1975.

The differential behavior of the 1963-1969 period relative to the 1969-1975 period is emphasized by the behavior of the manufacturing sector. After increasing by 3,172,000 jobs between 1963 and 1969, or at an annual average rate of 3.1%, manufacturing employment declined by 1,820,000 jobs between 1969 and 1975, which amounted to a negative annual average rate of 1.5%. Nationally only 285,000 more manufacturing jobs existed in 1975 than in 1965.[3] Even in 1977, when the nation was well into recovery from the recession of 1974–1975, 609,000 fewer jobs existed in manufacturing than in 1969. The effects of Vietnam in the late 1960s and of the recessionary conditions of the early 1970s had important implications for the manufacturing sector, which in turn had important implications for the spatial distribution of employment. Moreover, since manufacturing has historically been the single most important source of urban employment, the status of the manufacturing sector during the early 1970s had obvious implications for urban growth and for the intraurban location of economic activity.

Vernez *et al.* (1977) summarize their findings regarding the regional employment impacts of national economic fluctuations as follows:

> Areas that tend to be slow in recovery, with long cycles, are usually located in the North-East and North-Central census divisions and are characterized by a slow rate of employment growth or a large labor force. Slow growth and large size also characterize areas with the largest cyclical amplitudes. They are typically located in the North-East and East-North-Central areas.
>
>   . . . The severest cycles are more often found in areas of the North-East and North-West-Central census divisions and are characterized by slow employment growth [p.x].

Hence, according to the Vernez study, in terms of length, amplitude, and severity of cycle impacts, the Northeast and North Central regions tend to be the most seriously affected by national economic conditions.

During the period between 1947 and 1963 the national rate of employment growth appears clearly to have been dominated by the cyclical behavior of the economy. During the period between 1963 and 1975 the influence of cycles on the rate of employment growth is evident, but until 1974–1975 this influence does not seem dominant. One important cause of the observed differences between the two periods is the high rate of labor force entry since approximately 1963 caused by the aging of the war baby cohort. A second important cause is the coincident rise in labor force participation rates of women. Let us next turn to a more detailed discussion of these factors.

[3]The source of these figures is U.S. Department of Labor, *1977 Employment and Training Report of the President,* Table C-1. Other sources yield slightly different information. Data gathered from U.S. Department of Labor, Bureau of Labor Statistics, *Employment and Earnings, States and Areas 1939–75,* for example, indicate that manufacturing employment declined by 1,972,300 jobs between 1969 and 1975 and that nationally only 182,700 more manufacturing jobs existed in 1975 than in 1965. Note too that the choice of 1975 as the end point of the series has special implications for the manufacturing sector, which was especially impacted by the recession of 1974–1975, when manufacturing employment declined by 1,699,000 jobs, or by 8.5%. These latter two figures have been calculated from data presented in the *1977 Employment and Training Report of the President.*

The National Rate of Civilian Labor Force Growth

The period from approximately 1963 to and beyond 1975 is rather unusual in the recent history of the American economy, if only due to the high rate of labor force increase brought on by the aging of the war baby cohort and by the increased labor force participation rates of women. Table 2.2 reports the national rate of civilian labor force growth for each year from 1947–1948 to 1976–1977. The 31-year period is again divided into two subperiods. Selection of the subperiods has been dictated to correspond to those identified in the earlier examination of trends in the national rate of employment growth. Had the breakpoints in the civilian labor force series been selected independently of those in the employment series, they would have been slightly different. Either 1962–1963 or 1966–1967 might have been chosen as the beginning of Period II. Nevertheless, a close correspondence exists between the employment and civilian labor force periods as presented here.

Between 1947 and 1963 the civilian labor force increased by approximately 12.5 million persons, and the average annual rate of increase was 1.2%. Between

TABLE 2.2
Annual National Rates of Civilian Labor Force Growth, 1947–1977

Period I		Period II	
Year	Growth rate (%)	Year	Growth rate (%)
1947–1948	2.14	1963–1964	1.75
1948–1949	1.10	1964–1965	1.87
1949–1950	1.50	1965–1966	1.77
1950–1951	−0.31	1966–1967	2.08
1951–1952	0.20	1967–1968	1.80
1952–1953	1.41	1968–1969	2.54
1953–1954	1.00	1969–1970	2.46
1954–1955	2.17	1970–1971	1.69
1955–1956	2.35	1971–1972	2.89
1956–1957	0.57	1972–1973	2.51
1957–1958	1.06	1973–1974	2.59
1958–1959	1.08	1974–1975	1.76
1959–1960	1.84	1975–1976	2.33
1960–1961	1.19	1976–1977	2.77
1961–1962	0.22		
1962–1963	1.73		

Source: Calculated from data presented in U.S. Department of Labor, *1978 Employment and Training Report of the President* (Washington, D.C.: U.S. Government Printing Office, 1978), Table A-3.

1963 and 1977 the civilian labor force increased by over 25.6 million with an average annual rate of increase of 2.2%. Each yearly rate of increase during the most recent period was well in excess of the average rate for the earlier period, but only one rate for the earlier period (1955–1956) was greater than the average rate for the recent period. Note too that from 1969–1970 to 1976–1977 the average annual rate of increase was 2.4%, while between 1963–1964 and 1968–1969 the average rate was 2.0%.

Recall that we previously saw that between 1963–1964 and 1968–1969 the national rate of employment growth averaged 2.4% and never fell below 2.0%, but that between 1969–1970 and 1976–1977 the annual average rate was 1.9%. Over the same two periods the respective annual average rates of civilian labor force growth were 2.0 and 2.4%. The respective rates of growth are plotted in Figure 2.1, where the patterns described above can be seen. Clearly, then, with the labor force growing more rapidly and with employment growing less rapidly

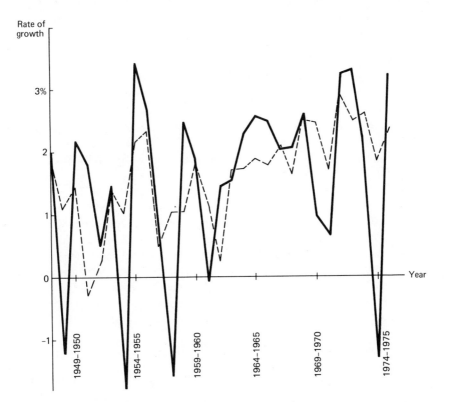

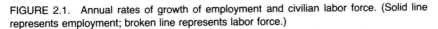

FIGURE 2.1.   Annual rates of growth of employment and civilian labor force. (Solid line represents employment; broken line represents labor force.)

after about 1969, the pressure of unemployment had to mount relative to the immediately preceding years.

Table 2.3 presents sex- and race-specific labor force data at 5-year intervals beginning in 1950 and ending in 1975. Moreover, the 16–24-year-old age group is partitioned out, and labor force participation rates are shown for each sex-age–race group at the various points in time. During the period from 1965 to 1975 the labor force aged 16 to 24 increased by 8.10 million, which amounts to an annual rate of 5.7%, compared to an annual average rate of increase of 2.3% over the previous 15 years. Moreover, labor force entry of women 25 and over accounted for another 6.57 million workers between 1965 and 1975.

The 1965–1975 increase in the young labor force was due not only to the larger number of persons aged 16–24 in the population, but also to increased labor force participation rates of this group. Approximately 35.7% of the increase in the labor force aged 16 to 24 can be attributed to increased labor force participation rates, with the remainder due to increased size of the underlying population.[4] Whereas young persons in general experienced increased participation rates, those for young women increased somewhat more than those for young men (44.0 to 57.1% for women versus 69.0 to 72.4% for men, as shown in Table 2.3).

The racial composition of the labor force has changed relatively little in recent years. In 1965 blacks accounted for 11.2% of the labor force, and in 1975 they accounted for 11.4%. The most conspicuous change along racial lines has been the appreciable decline in black male labor force participation rates, especially among the young. In 1960 black males, 16 to 24 years of age, had a participation rate of 74.0%, compared to a corresponding rate for whites of 71.3%. In 1975 the participation rate for black males in this age class was 60.1%, in contrast to a rate of 74.3% for comparable white males.[5] If black participation rates had been in 1975 what they were in 1965, an additional 208,000 young black males would have been in the labor force in 1975. Of course, if black rates had risen along with the corresponding white rates, this estimate would be somewhat higher. The 1975 unemployment rate of black males, 16 to 24, was 27.4%. A conservative estimate of the unemployment and underemployment rate among young black males is therefore 37.0%. Surely rates such as these have important implications for employment policy in the central cities of the nation's major metropolitan areas, where the 1975 black

[4]This estimate was derived by calculating the size of the 1975 labor force if 1965 participation rates had prevailed.

[5]A contributing factor in the decline of participation rates of young black males may be that this group is staying in school longer. In 1965 40.6% of the black males 16 to 24 years of age were enrolled in school, whereas in 1975 46.5% were enrolled. These figures have been calculated from data presented in U.S. Bureau of the Census (1967), Table 3, and U.S. Bureau of the Census (1976f), Table 1.

TABLE 2.3
Labor Force and Labor Force Participation Rates, 1950–1975, by Sex, Age, and Race[a]

Year	Males (in thousands)				Females (in thousands)			
	16 and over		16–24		16 and over		16–24	
	White	Nonwhite	White	Nonwhite	White	Nonwhite	White	Nonwhite
1950	43,819 [86.4]		7,136 [77.3]		18,389 [33.9]		4,387 [43.9]	
1955	40,196 (85.4) [85.3]	4,279 (85.0)	4,857 (72.0) [72.3]	732 (74.5)	17,886 (34.5) [35.7]	2,663 (46.1)	3,679 (43.5) [43.1]	489 (40.3)
1960	41,742 (83.4) [83.3]	4,645 (83.0)	5,992 (71.3) [71.6]	917 (74.0)	20,171 (36.5) [37.7]	3,069 (48.2)	4,071 (43.1) [42.9]	565 (41.2)
1965	43,400 (80.0) [80.7]	4,855 (79.6)	7,277 (68.9) [69.0]	1,012 (69.3)	22,736 (38.1) [39.3]	3,464 (48.6)	5,177 (44.3) [44.0]	700 (42.3)
1970	46,013 (80.0) [80.0]	5,182 (76.5)	8,533 (70.2) [69.4]	1,180 (64.4)	27,505 (42.6) [43.3]	4,015 (49.5)	7,135 (52.1) [51.3]	979 (46.2)
1975	49,881 (78.7) [77.9]	5,734 (71.5)	10,795 (74.3) [72.4]	1,363 (60.1)	32,203 (45.9) [46.3]	4,795 (49.2)	8,890 (59.0) [57.1]	1,216 (46.4)

Source: Data are from or are calculated from U.S. Department of Labor, *Employment and Training Report of the President: 1976* (Washington, D.C.: U.S. Government Printing Office, 1976), Tables A-3 and A-11.

[a] ( ) indicates sex-, age-, and race-specific labor force participation rate (%). [ ] indicates sex- and age-specific labor force participation rate (%).

unemployment and underemployment rate among the young was thought to be somewhat in excess of this figure.

The implications of changes in the age composition of the labor force and in labor force participation rates are crucial for interregional migration, and hence for regional economic growth and for the growth of urban areas in the nation's various regions. Lansing and Mueller (1967) point out that, of the population attributes associated with mobility, two are especially important, namely, age and education. Using data from the *Current Population Reports,* they go on to show that the peak years for mobility are the age bracket 22 to 24, for which the intercounty migration rate was 17.8%. The decline in mobility rates with age occurs rapidly. For the 30 to 34 and the 35 to 44-year-old age groups the respective intercounty migration rates were 8.8 and 4.8%.[6]

As might be expected due to the aging of the war baby cohort and the high migration rates for the age classes through which the cohort passed after 1965, the age composition of interregional migration streams changed somewhat. In 1965-1966, 40.9% of the migrants between Census regions were 18 to 34 years of age. During the 1970-1975 period 45.5% of the interregional migrants were 18 to 34, and during the 1975-1978 period 46.9% were 18 to 34.[7]

We saw previously that while in 1970 unemployment rates in Western metropolitan areas were relatively high, percentage point increases in unemployment rates between 1970 and 1975 tended to be larger in the metropolitan areas of the Northeast and North Central states, where manufacturing employment has also been more concentrated.[8] We also saw that migration rates decline

[6]The types of rates given by Lansing and Morgan are somewhat sensitive to the year of reference. The data reported by Lansing and Morgan refer to intercounty migration during the 12-month period ending in March, 1965. Intercounty migration rates for the 12-month period ending in March, 1976, were as follows: for the group aged 22-24, 15.9%; for the group aged 30-34, 7.5%; and for the group aged 35-44, 5.3%. Interstate migration rates taper off with age in much the same fashion. The respective rates for the 1964-1965 period are 9.5%, 4.3%, and 2.3%, and for the 1975-1976 period are 7.4%, 3.5%, and 2.7%. The source of these data are U.S. Bureau of the Census, *Current Population Reports,* Series P-20, No. 150, "Mobility of the Population of the United States: March 1964 to March 1965" (Washington, D.C.: U.S. Government Printing Office, 1966), and No. 305, "Geographical Mobility: March 1975 to March 1976" (Washington, D.C.: U.S. Government Printing Office, 1977).

[7]U.S. Bureau of the Census, *Current Population Reports,* Series P-20, No. 156, "Mobility of the Population of the United States: March 1965 to March 1966" (Washington D.C.: U.S. Government Printing Office, 1966); No. 285, "Mobility of the Population of the United States: March 1970 to March 1975" (Washington, D.C.: U.S. Government Printing Office, 1975); and No. 331, "Geographical Mobility: March 1975 to March 1978" (Washington, D.C.: U.S. Government Printing Office, 1978). Of course, these rates refer, respectively, to persons 1 year of age and over, 5 years of age and over, and 3 years of age and over.

[8]In 1975 the aggregate unemployment rate in the four Census regions was as follows: Northeast, 9.7%; West, 9.4%; North Central, 7.9%; and South, 7.8%. These rates have been calculated from data presented in the *1978 Employment and Training Report of the President,* Tables D3 and D4. Comparable data for 1970 are unavailable.

sharply with age. Similarly, unemployment rates decline sharply with age.[9] In 1977, for example, the unemployment rate among 18 and 19-year-old persons was 16.2%, among 20 to 24-year-old persons was 10.9%, among 25 to 34-year-old persons was 6.4%, and among 35 to 44-year-old persons was 4.4%. During the 9 years between 1969 and 1977 the unemployment rate of the 20 to 24-year-old group averaged 86.3% higher than that of the 25 to 34-year-old group.[10] The large, young, and mobile age group thus had an added incentive to migrate from the slower growing regions. DaVanzo (1978) has shown that higher local unemployment rates encourage out-migration of the unemployed. Hence, this group is likely to have acted on its unemployment incentive to migrate. Interregional migration after approximately 1965 was therefore of relatively great magnitude both because of the large increases in society's most mobile age classes and because underlying economic conditions were such as to encourage these age classes to have still higher migration rates.

Other Forces Contributing to Population Redistribution

To assume that unemployment rates and rates of employment growth are the only factors motivating interregional migration would be naive and contrary to the findings of many migration researchers. Many factors contribute to decisions to migrate.[11] Life-cycle considerations—such as marriage, divorce, completion of schooling, entry into the labor force, start of a career, birth and aging of children, and retirement—are important among these factors.

Mincer (1978) has shown that family ties tend to discourage migration. Moreover, such ties tend to reduce the employment and earnings of those wives who do migrate and to increase the employment and earnings of their husbands. He goes on to show that increased labor force participation rates of women cause an increase in migration ties, which results in both less migration and more marital instability.[12] Increased marital instability in turn encourages migration as well as increased women's labor force participation.

Mincer presents data from the *Current Population Reports* to show that husband–wife families migrate less frequently than persons without spouses. However, families in which the husband is between 20 and 24 years of age behave differently. These families have higher migration rates than persons

[9]This decline in unemployment rate with age continues to approximately 55 years of age, or perhaps slightly older, and thereafter the unemployment rate rises slightly.

[10]U.S. Department of Labor, Bureau of Labor Statistics, *1978 Employment and Training Report of the President*, Table A-19.

[11]For a detailed discussion of many of these factors, see Greenwood (1975b).

[12]Mincer (1978) defines "tied persons" in the family as "those whose gains from migration are (in absolute value) dominated by gains (or losses) of the spouse [p. 753]."

TABLE 2.4
Mobility Rates for 1970–1975 of Eighteen to Twenty-four-Year-
Old Males by Marital Status, 1975[a]

Type of mobility	Married, wife present (%)	Other (%)
Different house, same county	56.9	21.8
Different county, same state	20.0	7.7
Different state	18.7	7.8

Source: U.S. Bureau of the Census, *Current Population Reports,*
Series P-20, No. 285, "Mobility of the Population of the United
States: March 1970 to March 1975" (Washington, D.C.: U. S.
Government Printing Office, 1975), Table 20.
[a] Mobility refers to place of residence in 1970 by place of
residence in 1975. The number of persons abroad and the number
for whom mobility status was not reported were excluded from the
denominator in the rate calculation.

without spouses, which Mincer attributes to life-cycle events, such as completion of schooling, entry into the labor force, start of a career, and marriage itself.

Especially among the young, for whom marriage is a more frequent occurrence, change in marital status provides an appreciable inducement to move. The *Current Population Reports* present information on the reasons for male mobility between March, 1962, and March, 1963. Of males aged 18 to 24 who changed houses within a given county, 22.3% gave change in marital status as their reason for moving. Of those who migrated between counties but within a given state, 10.2% gave such a response, and of those who migrated between states, 4.3% (5.7% of nonmilitary-induced movers) gave this reason.[13]

The *Current Population Reports* indicate substantial differences in mobility rates between young married males with wife present and other young males. Table 2.4 reports these differences as they existed in 1975. Of the males aged 18 to 24 in 1975, 56.9% of those married with wife present had changed houses within a given county since 1970, whereas only 21.8% of the remaining male population had made a similar move. Migration rates also differ appreciably between the married and the other groups. Whereas married 18 to 24-year-old males with wife present had a 1970–1975 intercounty, intrastate migration rate of

[13]U.S. Bureau of the Census, *Current Population Reports,* Series P-20, No. 154, "Reasons for Moving: March 1962 to March 1963" (Washington, D.C.: U.S. Government Printing Office, 1966).

20.0%, other males in this age class had a comparably defined rate of 7.7%. The married group had a between-states migration rate of 18.7%, but the other group had a between-states rate of only 7.8%. As emphasized by Mincer, these differences, by and large, reflect life-cycle influences on the propensity to migrate.

Marriage rates among the young have been falling steadily for several years. In 1975, 56.0% of the females aged 20–24 were married, compared to 61.4% in 1970 and 68.8% in 1962. Comparable percentages for males are 38.6, 43.6, and 47.0.[14] Behavioral trends like these can have numerous consequences for location patterns.

In itself, the drop in marriage rates should have reduced mobility and migration among the young relative to what would have been and hence to some extent should have offset those factors contributing to increasing rates. However, according to Mincer's findings, if the fraction of this age cohort that is married remains lower than it might otherwise have been, then, as the cohort ages, its migration rates will be higher than they would otherwise be.

Since approximately 1970 divorce rates have risen dramatically.[15] As pointed out earlier, Mincer (1978) has shown that marital instability encourages migration as well as increased female labor force participation. According to Mincer, then, higher divorce rates are due in part to the increase in migration ties that results from increased labor market attachment of wives.

Information found in the *Current Population Reports* is consistent with the claim that changes in family composition may have contributed to greater interstate migration rates. For example, of married men 14 to 24 years of age with wife present, 20.3% of those with no children of their own changed their state of residence between 1970 and 1975, compared to 17.2% of those with children of their own. Comparable percentages for the 25 to 34-year-old age group are 25.4% for those with no children of their own and 17.6% for those with children

---

[14]U.S. Bureau of the Census, *Current Population Reports,* Series P-20, No. 287, "Marital Status and Living Arrangements: March 1975" (Washington, D.C.: U.S. Government Printing Office, 1975); also No. 212, "Marital Status and Family Status: March 1970" (1971), and No. 122, "Marital Status and Family Status: March 1962" (1963).

[15]A recent *Current Population Report* documents this upsurge in divorce rates as follows:

In March 1977, there were an estimated 8.1 million men and women who were divorced and who had not remarried compared to 48 million married couples; there were 84 divorced persons for every 1,000 persons in an intact marriage in 1977. The dramatic upsurge in divorce has been a relatively recent development; since 1970 the divorce ratio has increased by 79 percent, as compared with an increase of 34 percent during the entire decade from 1960 to 1970. . . . Persons under 45 had higher ratios (91 per 1,000) than those 45 years and over (76 per 1,000) [U.S. Bureau of the Census, *Current Population Reports,* Series P-20, No. 323, "Marital Status and Living Arrangements: March 1977" (Washington, D.C.: U.S. Government Printing Office, 1978), p.3].

TABLE 2.5
Percentage of Women, Twenty to Twenty-four, Ever Married with
No Children Ever Born, 1975, 1970, and 1960

	1975	1970	1960
All races	42.3	39.9	24.2
White	44.7	37.7	25.0
Black	20.2	20.8	17.0

Source: U.S. Bureau of the Census, *Current Population Reports,*
Series P-20, No. 301, ''Fertility of American Women, June 1975''
(Washington, D.C.: U.S. Government Printing Office, 1976), Table 17.

of their own.[16] Mincer has also shown that, holding many other relevant factors constant, the presence of school-aged children discourages migration.[17]

The influence of changes in fertility patterns on population movements from central cities to suburbs should not be overlooked. Young married couples with no children appear to have higher rates of movement from central cities to suburbs than young married couples with children. As of 1975, 24.7% of suburban married men 14 to 24 years of age with wife present and no children of their own had moved to the suburbs from the central city since 1970. Otherwise comparable men with children of their own constituted 19.9% of the relevant suburban population in 1975. For the 25 to 34-year-old group, corresponding percentages for men with no children of their own and with children of their own were, respectively, 35.6 and 26.4%.[18] A number of factors are responsible for higher rates of movement from central city to suburbs among married couples with no children. One of the most important of these is that couples with no children are more likely to have two wage earners, which makes suburban housing and other aspects of suburban living more affordable for them. Moreover, childless couples, to the extent that they need not make expenditures for child rearing, are better able to afford suburban residences.

[16]These percentages were calculated from data presented in U.S. Bureau of the Census, *Current Population Reports,* Series P-20, No. 285, Table 23. The numbers of persons abroad and for whom no information was available on mobility status were removed from the base population before the rates were calculated.

[17]Mincer (1978), Table 6.

[18]The source of this information is U.S. Bureau of the Census, *Current Population Reports,* Series P-20, No. 285, Table 22. The number of relevant suburban persons abroad and for whom no information was given on mobility status was removed from the denominator when the rates given above were calculated. The fractions of relevant 1970 central city married men who had moved to the suburbs by 1975 would be more appropriate, but the data do not allow the computation of mobility rates for the relevant base population as defined in 1970.

Table 2.5 indicates the percentage of women, 20 to 24 years of age, ever married with no children ever born. Note that between 1960 and 1975 a truly dramatic increase occurred in this percentage, from 24.2 to 42.3. Note too that white women experienced a far larger increase than black women, for whom the percentage increased from 17.0 to 20.2. Fertility and labor force participation behavior of women have been mutually dependent and have together permitted or encouraged many American families to move to the suburbs that under different circumstances would not have moved. Moreover, the differential behavior of white and black women is such as to discourage black mobility, both by reducing income per family member and by increasing local community ties.[19] In turn, black women tend to bear a higher cost of acquiring access to the labor market (e.g., the cost of day care).

Increased labor force participation rates of young married women may have acted as a permissive factor in the population dispersion out of the higher-income areas of the Northeast and the North Central states. The increased labor force participation of young women has meant that many young families now have multiple wage earners. Location in areas with historically low wages but desirable amenities—such as sunshine, mountains, and seashore—has been made possible at reasonably high levels of family income, when with a single wage-earner such location decisions would have been unlikely at early stages in the life cycle. This phenomenon reflects a relatively high income elasticity of demand for locational amenities, which is suggested by the work of Graves (1979).[20]

The U.S. Migration Experience, 1947–1975

To this point no data have been presented to show that in fact migration in general and migration rates among the young in particular have increased since

[19]A distinction between movements over short distances as opposed to long distances is necessary here. For a number of years blacks have had higher rates of intracounty movement than whites, but whites have had somewhat higher rates of intercounty and interstate migration. For example, as of 1975, 35.7% of the black population 5 years of age and over had since 1970 changed houses within a county, compared to 22.8% of the white population. On the other hand, over the same period 9.0% of the white population migrated between counties but within a state, and only 4.2% of the black population made a comparable move. Furthermore, 8.9% of the white population changed states, while 5.9% of the black population changed states. (These figures are reported in or are calculated from information presented in U.S. Bureau of the Census, *Current Population Reports*, Series P-20, No. 285, Table 29.)

[20]Actually, Graves's empirical results show that the net migration behavior of white persons aged 20 to 24 is not sensitive to climatic factors. The climate variables utilized by Graves are heating degree days, cooling degree days, annual temperature variance, humidity, and average wind speed. He makes no attempt to analyze the behavior of persons of different marital status.

TABLE 2.6
Annual Aggregate Mobility Rates, 1947–1948 to 1970–1971

Year	Between states Number	Rate (%)[a]	Within states Number	Rate (%)[a]	Within counties Number	Rate (%)[a]
1947–1948	4,638	3.02	4,370	3.21	19,202	13.28
1948–1949	3,992	3.02	4,344	2.78	18,792	13.08
1949–1950	4,360	2.66	3,889	2.98	19,276	13.17
1950–1951	5,276	3.50	5,188	3.56	20,694	13.97
1951–1952	4,854	3.41	5,112	3.24	19,874	13.26
1952–1953	4,626	3.63	5,522	3.04	20,638	13.55
1953–1954	4,947	3.25	5,034	3.20	19,046	12.31
1954–1955	5,511	3.10	4,895	3.50	21,086	13.37
1955–1956	5,859	3.15	5,053	3.65	22,186	13.82
1956–1957	5,192	3.10	5,076	3.18	21,566	13.19
1957–1958	5,656	3.35	5,584	3.39	22,023	13.21
1958–1959	5,419	2.99	5,070	3.19	22,315	13.14
1959–1960	5,724	3.18	5,523	3.30	22,564	13.00
1960–1961	5,493	3.26	5,753	3.11	24,289	13.77
1961–1962	5,461	3.11	5,562	3.05	23,341	13.05
1962–1963	5,712	3.66	6,640	3.15	23,059	12.70
1963–1964	6,191	3.28	6,047	3.36	24,089	13.06
1964–1965	6,597	3.29	6,147	3.53	25,122	13.43
1965–1966	6,275	3.31	6,263	3.31	24,165	12.76
1966–1967	6,308	3.43	6,553	3.30	22,339	11.70
1967–1968	6,607	3.64	7,035	3.42	22,960	11.88
1968–1969	6,316	3.39	6,625	3.23	22,993	11.78
1969–1970	6,250	3.58	7,066	3.17	23,225	11.76
1970–1971	6,197	3.47	6,946	3.10	23,018	11.51

Source: U.S. Bureau of the Census, Current Population Reports, Series P-20, "Mobility of the Population of the United States, . . . ," various years.
    [a] In the calculation of this rate the number of persons abroad has been deducted from the total U.S. population.

the early 1960s. Time series data on U.S. migration are sparse, which probably accounts for both the lack of studies concerning aggregate mobility behavior over time and the lack of attention to migration forecasting. The earliest source of annual mobility data is the Current Population Report, Series P-20, which yields a 24-year series beginning in 1947–1948 and continuing through 1970–1971, when the series was converted to reflect 1970 residence in each year until 1975. Because the CPR data give the longest time series and are superior for other reasons to data from alternative annual sources, such as the Social Security One Percent Continuous Work History, the CPR data are utilized in the following discussion.

Three types of mobility data are reported in the *CPR*: (*a*) persons who change house but not county of residence; (*b*) persons who change county but not state of residence; and (*c*) persons who change state of residence. The latter two measures are generally regarded as reflecting migration decisions.

For each mobility measure a rate was formed, where the rate is expressed as the number of movers relative to the resident U.S. population. Table 2.6 reports the three separate mobility rates for a 24-year period beginning in 1947–1948, as well as the absolute number of movers in each mobility category. Figure 2.2 plots the annual aggregate rate of interstate migration. If the period from 1947–1948 to 1962–1963 is again distinguished from the period 1963–1964 to 1970–1971, it is apparent that interstate migration rates have experienced a gradual rise over time. The mean rate for the earlier period is 3.21%, while that for the later period is 3.42%. This change is consistent with the hypotheses suggested previously.

After 1963 the average rate of within-state migration increased slightly from 3.22 to 3.30%, but the average rate of movement within counties declined somewhat from 13.24 to 12.24%. This decline in the rate of intracounty mobility may have been due in large part to the decreased marriage rates discussed earlier.

Because the *CPR* ceased giving annual migration data after the 1970–1971 information was reported, migration rates for the years since 1971 cannot be

FIGURE 2.2.   Annual aggregate rate of interstate migration.

TABLE 2.7
Annual Aggregate Interstate Migration Rates for Persons
Twenty to Twenty-four Years of Age, 1947–1948 to
1970–1971

Year	Rate (%)	Year	Rate (%)
1947–1948	6.40	1963–1964	8.21
1948–1949	5.88	1964–1965	8.60
1949–1950	5.69	1965–1966	9.38
1950–1951	6.71	1966–1967	9.56
1951–1952	8.10	1967–1968	9.22
1952–1953	10.50	1968–1969	9.54
1953–1954	9.56	1969–1970	9.06
1954–1955	9.02	1970–1971	8.87
1955–1956	10.57		
1956–1957	8.49		
1957–1958	9.24		
1958–1959	7.89		
1959–1960	9.23		
1960–1961	9.10		
1961–1962	8.48		
1962–1963	9.54		

Source: U.S. Bureau of the Census, Current Population
Reports. Series P-20, "Mobility of the Population of the United
States, . . . ," various years.

directly compared with those for earlier years. However, if the broad trends
described herein have had some impact on migration rates, these rates should
have risen during the period from 1970 to 1975. The CPR presents information
on mobility over the 1970–1975 period, where the data relate to 5-year flows
(i.e., place of residence in 1975 and place of residence in 1970).[21] This information can be compared with comparable data on 1965–1970 flows that are reported
in the 1970 Census.[22] Mobility data for the two periods are reported as
follows[23]:

	1965–1970	1970–1975
Between states	9.12%	9.28%
Within states	8.88	9.11
Within counties	24.59	26.09

[21]U.S. Bureau of the Census, Current Population Reports, Series P-20, No. 285.
[22]U.S. Bureau of the Census, Census of Population: 1970. Subject Reports, Final Report
PC (2)-2B, Mobility for States and the Nation (Washington, D.C.: U.S. Government Printing Office,
1973), Table 1.
[23]The number of persons abroad and the number of persons who moved but did not report
a place of residence have been deducted from the total U.S. population 5 years of age and over.

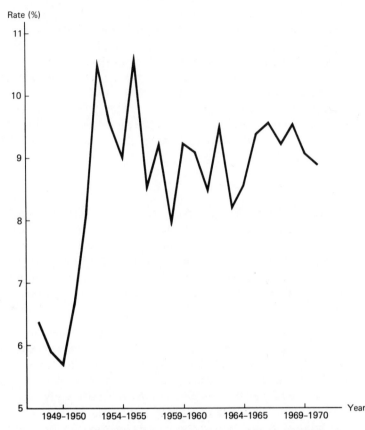

FIGURE 2.3.   Annual interstate migration rates of persons 20–24 years of age.

Note that these data indicate an increase in each type of mobility rate between 1965–1970 and 1970–1975. With a population of 200 million, the difference between the 1965–1970 between-states migration rate and that for 1970–1975 suggests that 320,000 more persons would have made an interstate move during the later period.[24]

The *Current Population Reports* also give data on age-specific movement for each of the three types of mobility previously distinguished. Table 2.7 indicates annual interstate migration rates for the 20-24-year-old age class, and Figure 2.3 shows the plot of these rates for the period from 1947–1948 to

---

[24]This figure of 320,000 refers to a rate of 9.28% and a base population of 200 million relative to a rate of 9.12% and base population of 200 million. Because of the size of the population base, even modest increases in migration rates can correspond to absolutely large numbers of migrants. Of course, as population rises over time, greater numbers of migrants would be expected even if the migration rate were constant.

1970–1971. Clearly, the interstate migration rate of this young age group tends to fluctuate somewhat more widely than the overall rate of interstate migration. Migration induced by military service is also particularly important for this age class, and the rapid rise in the rate from 1949–1950 to 1952–1953 was in part due to the military requirements of the Korean War. Differences in average rates of interstate migration of this young group for the 1947–1948 to 1962–1963 period relative to the period from 1963–1964 to 1970–1971 are again consistent with the broad hypothesis suggested earlier. The mean rate for the period from 1947–1948 to 1962–1963 is 8.40% while the mean rate for the period from 1963–1964 to 1970–1971 is 9.06%.

Summary

During the post-World-War-II Period a number of important national forces contributed to the changing spatial distribution of population and of economic activity. Moreover, the years from approximately 1965 to and beyond 1975 stand distinctly apart from the earlier post-war years as a period during which conditions were such as to encourage disproportionately much spatial redistribution. Three broad national forces distinguish the period following 1965 from the years immediately preceding 1965:

1. Due in part to the effects of the Vietnam War, to sizeable increases in the labor force, to the permanent tax cut of 1964, and to credit ease beginning in 1966, the national rate of employment growth altered sharply at about 1963, after which the rate averaged almost twice its prior average, and the rate of growth from 1963 to 1969 was particularly high relative to typical rates prevailing either before or since.
2. The aging of the war baby cohort brought an extremely large number of young persons into the labor force, and young persons tend to be quite mobile geographically. After about 1965 circumstances were ideal for the encouragement of much geographic movement, both because economic conditions offered the inducement for movement and because the age groups most responsive to such inducements were growing rapidly.
3. Substantial changes in fertility patterns and in family composition contributed to appreciable increases in the labor force participation rates of young white women. The ability of young couples to have two wage earners in the family allowed the location of many families in areas with historically low wages but desirable amenities. Moreover, the increased labor force participation of young women also allowed many young couples to afford suburban amenities, such as improved housing, and thereby encouraged their movement from central cities to suburbs. Especially since 1970, increased divorce rates have probably also contributed to migration.

One very important force operating in the direction of lower overall mobility rates among the young was the declining marriage rate. A great deal of geographic mobility occurs as a life-cycle phenomenon associated with marriage. Young married persons are over twice as likely as other young persons to have moved within a county or to have migrated either between counties or between states. In a little over 10 years prior to 1975 marriage rates among the young fell by about 12 percentage points.

After approximately 1963 rates of intercounty–intrastate migration and interstate migration increased slightly relative to their prior average levels. These changes are consistent with the broad societal trends previously discussed.

3

Interregional Shifts in the Location of Population and Employment

The Behavior of Regional Employment and Population Changes, 1947–1977: The Historical Record

Regional employment and population changes are expected to be, and indeed are, positively correlated. However, while a positive qualitative relationship exists between regional employment and population changes, the quantitative relationship between these variables is far from being clear. Available data suggest a highly unstable relationship between the variables over time as well as a relationship that differs considerably between regions.

Table 3.1 reports for each census region the average annual rate of growth of nonagricultural employment for the period 1947 to 1977 as well as for various subperiods within this time interval.[1] Over this period of time the West experienced an average annual rate of growth of 3.42%, which was over three times as high as the average annual rate of 1.03% in the Northeast and twice as high as the average rate of 1.77% in the North Central region. During the same period the South had an average annual rate of nonagricultural employment growth of 3.04%.

[1]The states and census divisions that make up each census region are indicated in the Appendix to this chapter.

TABLE 3.1
Average Annual Rates of Growth of Nonagricultural Employment, by Region, for Selected
Subperiods, 1947-1977

Period	Northeast (%)	North Central (%)	South (%)	West[a] (%)
1947–1948 to 1976–1977	1.03	1.77	3.04	3.42
1947–1948 to 1962–1963	0.76	1.22	2.43	3.26
1963–1964 to 1976–1977	1.35	2.39	3.73	3.60
1963–1964 to 1968–1969	2.70	3.61	4.54	4.15
1969–1970 to 1976–1977	0.33	1.48	3.13	3.18

Source: See Table 3.A1, in Appendix to this chapter.
[a] Alaska and Hawaii have been excluded from the West so as to maintain comparability for years when data are unavailable for these states.

Table 3.2 shows the average annual rate of population growth for each census region. For comparative purposes, the data of Table 3.2 are grouped into the same time periods shown in Table 3.1. As with nonagricultural employment growth, the West experienced the highest average annual rate of population growth between 1947 and 1977. The average rate of 2.53% in the West was considerably higher than the average rate of 1.47% in the South, which in turn had a rate somewhat higher than those prevailing in the North Central and Northeastern states. The latter two regions had respective average rates of 1.03 and 0.89%.

As a consequence of persistent, differentially higher rates of nonagricultural employment growth and of population growth in the West, between 1947 and 1977 this region experienced considerably greater relative employment and popu-

TABLE 3.2
Average Annual Rates of Growth of Population, by Region, for Selected Subperiods,
1947-1977

Period	Northeast (%)	North Central (%)	South (%)	West[a] (%)
1947–1948 to 1976–1977	0.89	1.03	1.47	2.53
1947–1948 to 1962–1963	1.29	1.38	1.60	3.26
1963–1964 to 1976–1977	0.43	0.63	1.34	1.69
1963–1964 to 1968–1969	0.80	1.17	1.06	1.74
1969–1970 to 1976–1977	0.16	0.40	1.46	1.66

Source: See Table 3.A2, in Appendix to this chapter.
[a] Alaska and Hawaii have been excluded from the West so as to maintain comparability for years when data are unavailable for these states.

lation gains than the other regions of the country. The percentage change in nonagricultural employment and in population follows for each region for the 1947–1977 period.

Region	Nonagricultural employment growth	Population growth
West[2]	172.1%	111.2%
South	143.5	55.1
North Central	67.3	36.0
Northeast	35.3	30.2

Note that in the West and in the South the absolute difference between the percentage change in employment and the percentage change in population is appreciable, and especially in the South the relative difference between the two variables is substantial. At a later point this observation will be discussed in more detail.

Tables 3.1 and 3.2 report average annual rates of growth for the same periods distinguished in Chapter 2. We saw in Chapter 2 that at the national level employment grew at somewhat higher rates between 1963 and 1977 than between 1947 and 1963. Hence, it is not surprising to find that each region experienced a higher average rate of growth after 1963 than before 1963. However, the growth experiences of the Northeast and North Central regions, and to a lesser extent that of the South, are in the sharpest contrast for the two periods. In the Northeast the nonagricultural employment growth rate averaged 78% higher during the later period. The average growth rate in the South was 53% higher after 1963, and in the West it was only 10% higher.

Just as the period from 1963 to 1969 stands out at the national level as a time of rapid employment growth compared to both preceding and succeeding periods, this period also stands out when the data are disaggregated to the regional level. What is quite remarkable about the behavior of nonagricultural employment growth during the late 1960s is the performance of the Northeast and North Central regions compared to their performance during earlier post-war years. Between 1963 and 1969 the average annual rate of nonagricultural employment growth in the Northeast was 255% higher than the average rate between 1947 and 1963. In the North Central states the rate was 196% higher. While the South (87% higher) and West (27% higher) experienced somewhat greater rates of nonagricultural employment growth during the late 1960s compared to the earlier post-war years, the relative performance of these regions over the two periods was nowhere near that of the Northeast and North Central states.

[2]Excludes Alaska and Hawaii.

In contrast to the performance of nonagricultural employment growth in the Northeast and North Central regions during the late 1960s, the early 1970s was characterized by extremely low average rates of growth. In the Northeast, after increasing at an average annual rate of 2.70% between 1963 and 1969, nonagricultural employment increased at an average annual rate of only 0.33% between 1969 and 1977. In the North Central region the average growth rate moderated from 3.61 to 1.48%.

The relative prosperity of the 1960s appears to have temporarily concealed the longer-term adjustments being experienced by the Northeast and North Central states. The recessions of 1969 and 1974 had particularly severe consequences in these regions, perhaps partially because the reimposition of the long-term relative decline of the Northeast coincided with cyclical phenomena. In the South and West, on the other hand, secular growth appears to have absorbed some of the impacts of recession such that these regions did not suffer the relative employment setbacks experienced in the Northeast and North Central states.

Previously we saw that in the West and in the South the absolute difference between the percentage change in employment and the percentage change in population has been appreciable, and especially in the South the relative difference has been substantial. Table 3.3 presents the ratios of average annual rates of nonagricultural employment growth to average annual rates of population growth for the various regions. The ratios are presented for the 1947–1977 period as well as for the subperiods previously distinguished. Over the entire period the ratio is highest for the South and lowest for the Northeast. Furthermore, due to the more rapid rates of labor force and employment increase after 1963, in combination with less rapid rates of population increase, the ratios are somewhat higher for the more recent period.

Moreover, note that for each region the ratio of the rate of employment to

TABLE 3.3
Ratio of Average Annual Rate of Nonagricultural Employment Growth to Average Annual Rate of Population Growth, by Region, for Selected Periods, 1947–1977

Period	Northeast	North Central	South	West[a]
1947–1948 to 1976–1977	1.16	1.72	2.07	1.35
1947–1948 to 1962–1963	0.59	0.88	1.52	1.00
1963–1964 to 1976–1977	3.14	3.79	2.78	2.13
1963–1964 to 1968–1969	3.38	3.09	4.28	2.39
1969–1970 to 1976–1977	2.06	3.70	2.14	1.92

Source: Calculated from data presented in Tables 3.1 and 3.2.
[a] Alaska and Hawaii have been excluded from the West so as to maintain comparability for years when data are unavailable for these states.

population growth has fluctuated fairly dramatically over time. The most obvious example is the Northeast, where the ratio was 3.38 for the 1963–1969 period, but 0.59 for the 1947–1963 period. The South, despite suffering substantial population losses due to net out-migration prior to about 1969, experienced relatively high rates of nonagricultural employment growth. Since approximately 1963 the South has experienced even more rapid rates of employment growth than the West, which was enjoying substantial population gains due to net in-migration.

The data of Table 3.3 suggest that far more than extra population lies behind additional employment. Among the other factors that contribute to regional employment growth, or that yield differentially high relationships between extra population and extra employment, are the demographic and socioeconomic composition of the population and of its changes, the composition of employment, the labor intensity of production processes, incremental regional income, technological factors, and the state of the national economy.

When labor demand is high, considerable employment can be drawn from a region's indigenous population through some combination of reduced unemployment and increased labor force participation. The responsiveness of labor force participation rates has, perhaps, been somewhat neglected relative to the responsiveness of population migration as a source of additional labor force members. Nevertheless, one of the most remarkable features of the period between 1947 and 1977 is the regional equalization of the ratio of nonagricultural employment to population. In 1947 this ratio was quite dissimilar across census regions—Northeast (0.374), North Central (0.316), West (0.297), and South (0.233). In 1977 the regions ranked in virtually identical fashion, but the differences were narrowed considerably—Northeast (0.389), North Central (0.389), West (0.383), and South (0.365).[3]

During the period between 1947 and 1969, the South was to some extent in a better position than other regions to experience more rapid rates of employment than population growth, and hence an increase in its nonagricultural employment to population ratio. At the beginning of the period under consideration, the South had an economy considerably more oriented toward agriculture than the other regions. Table 3.4 indicates that in 1950, 20.1% of the South's employment was in agriculture, forestry, and fishing, whereas in 1970 only 4.6% was in this broad industry category. In 1950 each of the other regions was substantially less oriented toward agriculture than the South, and, in fact, these other regions were already heavily nonagricultural. The North Central region, which after the South had the next highest fraction of its employment in agriculture, had 86.2% of its 1950 employment in nonagricultural pursuits, compared to 80.0% in the South. Hence, the other regions of the country were not in the initial position of the

[3]The ratio reported for the West excludes Alaska and Hawaii.

TABLE 3.4

Percentages of Regional Employment by Race and by Broad Industrial Classification, 1950, 1960, and 1970

	1950			1960			1970		
	White	Nonwhite	Total	White	Nonwhite	Total	White	Nonwhite	Total
Northeast									
Nonagriculture	90.0	6.6	96.6	91.1	6.8	97.9	90.2	8.4	98.6
Agriculture[a]	3.3	0.1	3.4	2.0	0.1	2.1	1.4	0.1	1.5
Total	93.3	6.7	100.0	93.1	6.9	100.0	91.6	8.5	100.0
North Central									
Nonagriculture	81.4	4.8	86.2	85.7	6.0	91.7	87.8	7.4	95.2
Agriculture[a]	13.7	0.1	13.8	8.3	0.1	8.4	4.8	0.1	4.9
Total	95.1	4.9	100.0	94.0	6.1	100.0	92.6	7.5	100.0
South									
Nonagriculture	64.3	15.7	80.0	74.1	16.3	90.4	79.4	16.1	95.5
Agriculture[a]	13.9	6.2	20.1	6.7	2.9	9.6	3.5	1.1	4.6
Total	78.2	21.9	100.0	80.8	19.2	100.0	82.9	17.2	100.0
West									
Nonagriculture	85.0	4.1	89.1	87.0	6.7	93.7	87.6	8.3	95.9
Agriculture[a]	10.0	0.9	11.0	5.7	0.6	6.3	3.8	0.4	4.2
Total	95.1	5.0	100.0	92.7	7.3	100.0	91.4	8.7	100.0

Source: U.S. Bureau of the Census, *U.S. Census of Population: 1950*, Vol. II, *Characteristics of the Population*, Part 1, United States Summary (Washington, D.C.: U.S. Government Printing Office, 1953), Table 161; U.S. Bureau of the Census, *U.S. Census of Population: 1960*, Vol. I, *Characteristics of the Population*, Part I, United States Summary (Washington, D.C.: U.S. Government Printing Office, 1964), Table 260; and U.S. Bureau of the Census, *U.S. Census of Population: 1970*, Vol. I, *Characteristics of the Population*, Part I, United States Summary—Section 2 (Washington, D.C.: U.S. Government Printing Office, 1973), Table 300.

[a] Refers to agriculture, forestry, and fishing

South to experience the sizeable shift away from agricultural and toward nonagricultural pursuits. This transformation in itself accounts for a large fraction of the South's increase in its employment to population ratio; labor resources were transferred out of an industry and areas where they were underutilized and into industries and areas where they were more fully utilized. Note that by 1970 the South's orientation toward nonagricultural employment was approximately equal to that of the other regions.

Changes in the racial composition of employment were also of some importance in the rise in the South's employment to population ratio, though this factor was probably of somewhat less importance than the transformation away from agriculture. Due to generally lower labor force participation rates and higher unemployment rates among nonwhites, the nonwhite employment to population ratio is lower than that for whites. Moreover, the age composition of the non-white population is more heavily weighted with young persons than the white population, which further contributes to the lower ratio for nonwhites. While between 1950 and 1970 the South was experiencing a decrease in the fraction of its employment that was nonwhite (from 21.9 to 17.2%, as shown in Table 3.4), each of the other regions was experiencing an increase. Because nonwhite persons were so heavily weighted in Southern agricultural employment in 1950, changes in Southern industrial composition were not independent of changes in Southern racial composition.

One consequence of interregional shifts of population and employment has been a more equitable distribution of employment opportunities relative to population. Table 3.5 indicates that in 1947 the Northeast held 32.6% of the nonagricultural jobs (the highest share) and 26.4% of the population (the third-highest share), while the South contained 24.1% of the jobs (the third-highest share) but 31.4% of the population (the highest share). By 1977 regional employment shares had changed somewhat, with the South containing 31.2% of the nonagricultural employment (the highest share) and the Northeast containing 23.4% (the third-highest share). In 1977 employment shares ranked identically with population shares, and the share of each was quite similar for every region.

During the period following 1977, the rate of employment growth is unlikely to remain as much above the rate of population growth as characterized the period between 1963 and 1977. A number of factors probably will be responsible for this reversal. The labor transfer out of agriculture appears to be near completion. The war baby cohort will have entered the labor force, and the rate of

TABLE 3.5
Regional Nonagricultural Employment and Population Shares, 1947 and 1977 (in percentages)

	1947		1977	
Region	Employment share	Population share	Employment share	Population share
Northeast	32.6	26.4	23.4	22.9
North Central	31.0	29.7	27.6	26.9
South	24.1	31.4	31.2	32.5
West[a]	12.3	12.5	17.8	17.7
	100.0	100.0	100.0	100.0

Source: See Tables 3.A1 and 3.A2, in Appendix to this chapter.
[a] Excludes Alaska and Hawaii.

increase in female labor force participation will taper off.[4] The most important potential sources of labor force and employment increases among the indigenous population are, over the next decade or two, increased labor force participation rates of blacks and women, but these sources are unlikely to yield increases that remotely approach those of the late 1960s and early 1970s. What this observation means is that population migration is likely to reassert itself as the major vehicle through which relative employment gains are transmitted from the less rapidly growing regions to the more rapidly growing regions.

Regional Shifts in Manufacturing Employment

Much has been written about the relative decline of the manufacturing sector in the Northeast and the rise of this sector in the South and the West. This phenomenon has, however, not been limited to the post-World-War-II period. Fuchs (1962a) offers a detailed description of changes in the location of manufacturing employment in the United States between 1929 and 1954. He summarizes his findings in the following way:

> The South and the West grew much more rapidly than the nation as a whole; the North Central region just held its share, and the Northeast showed a large comparative loss. In 1929 the South and the West together accounted for less than one out of every four manufacturing jobs and for only one-fifth of value added by manufacture. By 1958 their share had increased to one-third, as measured by either variable. The direction of change since 1947 was substantially the same as in the longer period, but the comparative gains of the West were conspicuously greater than those of the South [p.9].

The trends distinguished by Fuchs actually began unfolding somewhat earlier in the century than 1929.

As shown in Table 3.6, since 1958 the broad trends described by Fuchs have continued. The South and the West have gained an increasing share of national manufacturing employment, from 33% in 1958 to almost 43% in 1977. The North Central region has held its share, and the Northeast has experienced a large comparative loss. However, two important differences are apparent in the behavior of manufacturing employment since 1958 relative to the periods described by Fuchs. First, between 1929 and 1958, while suffering a comparative loss of manufacturing employment, the Northeast gained 1,287,900 manufacturing jobs, which amounted to over a 23% increase. Northeastern manufacturing employment continued to grow until 1967, but between 1967 and 1975 this region

---

[4]Fullerton and Flaim (1976) present labor force projections suggesting that between 1975 and 1990 the labor force participation rate of women 16 and over will rise from 46.3% to 51.4% while that for women 16 to 24 will rise from 57.1% to 66.6%. These rates can be compared with those presented previously in Table 2.3.

TABLE 3.6
Regional Manufacturing Employment and Regional Shares of Manufacturing Employment 1947-1977

Year	Northeast Employment (in thousands)	Regional share (%)	North Central Employment (in thousands)	Regional share (%)	South Employment (in thousands)	Regional share (%)	West[a] Employment (in thousands)	Regional share (%)	Total Employment (in thousands)	Share (%)
1947	5,879.7	(37.9)	5,423.2	(35.0)	2,999.7	(19.4)	1,195.1	(7.7)	15,497.7	(100.0)
1954	5,773.7	(35.4)	5,618.5	(34.5)	3,332.1	(20.4)	1,576.2	(9.7)	16,300.5	(100.0)
1958	5,426.8	(34.1)	5,194.4	(32.6)	3,511.0	(22.0)	1,803.0	(11.3)	15,935.2	(100.0)
1963	5,437.6	(32.1)	5,516.7	(32.5)	3,952.0	(23.3)	2,053.5	(12.1)	16,959.8	(100.0)
1965	5,627.8	(31.2)	5,981.4	(33.2)	4,346.2	(24.1)	2,087.7	(11.6)	18,043.1	(100.0)
1967	5,894.7	(30.3)	6,383.1	(32.8)	4,811.5	(24.7)	2,358.3	(12.1)	19,447.6	(100.0)
1969	5,893.2	(29.2)	6,615.6	(32.8)	5,204.9	(25.8)	2,483.1	(12.3)	20,196.8	(100.0)
1970	5,608.0	(29.1)	6,260.8	(32.5)	5,042.1	(26.2)	2,334.9	(12.1)	19,245.8	(100.0)
1972	5,232.5	(27.4)	6,164.7	(32.3)	5,332.9	(28.0)	2,346.2	(12.3)	19,076.3	(100.0)
1974	5,303.3	(26.4)	6,499.4	(32.4)	5,663.7	(28.2)	2,594.5	(12.9)	20,060.9	(100.0)
1975	4,806.1	(26.3)	5,839.4	(31.9)	5,212.3	(28.5)	2,435.2	(13.3)	18,293.0	(100.0)
1977	4,960.4	(25.4)	6,242.9	(31.9)	5,707.4	(29.2)	2,640.9	(13.5)	19,551.6	(100.0)

Source: U.S. Department of Labor, Bureau of Labor Statistics, *Handbook of Labor Statistics 1978* (Washington, D.C.: U.S. Government Printing Office, 1979), Table 52.

[a] Alaska and Hawaii have been excluded from the West so as to maintain comparability for years when data are unavailable for these states.

lost 1,088,600 jobs. During the same period the North Central region lost 543,700 manufacturing jobs. Second, the locus of growth shifted from the West to the South. Between 1958 and 1977 the West's share of national manufacturing employment increased from 11.3 to 13.5%, while the South's share increased from 22.0 to 29.2%.

Between 1969 and 1975 national manufacturing employment declined by 1,903,800 jobs. As is clear in Table 3.6, this decline occurred in two steps associated with the recessions of 1969–1970 and 1974–1975. By 1974 national manufacturing employment had almost recovered to its 1969 level, but between 1974 and 1975 alone employment fell by 1,767,900 jobs. No region was immune from the absolute manufacturing employment declines of the 1974–1975 recession. The relative declines in the North Central states (10.2%) and in the Northeast (9.4%) were greater than in the West (6.1%) and in the South (8.0%). What made the decline in Northeastern manufacturing employment particularly severe was that this sector never fully recovered from the recession of 1969–70 and, moreover, had been declining rather steadily since approximately 1967. Note that even in 1977 manufacturing employment in the Northeast and North Central regions remained well below its 1974 level.

These data suggest two conclusions. First, the increase in Northeastern manufacturing employment during the 1960s, due in part to the consequences of the Vietnam War, served to mask the longer-term plight of this sector in the Northeast. Somewhat the same conclusion can be applied to the North Central region. Second, the general state of the economy has much to do with the performance of the manufacturing sector, as indicated by the 1975 decline even in the South and the West.

The long-term trends in the locus of manufacturing employment have been attributed to a number of factors. Among the factors generally regarded to be important are the growth of markets, the lack of unionization, relatively low wages, and the availability of sunshine in the South and the West. Thompson and Matilla (1959), Burrows, Metcalf, and Kaler (1971), and Wheat (1973), for example, place particular emphasis on the growth of markets, while Fuchs (1962a) argues that the lack of unionization and relatively low wages, in combination with climatic factors, have attracted manufacturing employment to the South and the West. Others, such as Vaughan (1977), place more emphasis on technological change. They attribute the Southward and Westward shifts of the manufacturing sector to factors like the decreasing raw material content of manufacturing output, the rising importance of truck transportation, and the general availability of air conditioning.

Moreover, it is argued that the old vintage of the manufacturing capital stock in the Northeast and North Central regions places the manufacturing sector of these regions at a competitive disadvantage that is particularly severe in light of the strong and growing foreign competition. Finally, the growth of manufacturing employment in the South and West is sometimes seen as a cumulative phenomenon since manufacturing firms have a tendency to cluster in order to enjoy agglomeration economies.

The debate over the relative importance of these various factors in explaining broad interregional shifts in the locus of manufacturing employment can be placed in the context of the debate over the direction of the causal relationship between regional population and regional employment growth. Do jobs follow people, or do people follow jobs? Suppose we consider in slightly more detail the results of certain studies dealing with manufacturing employment that can be placed in this framework.

A good deal of evidence can be cited in favor of the jobs follow people hypothesis. Thompson and Matilla (1959), for example, studied the absolute growth of state-specific manufacturing employment in 20 industries for the period 1947–1954. They found that, in the durable goods industries, prior growth of the local market was the chief determinant of employment growth. Growth of the local market was measured by 1940–1947 population and income changes. Low wages and lack of unionization were also found to be important for certain industries, such as apparel.

More recently, Burrows, Metcalf, and Kaler (1971) studied employment in 22 industries that included agricultural and service industries as well as manufacturing. The county was the basic unit of analysis and the period of interest was essentially that from 1950 to 1960. Population growth was found to be the "most effective" variable in explaining employment, and the general conclusion was that "those counties with a high growth in population in the past are likely to exhibit a high growth in employment in the future [p.76]." On the average it appeared that doubling population would increase future employment by a factor of 2.72.

Wheat (1973) has also studied the regional distribution of manufacturing employment growth. He considers three variables—absolute, per capita, and percentage growth—each defined for states over the 1947–1963 period. These variables are related to a number of "locational influences," including markets, climate, labor, development thresholds, resources, urban attraction, and agglomeration. Wheat (1973) concludes that "markets and climate are far ahead as the leading influences affecting manufacturing growth in the United States [p. 183]." Labor and development thresholds are found to be of secondary importance, and resources and urban attraction are of tertiary influence. The tendency for manufacturing firms to cluster around one another is not evident in Wheat's work.

Fuchs (1962a), on the other hand, does not find the influence of markets to be a particularly important determinant of the location of manufacturing employment. Rather, he concludes that over the period 1929–1957 the rapid expansion of the aircraft industry in temperate climates was an important factor in the regional distribution of incremental manufacturing employment. He further suggests that unionization discouraged, and the availability of space encouraged, the relocation of manufacturing industries. These latter two factors vary systematically between regions in such a way as to encourage manufacturing employment in the South and the West relative to the Northeast and North Central states. An implication that can be drawn from Fuchs' work is that people follow employment.

The Causal Linkages between Population and Employment

THE CONCEPTUAL UNDERPINNINGS

Of the sources of spatial population change, migration is likely to have the most immediate implications for employment, and the primary focus of this section is therefore on the relationship between migration and employment growth. At the extremes, two theoretical approaches have been developed to characterize the relationship between migration and employment change. One approach hypothesizes a one-way causation running from employment change to migration, while the other hypothesizes a one-way causation running from migration to employment change.

The work of Blanco (1962, 1963, 1964) provides one of the best examples of those studies hypothesizing that causation runs from employment change to migration. She argues that "prospective unemployment," rather than the level of unemployment or the unemployment rate, is critical in determining (net interstate) migration. Blanco (1964) defines prospective unemployment as "the annual rate of change in unemployment which would be expected to occur if workers were not able to migrate between states [p.221]." The variable is measured "by the difference between the actual rate of change of employment and the natural rate of increase of the working-age population in each state [p.221]."

Basic to Blanco's concept of prospective unemployment is the notion that the actual change in civilian labor force in a given region (ΔCLF) must be identically equal to the sum of its component changes in employment (ΔEMP) and unemployment ($\Delta UNEMP$), and in turn identically equal to the sum of net (in) migration of civilian labor force members ($NETMIG$) and natural change of the civilian labor force (NAT):

$$\Delta CLF \equiv \Delta EMP + \Delta UNEMP \equiv NETMIG + NAT.$$

If we set $NETMIG = 0$, we get

$$\Delta UNEMP = NAT - \Delta EMP.$$

So defined, $\Delta UNEMP$ is the change in the level of prospective unemployment. If NAT is assumed to be determined exogenously, then prospective unemployment is largely determined by the growth of employment. Given natural increase, the greater the growth of employment, the smaller will be prospective unemployment, and hence presumably the greater will be net (in) migration.

Borts and Stein (1964) best characterize the notion that migration causes changes in employment. A number of critical assumptions underlie the Borts and Stein argument, and from these flow the implication that the labor demand curve for a given locality is perfectly elastic. Hence, any increase in labor supply that results from migration must result in increased employment. Moreover, migration may induce increased investment expenditures in receiving localities, which causes the demand curve for labor to shift upward, and thus gives rise to higher wages. The higher wages induce increased labor force participation, which results in further increases in employment.

Muth (1968, 1971) has attempted to reconcile the opposing views of the causal relationship between migration and employment growth by specifying a simultaneous-equations model of net migration and employment change. He argues that employment growth and migration are mutually dependent. Muth estimates his model by means of appropriate simultaneous-equations techniques and finds some support for each of the opposing hypotheses, although his results tend to favor the Borts and Stein hypothesis. Subsequent work by Olvey (1972) and Greenwood (1973, 1975a, 1976) have further substantiated the mutual causality exerted by employment growth and migration.

The basic idea behind the simultaneous-equations models is that the migration of labor force members is responsive to job opportunities. Areas in which the rate of employment growth, and hence presumably the rate of growth of job opportunities, is greatest are those that will experience the highest rates of in-migration and the lowest rates of out-migration. Furthermore, the migrants themselves influence both the supply of, and demand for, local labor. Employment should grow most rapidly in those areas that are attractive to migrants and least rapidly in those areas that are suffering population and labor force losses due to migration.

Although little attention has been paid to this idea in the migration literature, it is important to recognize that the labor supply effects of migration are dependent not only on the numbers of persons migrating, but also on the characteristics of the migrants. Clearly, in- and out-migration of labor force members have immediate impacts on local labor supply. As long as local labor demand is not perfectly inelastic, employment will tend to grow in areas of in-migration and decline in areas of out-migration. Moreover, labor force participation rates differ between age, racial, education, and earnings classes. Bowen and Finegan (1969), for example, demonstrate a strong tendency for participation rates of prime-age (25–54) males to rise with education. Table 2.3 of this study shows that such rates are higher for white males than for black males. Since prime-age population groups, whites, and the better-educated tend to have higher labor force participation rates, migration streams composed of relatively high numbers of these persons will therefore tend to have greater impacts on labor supply in sending and receiving areas. Other things being equal, employment should grow most rapidly in localities experiencing relatively high rates of (net) in-migration as well as relatively high rates of in-migration of prime-age, white, and well-educated persons.

Like the labor supply effects, the labor demand effects of migration are dependent on both the numbers and the characteristics of the migrants. It is useful to distinguish two types of labor demand that are affected by migration—the demand for labor in the production of private goods and the demand for labor in the production of public goods. The demand for locally produced and consumed commodities will tend to rise with the population increase brought on by in-migration. Furthermore, other things being equal, the higher the income or wealth of the migrants and the better their education, the greater will be the increase in the derived demand for local labor.

Another factor that may be of substantial importance is the entrepreneurial ability embodied in the migration stream. Allaman and Birch (1975) argue that relatively little interstate migration of firms occurs. What distinguishes states and regions with rapidly growing employment is their rates of birth of new firms. They conclude by emphasizing the role of entrepreneurial activity in encouraging employment expansion and by suggesting that the locational choices of persons with entrepreneurial ability are therefore critical for differential employment growth, such as has recently occurred in the South, for example.

Net in-migration of retired persons is clearly concentrated in a few states, such as Florida and Arizona. Although the destinations of retired persons are largely chosen for reasons other than job opportunities, retirement migration has important implications for employment growth and subsequently induced labor force migration. The in-migration of retired persons increases local labor demand without coincidentally increasing labor supply. The increased demand for local labor may be satisfied in part by increased local labor force participation rates, but immediate local demands, such as in the construction industry, are unlikely to be completely satisfied by local sources. In-migration of labor force members is thus likely to occur, which further fuels the growth of the area.

In some ways retirement migration is likely to induce greater labor force migration than would be induced by labor force migration itself. The reason is that if family composition, income, wealth, etc., were controlled for, the labor force migrant to some extent himself satisfies the increase in local labor demand that his migration causes, while the retired migrant does not. In other words, other things being equal, greater excess labor demand is created by the retired migrant than by the labor force migrant. This factor may help explain the observation that areas of retirement in-migration also experience appreciable nonretirement migration. Much of the nonretirement migration may be caused by the same amenities that cause retirement migration, but a great deal of nonretirement migration also appears to be responsive to growing job opportunities.

Both migrant numbers and characteristics importantly influence the demand for public services, as well as the revenues that support their provision. The extra local revenue provided by many low-income migrants it likely to fall short of the extra cost of the public services they consume. Just the opposite is true for many high-income migrants. The fiscal sectors of areas that experience proportionate in- or out-migration of high- and low-income groups are probably not seriously imperiled by migration. However, fiscal plight is expecially likely when a locality simultaneously experiences net in-migration of low-income persons and out-migration of high-income persons. This situation is typical of many of the central cities of the nation's major metropolitan areas.

INTERREGIONAL MIGRANT NUMBERS AND CHARACTERISTICS

As indicated in Table 3.7, during the years between 1940 and 1969, the North Central region and the South generally experienced net out-migration, while the West experienced net in-migration. Note that in most years net migration is a small fraction of gross migration, and thus that relatively small changes in gross in- or out-migration, or in both, can cause relatively large year-to-year changes in regional net migration. Especially for the regions experiencing net out-migration, substantial year-to-year fluctuations are evident in the volume of net migration. However, as noted in Table 3.2, regional population has continued to rise in spite of the net out-migration that occurred from the Northeast, North Central, and Southern regions. These population increases are, of course, due to natural increase and to net immigration (from abroad). As pointed out by Alonso (1978) and others, during a period when the natural rate of population increase is quite low, natural population increase in particular cities and even in broader regions may fail to compensate for net out-migration, such that population in these areas declines absolutely. In this way migration becomes a more obvious mechanism through which area-specific population gains and losses occur.

The observation has frequently been made that migration rates rise with education. From the point of view of regions of net out-migration, this observation has relevance because it may mean that these regions suffer disproportionately heavy losses of their best-educated manpower. Similarly, regions of net in-migration may experience disproportionately heavy gains of such persons. The present value of the expected stream of future earnings is greater for the better educated, which has important implications for regional development.[5] Moreover, important spillover benefits accrue to areas in which the better-educated reside. Among other factors, the educated may contribute to technolog-

[5]Wertheimer (1970) makes present value estimates of the returns to migration of the more educated relative to the less educated and confirms this point.

TABLE 3.7
Gross In- and Out-Migration and Net Migration of the Population One Year Old and Over, by Region, 1940-1978 (in thousands)

Year	Northeast			North Central			South			West		
	In	Out	Net	In	Out	Net	In	Out	Net	In	Out	Net
1940–1947	819	1,084	−265	1,817	2,099	−282	1,280	2,803	−1,523	2,767	697	2,070
1949–1950	256	391	−135	515	569	−54	688	574	114	470	395	75
1953–1954	364	408	−44	827	654	173	682	1,083	−401	671	399	272
1954–1955	360	439	−79	724	683	41	814	993	−179	752	535	217
1955–1956	398	418	−20	778	651	127	811	1,091	−280	687	514	173
1956–1957	388	445	−57	575	968	−393	961	821	140	734	424	310
1957–1958	551	465	86	672	944	−272	984	1,003	−19	738	533	205
1958–1959	419	522	−103	748	719	29	759	985	−226	739	439	300
1959–1960	466	463	3	662	797	−135	867	1,078	−211	877	534	343
1960–1961	433	524	−91	677	994	−317	1,008	1,027	−19	979	552	427
1961–1962	479	493	−14	723	874	−151	806	1,089	−283	969	521	448
1962–1963	451	594	−143	962	1,170	−208	1,002	1,216	−214	1,163	598	565
1963–1964	517	611	−94	671	985	−314	1,036	1,143	−107	1,101	586	515
1964–1965	582	623	−41	687	854	−167	1,115	1,082	33	998	823	175
1965–1966	569	509	60	838	860	−22	1,036	1,214	−178	905	765	140
1966–1967	514	652	−138	943	919	24	1,056	1,307	−251	1,022	657	365
1967–1968	545	717	−172	1,038	1,055	−17	1,283	1,311	−28	944	777	217
1968–1969	557	594	−37	887	899	−12	1,079	1,313	−234	961	678	283
1969–1970	521	827	−306	868	1,007	−139	1,297	1,247	50	1,085	690	395
1970–1971	609	804	−195	870	1,183	−311	1,425	1,171	254	1,032	780	252
1970–1975[a]	1,057	2,399	−1,342	1,731	2,926	−1,195	4,082	2,253	1,829	2,347	1,639	708
1975–1978[b]	876	1,575	−699	1,484	2,171	−687	2,881	1,872	1,009	1,900	1,524	376

Source: U.S. Bureau of the Census, *Current Population Reports*, Series P-20, "Mobility of the Population of the United States,...," various years.
[a] Refers to persons 5 years of age and over.
[b] Refers to persons 3 years of age and over.

TABLE 3.8
Interdivisional Net Migration Rates of College Graduates, 1965–1970 (in percentages)[a]

	All persons 25–64	College graduates 25–64	College graduates 25–34
New England	−0.34	1.00	0.61
Middle Atlantic	−1.96	−3.91	−5.14
East North Central	−0.89	−3.57	−5.37
West North Central	−2.27	−5.34	−9.41
South Atlantic	2.47	6.10	8.72
East South Central	−2.34	−3.72	−9.90
West South Central	−0.54	−1.18	−2.07
Mountain	2.95	3.24	4.20
Pacific	3.39	5.87	11.12

Source: U.S. Bureau of the Census, Census of Population: 1970, Subject Reports PC(2)-2D, Lifetime and Recent Migration (Washington, D.C., U.S. Government Printing Office, 1973), Table 12.

[a] Refers to persons who were residing in one Census division in 1965 and in another in 1970 and who were not returning to the division of their birth. Rates are expressed relative to the relevant 1970 Census division population. "College graduates" refers to persons with 4 or more years of college in 1970.

ical change and may breed entrepreneurship, both of which would tend to foster more rapid employment growth.

For each of the nine census divisions Table 3.8 shows 1965–1970 interdivisional net migration rates of nonnative college graduates. With the exception of New England, each division that experienced net out-migration during the period had a substantially higher rate of out-migration of college graduates than the overall rate of out-migration. Furthermore, again with the exception of New England, each division had a considerably higher rate of net out-migration of young college graduates (25–34 years of age) than of college graduates as a whole. Similarly, the three divisions (South Atlantic, Mountain, and Pacific) that experienced net in-migration enjoyed especially high in-migration rates of college graduates. Such a pattern of rates suggests a "brain drain" from the Middle Atlantic, East and West North Central, and East South Central divisions to the South Atlantic, Mountain, and Pacific divisions.[6]

The South Atlantic division is particularly noteworthy in this respect. The rate of 1965–1970 net in-migration was 2.47%, whereas the rate for college

[6]The brain-drain argument is typically focused on the drain of talent from less-developed to developed countries or from less to more prosperous regions within a country. In this context, the net migration of the better-educated from more to less prosperous (in terms of income levels) regions does not fit the conditions established for the brain-drain argument.

graduates was 6.10% and that for young college graduates was 8.72%. Net in-migration of college graduates to the South Atlantic Census division is not a recent phenomenon. Whereas this division received 93,680 nonnative net in-migrant college graduates between 1965 and 1970, it experienced a net gain of 43,203 such persons between 1955 and 1960, when the South in general had reasonably heavy out-migration, as indicated in Table 3.7. Note that the Pacific division also had a quite substantial net gain of nonnative college graduates and especially of young college graduates.

Despite relatively heavy net out-migration during the years between 1940 and 1969, the South enjoyed sizeable increases in employment—increases that during the 15 years between 1960 and 1975 not only kept pace with, but frequently exceeded, those of the West, which experienced considerable in-migration during the period. Labor force participation rates were low in the South to begin with, and hence a fraction of the Southern employment increase can be attributed to the rising labor force participation of indigenous residents. Moreover, gross in-migration to the South was substantial during the entire period— so substantial, in fact, that in most years the volume of Southern in-migration exceeded that of the other regions. Given the favorable balance of migration of the best educated, these observations suggest, but do not prove, that migration may have contributed to changing the South's population composition in a fashion conducive to employment growth.

Kain and Persky (1971) go a step further in arguing that historically South to North migration has contributed to the problems of the metropolitan North. Rural areas of the South have underinvested in human capital, and when persons raised in the rural South migrate to the urban North, they are ill-equipped to compete effectively for the available jobs.

Summary

During the period from 1947 to 1977 the West experienced an average annual rate of nonagricultural employment growth of 3.42%, which was over three times as high as the average annual rate of 1.03% in the Northeast, and twice as high as the average rate of 1.77% in the North Central region. During the same period the South had an average annual rate of nonagricultural employment growth of 3.04%.

At the national level nonagricultural employment grew at somewhat higher annual rates between 1963 and 1969 than during the periods between 1947 and 1963 and between 1969 and 1977, and these differences are clearly reflected in patterns of regional employment growth. The Northeast and North Central states stand out because their growth performance during the period from 1963 to 1969 was extremely good compared to their performance between 1947 and 1963. The average annual rate of nonagricultural employment growth in the Northeast was

255% higher during the later period than during the earlier, and in the North Central states the rate was 196% higher. However, in contrast to the performance of nonagricultural employment growth in these regions during the late 1960s, the growth performance during the period from 1969 to 1977 was poor. In the Northeast, after increasing at an average annual rate of 2.70% between 1963 and 1969, nonagricultural employment increased at an annual rate of only 0.33% between 1969 and 1977. In the North Central region the average growth rate moderated from 3.61 to 1.48%. The manufacturing sectors of these regions were particularly sluggish in their performance during the later period, in large part due to the impacts of two recessions.

Regional rates of population growth behaved in much the same fashion as regional rates of nonagricultural employment growth during the post-World-War-II period. Population grew most rapidly in the West, followed by the South, the North Central region, and the Northeast. However, though regional population and employment changes are positively correlated, they are not as highly correlated as might be expected. Changes in labor force participation rates also appear to be an important source of additional employment, and particularly in the South increases in labor force participation rates were dramatic.

Increased labor force participation rates and increased employment in the South were due to a number of factors. The shift of population out of agricultural pursuits and the associated migration of black persons out of the South were important. Moreover, the South experienced a favorable balance of migration of the best-educated and perhaps of the entrepreneurial class. Each of these factors appears to have contributed to a sharp increase in the South's employment to population ratio.

Appendix

The states and Census divisions that make up each Census region are indicated below:

Northeast

New England Division: Connecticut, Maine, Massachusetts, New Hampshire, Rhode Island, Vermont

Middle Atlantic Division: New Jersey, New York, Pennsylvania

North Central

East North Central Division: Illinois, Indiana, Michigan, Ohio, Wisconsin

West North Central Division: Iowa, Kansas, Minnesota, Missouri, Nebraska, North Dakota, South Dakota

South

South Atlantic Division: Delaware, District of Columbia, Florida, Georgia, Maryland, North Carolina, South Carolina, Virginia, West Virginia

East South Central Division: Alabama, Kentucky, Mississippi, Tennessee
West South Central Division: Arkansas, Louisiana, Oklahoma, Texas
West
Mountain Division: Arizona, Colorado, Idaho, Montana, Nevada, New
                          Mexico, Utah, Wyoming
Pacific Division: Alaska, California, Hawaii, Oregon, Washington

TABLE 3.A1
Nonagricultural Employment, 1947–1977, by Region (in thousands)

Year	Northeast	North Central	South	West[a]
1977	19,147.0	22,513.0	25,509.7	14,527.5
1976	18,821.8	21,811.5	24,704.3	13,867.2
1975	18,619.8	21,175.1	23,747.1	13,310.8
1974	19,182.4	21,750.1	24,053.7	13,255.1
1973	19,149.8	21,409.8	23,362.6	12,845.7
1972	18,686.4	20,440.7	22,022.9	12,104.1
1971	18,401.9	19,849.3	20,883.3	11,496.3
1970	18,664.9	19,952.8	20,401.5	11,399.5
1969	18,671.7	20,069.3	19,971.7	11,327.4
1968	18,175.1	19,445.9	19,178.2	10,854.3
1967	17,778.3	18,961.2	18,438.3	10,402.4
1966	17,347.7	18,332.3	17,757.4	10,054.0
1965	16,696.2	17,501.8	16,723.1	9,477.4
1964	16,184.8	16,694.6	15,900.8	9,142.6
1963	15,912.0	16,229.9	15,319.2	8,877.2
1962	15,844.7	15,932.7	14,827.2	8,606.9
1961	15,540.9	15,552.5	14,323.2	8,250.3
1960	15,612.3	15,836.5	14,239.7	8,090.7
1959	15,423.9	15,606.7	14,003.8	7,883.0
1958	15,128.0	15,126.0	13,542.7	7,473.7
1957	15,636.3	15,782.8	13,647.4	7,493.3
1956	15,499.4	15,781.7	13,388.6	7,253.6
1955	15,080.9	15,446.7	12,825.5	6,864.2
1954	14,834.5	14,935.9	12,330.9	6,525.7
1953	15,283.8	15,515.2	12,557.9	6,572.7
1952	14,998.9	14,949.9	12,325.7	6,393.6
1951	14,868.7	14,737.5	11,961.9	6,030.7
1950	14,222.3	13,976.0	11,144.2	5,607.1
1949	13,857.8	13,428.8	10,702.6	5,399.0
1948	14,352.6	13,851.4	10,887.0	5,501.3
1947	14,147.6	13,453.5	10,475.3	5,340.0

Source: U.S. Department of Labor, Bureau of Labor Statistics, *Handbook of Labor Statistics 1978* (Washington, D.C.: U.S. Government Printing Office, 1979), Table 51.
[a] Excludes Alaska and Hawaii.

TABLE 3.A2
Total Resident Population, 1947–1977, by Region (in thousands)

Year	Northeast	North Central	South	West[a]
1977[b]	49,280	57,941	69,849	37,961
1976	49,400	57,715	68,984	37,278
1975	49,422	57,583	68,141	36,654
1974	49,397	57,527	67,179	36,087
1973	49,528	57,434	66,196	35,524
1972	49,663	57,308	65,159	34,954
1971	49,568	57,023	64,038	34,473
1970	49,151	56,659	63,018	33,900
1969	48,678	56,106	62,190	33,286
1968	48,435	55,692	61,489	32,677
1967	48,106	55,289	60,771	32,206
1966	47,788	54,840	60,205	31,686
1965	47,451	54,225	59,579	31,230
1964	46,953	53,655	58,853	30,661
1963	46,402	53,073	58,008	30,017
1962	45,833	52,583	57,179	29,212
1961	45,384	52,185	56,158	28,349
1960	44,802	51,715	55,174	27,413
1959	44,193	51,147	54,324	26,627
1958	43,373	50,547	53,532	25,787
1957	42,673	49,860	52,657	25,104
1956	42,267	49,163	51,533	24,298
1955	41,986	48,360	50,548	23,409
1954	41,591	47,497	49,458	22,644
1953	40,787	46,379	49,172	21,974
1952	40,135	45,472	48,961	21,194
1951	39,677	44,941	48,422	20,344
1950	39,609	44,645	47,268	19,711
1949	39,551	44,175	45,981	18,958
1948	38,790	43,437	45,414	18,452
1947	37,835	42,597	45,041	17,973

Sources: U.S. Bureau of the Census, *Current Population Reports,* Series P-25: 1947–49, No. 72; 1950–59, No. 229; 1960–69, No. 460; 1970–77, No. 727.

[a] Excludes Alaska and Hawaii.
[b] Preliminary.

4

Metropolitan Growth
and Migration:
The Patterns Since 1950

A distinction is frequently made between urban economic growth and urban economic development. When viewed from a rather narrow perspective, urban economic growth refers to changes in the scale of various urban economic phenomena, such as labor force, employment, value of goods and services produced, and total income generated. Urban economic development, on the other hand, usually refers to increases in the standard of living, which standards are typically gauged in terms of some central-tendency measure of income growth and/or some measure of the change in the distribution of income. Recently, certain "quality of life" measures of economic and social well-being have also been formed as indicators of the standard of living in various urban areas.[1]

The concept of urban economic growth can, however, be interpreted in a somewhat broader sense to embrace changes in average and in per capita measures of various economic phenomena, in which case the meanings of the concepts of urban economic growth and urban economic development are much closer. When the narrower connotation of urban growth is adopted, situations can be conceptualized in which growth occurs without development or in which development occurs in the absence of growth and even in the presence of decline.

[1]See, for example, Liu (1975).

However, when average and per capita measures of growth are adopted, economic growth and economic development are more likely to move together.

In any case, changes in the scale of urban population and employment, whether increases or decreases, impose on urban areas problems that are frequently severe. Human and capital resources must adapt to these changes, and the process of adaptation often involves long periods of time during which severe hardships may be borne by certain members of society. Local governments also tend to be sluggish in their reaction to changes in the scale of activity. This sluggishness is especially apparent when the scale of activity is declining with the consequence that excess capacity exists in public facilities, and yet the governments choose to maintain these facilities to satisfy former levels of demand. The processes of adaptation and resource reallocation associated with growth thus give rise to problems whose severity is likely to be closely related to the rate of change that is occurring. Hence, a fairly detailed descriptive examination of urban growth rates provides a reasonable starting point for the subsequent specification and estimation of models of urban growth and of intraurban location.

A detailed analysis of the factors behind urban economic growth and migration is beyond the scope of this chapter. Such an analysis is, however, undertaken in later chapters. Rather, the major goal here is to describe patterns of urban economic growth in the United States over the period from 1950 to 1975 for a fairly large sample of metropolitan areas.

The Sample Metropolitan Areas and the Data

In 1970, 64 of 242 Standard Metropolitan Statistical Areas (SMSAs) in the continental United States had a population in excess of 500,000. In 1960, 100 of 211 SMSAs in the continental United States had a population in excess of 250,000. These SMSAs are the only ones for which detailed published census migration data exist for the respective periods.[2] The census also reports comparable information on intrametropolitan relocations between the central city (suburban ring) and suburban ring (central city) of each of these SMSAs. Finally, SMSA in-migrants are distinguished as locating in either the central city or the suburbs. In each case the central city or cities of the SMSA correspond to the political boundaries of the cities indicated in the SMSA title, while the suburban ring consists of the remaining land area in the SMSA.

A summary definition of SMSA given by the census is as follows:

> Except in the New England States, a standard metropolitan statistical area is a county or group of contiguous counties which contains at least one city of 50,000 inhabitants or more, or twin cities with a combined population of at least 50,000. In addition to the

[2]See U.S. Bureau of the Census (1963b, 1973d).

county, or counties, containing such a city or cities, contiguous counties are included in
an SMSA, if, according to certain criteria, they are socially and economically integrated
with the central city or cities. In the New England States, SMSAs consist of towns and
cities instead of counties. Each SMSA must contain at least one central city, and the
complete title of an SMSA identifies the central city or cities [1973d, pp. App-3,4].

The sample SMSAs employed in this study consist of 62 that are common to
the sets on which comparable migration and intrametropolitan relocation data are
reported in the 1960 and 1970 censuses. These SMSAs are indicated in Table
4.1, where they are also ranked according to 1970 population. The availability of
more and better data for population census years makes it convenient to examine
SMSA growth patterns over 10-year intervals. This study especially focuses on
growth patterns for two time periods, namely, 1950 to 1960 and 1960 to 1970,
but more recent data are not ignored.

Between the 1960 and 1970 censuses the Los Angeles–Long Beach SMSA,
as defined in 1960, was split into two components (Anaheim–Santa Ana–Garden
Grove and Los Angeles–Long Beach), both of which are included in the data set
for the 1960–1970 period. Hence, for the 1950–1960 period only 61 observations
exist for migration data, though the geographic area covered by the divided
SMSA is identical for the two periods. As defined in 1970, the Los Angeles–
Long Beach SMSA is Los Angeles County, while the Anaheim–Santa Ana–
Garden Grove SMSA is Orange County, California. Data other than that on
migration can in some instances be adjusted back through time on a county basis,
and therefore the SMSAs can sometimes be distinguished for years other than
1970.

Although data on the Jacksonville SMSA are available for each period, the
Jacksonville observation was eliminated from the data set due to the fact that no
suburban ring existed in 1970 after the city of Jacksonville merged with Duval
County, Florida. If the information on Jacksonville were utilized, the set of
SMSAs employed to examine urban growth issues would have differed from that
used to examine intrametropolitan location issues. Because the growth and location issues are closely related, this possibility was regarded as undesirable.
Whereas a 1970 observation is available on the Greensboro–Winston–Salem–
High Point SMSA, none is available in 1960, and thus this SMSA was not
included in the data set. Likewise, although an observation on Honolulu is
available for each period, this SMSA has been eliminated from the data set due to
its lack of proximity to other SMSAs. Honolulu's location is such as to suggest
an entirely different type of spatial relationship with other areas than holds for the
SMSAs within the continental United States.

Between 1950 and 1970 a number of SMSAs included in the sample experienced a change in their geographic scope as new counties were added to their
definitions or, in some instances, counties were deleted. For most of the descriptive purposes of this study, all data have been adjusted where possible to reflect

TABLE 4.1
Sample SMSAs Ranked by 1970 Population

Rank	SMSA	1970 Population
1	New York	11,571,899
2	Los Angeles–Long Beach	7,032,075
3	Chicago	6,978,947
4	Philadelphia	4,817,914
5	Detroit	4,199,931
6	San Francisco–Oakland	3,109,519
7	Washington, D.C.	2,861,123
8	Boston	2,753,700
9	Pittsburgh	2,401,245
10	St. Louis	2,363,017
11	Baltimore	2,070,670
12	Cleveland	2,064,194
13	Houston	1,985,031
14	Newark	1,856,556
15	Minneapolis–St. Paul	1,813,647
16	Dallas	1,555,950
17	Seattle–Everett	1,421,869
18	Anaheim–Santa Ana–Garden Grove	1,420,386
19	Milwaukee	1,403,688
20	Atlanta	1,390,164
21	Cincinnati	1,384,851
22	Paterson–Clifton–Passaic	1,358,794
23	San Diego	1,357,854
24	Buffalo	1,349,211
25	Miami	1,267,792
26	Kansas City	1,253,916
27	Denver	1,227,529
28	San Bernardino–Riverside–Ontario	1,143,146
29	Indianapolis	1,109,882
30	San Jose	1,064,714
31	New Orleans	1,045,809
32	Tampa–St. Petersburg	1,012,594
33	Portland	1,009,129
34	Phoenix	967,522
35	Columbus	916,228
36	Providence–Pawtucket–Warwick	910,781
37	Rochester	882,667
38	San Antonio	864,014
39	Dayton	850,266
40	Louisville	826,553
41	Sacramento	800,592
42	Memphis	770,120

(cont'd.)

TABLE 4.1 (cont'd.)

Rank	SMSA	1970 Population
43	Fort Worth	762,086
44	Birmingham	739,274
45	Albany–Schenectady–Troy	721,910
46	Toledo	692,571
47	Norfolk–Portsmouth	680,600
48	Akron	679,239
49	Hartford	663,891
50	Oklahoma City	640,889
51	Syracuse	636,507
52	Gary–Hammond–East Chicago	633,367
53	Fort Lauderdale–Hollywood	620,100
54	Jersey City	609,266
55	Salt Lake City	557,635
56	Allentown–Bethlehem–Easton	543,551
57	Nashville–Davidson	541,108
58	Omaha	540,142
59	Grand Rapids	539,225
60	Youngstown–Warren	536,003
61	Springfield–Chicopee–Holyoke	529,922
62	Richmond	518,319

Source: U.S. Bureau of the Census (1973d), List B, p. XIV.

1970 SMSA definitions.[3] These adjustments consist of including the appropriate data for the added counties in the earlier SMSA totals. In the cases of the four New England SMSAs (Boston, Hartford, Providence–Pawtucket–Warwick, and Springfield–Chicopee–Holyoke) the adjustments were somewhat more difficult to make and were somewhat less exact since they had to be estimated. Population is the only reported characteristic of towns that were subsequently included in the various SMSA definitions. The adjustments consisted of calculating per capita suburban values of variables of interest, such as employed and unemployed residents, assuming that the added towns had per capita values equal to those calculated for the old suburban definition, and multiplying the earlier per capita values by the corresponding earlier population of the towns subsequently included in the SMSAs. The resulting values were then added to former SMSA totals. In no instance was an adjustment to a New England SMSA of either absolute or relative magnitude sufficient to appreciably affect metropolitan or even suburban values of the affected variables.

[3]The Appendix to this chapter reports both the 1970 and 1960 county components of each SMSA.

Different and less comprehensive data than those found in the *Census of Population* are available in the *Censuses of Business* and *of Manufactures*. Since these censuses are taken in different years than the *Census of Population*, they yield somewhat different and shorter time intervals. These two data sources have also been extensively utilized in this study, especially for the examination of changes in intraurban employment location patterns. Data from the *Censuses of Business* and *of Manufactures* will be discussed in more detail at a later point in the study.

Unless otherwise indicated in the discussion of urban growth, data are from the various *Censuses of Population,* and therefore employment data refer to the place of residence of employed persons, not to their place of work. In 1970, 4.9% of the employed residents of the sample SMSAs worked outside of the SMSA in which they resided. Of course, other persons residing outside the various SMSAs worked in them, so the use of employment data referring to place of residence overstates actual SMSA employment by somewhat less than 4.9%.

The SMSAs included in the sample account for a sizeable percentage of national employment. In 1970 their residents accounted for 51.9% of national total employment, which then stood at approximately 77.31 million persons employed. They contained 55.0% of the 18.88 million persons employed in the nation's manufacturing sector. The percentages of national total employment and of national manufacturing employment contained in the sample SMSAs (as defined by their 1970 geographic areas) have changed relatively little since 1950, when the respective percentages were 48.2 and 55.1. Nationally, 24.4% of 1970 employment was in manufacturing, while in the sample SMSAs 25.9% was in manufacturing. In 1950 these percentages stood, respectively, at 25.9 and 29.6.

Table 4.2 shows the growth experience of the sample SMSAs as a whole

TABLE 4.2
Percentage Rates of Total, Manufacturing, and Government Employment Growth in Sample SMSAs and outside of Sample SMSAs 1950-1960 and 1960-1970

	1950–1960	1960–1970
National total employment	14.9	19.6
In sample SMSAs	21.6	21.8
Outside of sample SMSAs	8.8	17.3
National manufacturing employment	20.2	7.8
In sample SMSAs	20.2	7.6
Outside of sample SMSAs	20.1	8.1
National government employment	43.0	56.4
In sample SMSAs	38.9	61.1
Outside of sample SMSAs	47.3	52.5

Sources: See Tables 4.3 and 4.6.

relative to both the growth experience of the nation as a whole and the growth experience of spatial areas other than those included in the sample SMSAs. Note that during the 1950s employment grew somewhat more rapidly in the sample SMSAs than in the nation as a whole and considerably more rapidly than in nonsample areas. However, during the 1960s the growth experience of the non-sample and sample areas were much more similar, due primarily to a substantial increase in the rate of employment growth in nonsample areas. Manufacturing employment growth was quite comparable during each period for sample as compared to nonsample areas.

Urban Employment Growth, 1950–1970

The most comprehensive and best data to utilize in examining patterns of urban employment growth are from the *Census of Population: 1950, 1960,* and *1970.* These data are particularly useful because they can be corrected for changes in the spatial areas covered by the various SMSAs. The major shortcoming associated with utilizing census data is that they are not current. The most recent year on which an observation is available is 1970. Data on nonagricultural employment from *Employment and Earnings* are more current, but data from this source cannot be corrected for changes in SMSA definitions and must therefore be interpreted with caution. In the discussion that follows each data source has been employed.

Table 4.3 reports rates of growth of total employment in each sample SMSA for both the 1950–1960 and 1960–1970 periods. As reported in the table, the SMSAs are organized by region and within each region are ranked from that with the largest 1970 population to that with the smallest. Moreover, SMSAs have been ranked in terms of rates of employment growth, and each SMSA's rank is indicated both within its region and within the national sample of SMSAs. The column labeled "relative performance" indicates whether the SMSA had a growth rate during the period that was above (A) or below (B) the regional rate of growth and above or below the national rate. An entry of AB, for example, suggests that the SMSA had a rate above the regional rate but below the national rate.

During the 1950–1960 period only three Northeastern SMSAs had employment growth rates above the national average rate of growth, Paterson–Clifton–Passaic, Hartford, and Syracuse. The former two had particularly high rates relative to the regional rate. The rate for Paterson–Clifton–Passaic was 27.2% and that for Hartford was 25.3%, both of which were substantially higher rates than that for Syracuse, which had a rate of 15.5%. During the 1960–1970 period both Paterson–Clifton–Passaic and Hartford maintained relatively high rates of growth, but Rochester replaced Syracuse as the third SMSA with a rate of growth higher than the national rate. Rochester was, moreover, the fastest growing

TABLE 4.3
Rates of Employment Growth and Regional and National Rankings of SMSAs by Rates of
Employment Growth, 1950-1960 and 1960-1970

	1950-1960[a]				1960-1970[a]			
	Growth rate (%)	Relative performance[b]	Rank region	Rank U.S.	Growth rate (%)	Relative performance[b]	Rank region	Rank U.S.
Northeast	10.7				13.6			
New York	11.7	AB	8	50	5.6	BB	13	60
Philadelphia	14.4	AB	5	44	14.9	AB	8	50
Boston	10.1	BB	9	54	12.0	BB	11	57
Pittsburgh	2.9	BB	14	61	5.2	BB	14	61
Newark	12.0	AB	7	49	12.7	BB	10	56
Paterson–	27.2	AA	1	23	23.0	AA	3	33
Buffalo	12.4	AB	6	47	7.8	BB	12	59
Providence–	3.9	BB	13	60	18.8	AB	4	40
Rochester	14.5	AB	4	43	26.3	AA	1	24
Albany–	4.3	BB	12	59	16.3	AB	6	45
Hartford	25.3	AA	2	25	25.9	AA	2	25
Syracuse	15.5	AA	3	40	15.8	AB	7	47
Jersey City	– 7.3	BB	15	62	1.3	BB	15	62
Allentown–	8.5	BB	10	56	17.3	AB	5	44
Springfield–	6.9	BB	11	57	14.0	AB	9	52
North Central	9.7				15.9			
Chicago	12.3	AB	13	48	14.7	BB	14	51
Detroit	11.4	AB	14	51	19.5	AB	8	38
St. Louis	10.8	AB	15	52	16.0	AB	11	46
Cleveland	14.8	AB	12	41	13.6	BB	16	54
Minneapolis–	21.7	AA	5	28	33.8	AA	1	17
Milwaukee	16.3	AA	10	37	15.3	BB	13	49
Cincinnati	16.1	AA	11	39	13.7	BB	15	53
Kansas City	20.5	AA	7	30	23.8	AA	5	31
Indianapolis	23.1	AA	4	27	20.9	AA	7	36
Columbus	27.9	AA	1	20	32.0	AA	2	18
Dayton	25.6	AA	3	24	24.8	AA	3	28
Toledo	10.4	AB	16	53	18.3	AB	10	42
Akron	21.4	AA	6	29	18.6	AB	9	41
Gary–	27.3	AA	2	22	15.6	BB	12	48
Omaha	17.8	AA	9	36	21.0	AA	6	35
Grand Rapids	18.1	AA	8	35	23.8	AA	4	30
Youngstown–	9.3	BB	17	55	13.2	BB	17	55
South	12.8				23.5			
Washington, D.C.	28.2	AA	9	19	46.3	AA	5	8
Baltimore	16.3	AA	15	38	22.8	BA	15	34
Houston	42.7	AA	4	13	52.5	AA	2	5
Dallas	39.3	AA	5	14	47.8	AA	4	7
Atlanta	35.4	AA	7	16	49.9	AA	3	6
Miami	80.2	AA	2	7	43.6	AA	7	10

(cont'd.)

TABLE 4.3 (cont'd)

	1950-1960[a]				1960-1970[a]			
	Growth rate (%)	Relative performance[b]	Rank region	Rank U.S.	Growth rate (%)	Relative performance[b]	Rank region	Rank U.S.
New Orleans	19.7	AA	11	31	17.9	BB	17	43
Tampa–	77.3	AA	3	8	36.6	AA	8	14
San Antonio	27.5	AA	10	21	29.2	AA	10	21
Louisville	13.8	AB	17	45	26.6	AA	11	23
Memphis	14.6	AB	16	42	19.1	BB	16	39
Fort Worth	36.2	AA	6	15	46.1	AA	6	9
Birmingham	6.1	BB	18	58	11.8	BB	18	58
Norfolk–	19.0	AA	13	33	24.8	AA	14	29
Oklahoma City	28.4	AA	8	18	34.5	AA	9	15
Ft. Lauderdale–	264.1	AA	1	1	96.7	AA	1	2
Nashville–	19.3	AA	12	32	25.3	AA	13	27
Richmond	18.4	AA	14	34	25.3	AA	12	26
West	41.7				29.6			
Los Angeles–	46.8	AA	8	11	19.9	BA	12	37
San Francisco–	24.7	BA	11	26	23.2	BA	11	32
Seattle–	31.7	BA	10	17	33.9	AA	7	16
Anaheim–	230.0	AA	1	2	127.4	AA	1	1
San Diego	84.8	AA	4	5	39.6	AA	6	13
Denver	50.8	AA	7	10	41.2	AA	4	11
San Bernardino–	84.2	AA	5	6	40.6	AA	5	12
San Jose	126.3	AA	2	3	81.2	AA	2	3
Portland	13.7	BB	12	46	29.6	BA	9	20
Phoenix	115.5	AA	3	4	56.4	AA	3	4
Sacramento	68.9	AA	6	9	27.1	BA	10	22
Salt Lake City	44.2	AA	9	12	31.4	AA	8	19

Sources: U.S. Bureau of the Census (1952), Tables 35 and 43; (1963a), Tables 73 and 83; and (1973b), Tables 85 and 121.

[a] All data have been corrected to correspond to 1970 definitions of the geographic area covered by the various SMSAs.

[b] "A" refers to above average and "B" to below average. The first letter relates to the region and the second to the nation.

sample SMSA in the Northeast during the period, with a rate of employment growth of 26.3%.

At the other extreme, during the 1950s 7 of the 15 Northeastern sample SMSAs (Boston, Pittsburgh, Providence–Pawtucket–Warwick, Albany–Schenectady–Troy, Jersey City, Allentown–Bethlehem–Easton, and Springfield–Chicopee–Holyoke) not only failed to meet the national average rate of employment growth but also failed to meet the regional average rate. During the 1960s 6 Northeastern sample SMSAs (New York, Boston, Pittsburgh, Newark, Buffalo, and Jersey City) had rates of growth below both the regional and the national average rates.

Growth rates during the two decades are correlated, though perhaps not as highly as might be thought. The rank correlation coefficient between the regional ranking for the 1950–1960 and that for the 1960–1970 period is 0.54, which is significant at well over the 5% level. The rate of growth in Providence increased from 3.9 to 18.8%, which accounted for the fact that this SMSA enjoyed the greatest improvement in its rank within the Northeast, from 13 to 4. Buffalo, whose growth rate fell from 12.4 to 7.8%, suffered the largest decrease in rank position, from 6 to 12. New York dropped from 8 to 13 when its rate of growth declined from 11.7 to 5.6%.

Within the Northeast a particularly high correlation does not exist between 1970 rank size of the sample SMSAs and either the 1950–1960 or the 1960–1970 growth rates. The rank correlation coefficient between 1970 size and the 1950–1960 growth rate is 0.15, whereas that between 1970 size and the 1960–1970 growth rate is −0.30. Neither rank correlation coefficient is significant at 10%. Note, however, that the relative position of the larger SMSAs appears to have shifted in the direction of lower growth rates during the decade of the 1960s compared to the decade of the 1950s.

During the 1950–1960 period 6 of the 17 sample SMSAs in the North Central region (Chicago, Detroit, St. Louis, Cleveland, Toledo, and Youngstown–Warren) had rates of employment growth below the national average rate of growth, and only one SMSA (Youngstown–Warren) had a rate of growth below the regional average rate. During the 1960–1970 decade these 6 SMSAs were joined by 4 more (Milwaukee, Cincinnati, Akron, and Gary–Hammond–East Chicago) with rates below the national rate. Moreover, in addition to Youngstown–Warren, 5 other SMSAs (Chicago, Cleveland, Milwaukee, Cincinnati, and Gary–Hammond–East Chicago) slipped below the regional average rate of growth. Clearly, during the decade of the 1950s a major locus of growth in the North Central states was the relatively large metropolitan areas. While during the 1960s the sample SMSAs also tended to grow at somewhat faster rates than the region, their position had eroded somewhat compared to the previous decade.

Seven North Central SMSAs (Minneapolis–St. Paul, Kansas City, Indianapolis, Columbus, Dayton, Akron, and Gary–Hammond–East Chicago) had rates of employment growth above 20% during the 1950s; these rates were better than twice the regional average rate. Five of these SMSAs also maintained a rate of employment growth of over 20% during the 1960s. Akron and Gary–Hammond–East Chicago slipped from the group and were replaced by Omaha and Grand Rapids.

During the 1950s Columbus had the highest rate of growth among the North Central sample SMSAs (27.9%), and during the 1960s Minneapolis–St. Paul had the highest rate (33.8%) although Columbus also maintained a relatively high rate (32.0%) within the region. Between the two periods Detroit, which moved from 14th to 8th, and Toledo, which moved from 16th to 10th, experienced the largest improvements in their rank positions within the region, while Gary–Hammond–East Chicago, which fell from the 2nd to the 12th position, experienced the largest loss in its rank.

Among the North Central SMSAs growth rates were fairly highly correlated during the two periods. The rank correlation coefficient between the regional ranking for the 1950-1960 and that for the 1960-1970 period is 0.64. In spite of the fact that none of the four largest SMSAs in the North Central region ranked higher than 8th during either decade, a strong relationship did not exist between 1970 rank size and either the 1950-1960 or the 1960-1970 growth rate. The rank correlation coefficient between 1970 size and the 1950-1960 growth rate is −0.24, and that between 1970 size and the 1960-1970 growth rate is −0.14. Neither rank correlation coefficient is significant at 10%.

Only three Southern sample SMSAs (Louisville, Memphis, and Birmingham) failed to grow at a rate higher than the national rate during the 1950s, and only one of these (Birmingham) failed to grow at a rate in excess of the regional rate. During the 1960s three Southern SMSAs also failed to grow at the national rate, with New Orleans replacing Louisville on the previous list.

The employment growth experience of Birmingham especially stands out among the major metropolitan areas of the South. Among the 62 sample SMSAs Birmingham ranked 58th nationally during each decade. Its growth rate was far below the next lowest in the South. During the decade of the 1950s Louisville's growth rate, which was 13.8%, ranked just ahead of Birmingham's, which was 6.1%. During the 1960s, when Birmingham's rate of growth was 11.8%, New Orleans had a growth rate of 17.9%, which was just ahead of Birmingham among Southern SMSAs.

During the 1950s Fort Lauderdale–Hollywood experienced the highest rate of employment growth among the 62 sample SMSAs (264.1%), and during the 1960s it experienced the second highest rate of growth (96.7%). During the earlier decade Florida had 3 SMSAs (Fort Lauderdale–Hollywood–1st, Miami–7th, and Tampa–St. Petersburg–8th) among the nation's top 10, while during the later decade Texas had 3 (Houston–5th, Dallas–7th, and Fort Worth–9th) among the top 10. Hence, in the South the locus of growth spread toward the Southwest. Moreover, more rapid growth was common in the South as 12 of the 18 Southern sample SMSAs improved their position in the national ranking, while only four slipped.

For the South the correlation between the rank position of the various SMSAs during the two decades is somewhat higher than for the Northeast or the North Central regions. The rank correlation coefficient between the two rankings is 0.83. Furthermore, a positive but not highly significant relationship exists between the 1970 rank size of the various Southern SMSAs and their growth rates during the two periods. The rank correlation coefficient between size and growth rate during the 1950s is 0.23, while that between size and growth rate during the 1960s is 0.30.

Among the 12 Western sample SMSAs only Portland during the 1950s failed to grow at the national rate or better. During the 1950s three Western metropolitan areas (Anaheim–Santa Ana–Garden Grove, San Jose, and Phoenix) experienced rates of employment growth in excess of 100%. Only two SMSAs (San Francisco–Oakland and Portland) were below the regional average rate of employment growth during both decades.

A fairly high rank correlation (0.78) exists between employment growth in Western SMSAs during the 1950s and the 1960s. As with the other regions, a strong relationship does not exist in the West between 1970 rank size and growth rate. The corresponding rank correlation coefficient for the 1950s is 0.13, and that for the 1960s is 0.18.

Within the national system of large metropolitan areas a very high, but by no means a perfect, rank correlation exists between employment growth rates during the two decades. The rank correlation coefficient between the national rankings for employment growth rates over the two periods is 0.84. The SMSAs that slipped farthest in the rankings between the 1950s and 1960s were Gary–Hammond–East Chicago and Los Angeles–Long Beach, both of which fell 26 positions. Those that gained the most were Portland (26 positions), Louisville (22 positions), and Providence–Pawtucket–Warwick (20 positions).

For neither decade is the relationship between size and rate of employment growth statistically significant within the national system. The rank correlation coefficient between 1970 size and rate of employment growth over the decade of the 1950s is 0.06, while that between 1970 size and rate of growth over the decade of the 1960s is −0.04. Two different but related causes appear to be somewhat responsible for the lack of a strong relationship between size and rate of growth. The first is that the growth experience of the various metropolitan areas is more closely related to the growth experience of the region in which the metropolitan area is located than to size of the metropolitan area itself. The second is that metropolitan areas in the intermediate size class generally experienced somewhat higher rates of employment growth during both decades than did those in the higher and lower size classes. This observation is evident in Table 4.4.

Urban Nonagricultural Employment Growth, 1970–1975

Table 4.5, which is constructed from data in *Employment and Earnings,* allows the assessment of the performance of nonagricultural employment growth

TABLE 4.4
Average Rates of Metropolitan Employment Growth, by Size Class,
1950–1960 and 1960–1970 (in percentages)[a]

	Over 2,000,000	1,999,999 to 1,000,000	999,999 to 500,000
1950–1960			
Northeast	9.8(4)	17.2(3)	9.0(8)
North Central	12.3(4)	19.5(5)	19.7(8)
South	22.3(2)	49.1(6)	44.7(10)
West	35.8(2)	88.8(7)	76.2(3)
U.S.	17.0(12)	50.7(21)	31.2(27)
1960–1970			
Northeast	9.4	14.5	17.0
North Central	16.0	21.5	20.9
South	34.6	41.4	33.9
West	21.6	56.2	38.3
U.S.	17.8	37.8	26.1

Source: Calculated from data presented in Table 4.3.
[a] Numbers in parentheses indicate the number of SMSAs in each size class.

over the 1970–1975 period. These data differ from those reported in the census in two important ways. First, they cannot be corrected for changes over time in the geographic area included in the various SMSAs, which requires that changes be interpreted with caution. For example, the data show that during the 1970–1975 period nonagricultural employment grew more rapidly in the Salt Lake City SMSA than in any other. This observation, however, is due to the fact that in 1972 Ogden, Utah (Morgan, Tooele, and Weber Counties), was included in the Salt Lake City SMSA. Due to this type of data shortcoming, the behavior of employment over the 1970–1975 period is not considered in as much detail as the changes discussed previously.

Second, data from *Employment and Earnings* relate to the number of jobs rather than to the number of employed persons. As such, multiple job holders are counted multiple times, and areas in which commuting into or out of the SMSA is sizeable may appear to behave somewhat differently than they would if place of residence data were utilized. The Paterson–Clifton–Passaic SMSA, which in 1970 ranked 7th largest among sample Northeastern SMSAs on the basis of census employment data but 15th largest on the basis of nonagricultural employment data from *Employment and Earnings,* reflects this latter point.

The national rate of nonagricultural employment growth over the 1970–1975 period was 8.5%. None of the 15 Northeastern sample SMSAs grew at a rate this high, and only 4 of 17 North Central SMSAs (Minneapolis–St. Paul,

TABLE 4.5

Five-Year Rates of Nonagricultural Employment Growth in Major SMSAs, 1960–1975

	Number of jobs (in thousands)				Percentage of change		
	1960	1965	1970	1975	1960–1965	1965–1970	1970–1975
Northeast	15,609.8	16,693.1	18,654.0	18,571.5	6.9	11.7	−0.4
New York	3,810.1	3,894.9	4,119.9	3,665.7	2.2	5.8	−11.0
Philadelphia	1,502.9	1,592.7	1,794.9	1,777.8	6.0	12.7	−1.0
Boston	1,704.7	1,140.3	1,294.7	1,262.0	6.1	13.5	−2.5
Pittsburgh	776.3	795.4	873.0	880.2	2.5	9.8	0.8
Newark	696.0	770.6	855.1	845.3	10.7	11.0	−1.1
Paterson–	151.7	167.9	184.4	174.3	10.7	9.8	−5.5
Buffalo	441.7	455.5	497.5	481.2	3.1	9.2	−3.3
Providence–	298.8	323.7	354.0	354.5	8.3	9.4	0.1
Rochester	274.6	315.0	366.9	383.5	14.7	16.5	4.5
Albany–	242.5	263.4	297.9	305.3	8.6	13.1	2.5
Hartford	237.1	270.6	322.4	336.8	14.1	19.1	4.5
Syracuse	182.5	198.7	225.2	234.0	8.9	13.3	3.9
Jersey City	256.2	255.3	259.5	232.1	−0.4	1.6	−10.6
Allentown–	182.2	197.2	232.1	249.7	8.2	17.7	7.6
Springfield–	172.6	182.5	203.7	209.7	5.7	11.6	2.9
North Central	15,836.5	17,501.8	19,952.9	21,105.8	10.5	14.0	5.8
Chicago	2,471.2	2,683.5	2,971.7	2,985.7	8.6	10.7	0.5
Detroit	1,199.5	1,366.4	1,551.0	1,566.9	13.9	13.5	1.0
St. Louis	737.4	814.3	906.0	894.2	10.4	11.3	−1.3
Cleveland	700.3	766.1	855.1	849.4	9.4	11.6	−0.7
Minneapolis–	560.6	644.4	785.8	895.3	14.9	21.9	13.9
Milwaukee	457.8	500.1	568.6	594.5	9.2	13.7	4.6
Cincinnati	402.6	430.8	507.6	532.1	7.0	17.8	4.8
Kansas City	388.0	446.3	512.2	540.0	15.0	14.8	5.4
Indianapolis	330.4	368.7	419.1	448.3	11.6	13.7	7.0
Columbus	256.7	332.7	403.0	446.2	29.6	21.1	10.7
Dayton	247.7	282.1	331.2	318.9	13.9	17.4	−3.7
Toledo	159.6	224.6	262.3	273.2	40.7	16.8	4.2
Akron	176.0	210.2	244.5	246.3	19.4	16.3	0.7
Gary–	NA	204.8	223.3	233.1	NA	9.0	4.5
Omaha	163.0	176.2	208.9	232.0	8.1	18.6	11.1
Grand Rapids	144.9	164.5	192.0	210.3	13.5	16.7	9.5
Youngstown–	164.9	172.3	195.6	201.1	4.5	13.5	2.8
South	14,242.8	16,725.3	20,377.3	23,449.0	17.4	21.8	15.1
Washington, D.C.	744.3	933.5	1,182.6	1,329.8	25.4	26.7	12.4
Baltimore	629.3	692.4	806.0	843.9	10.0	16.4	4.7
Houston	464.7	567.7	769.1	996.6	22.2	35.5	29.6
Dallas							
Atlanta	370.0	477.0	651.9	733.7	28.9	36.7	12.5
Miami	307.6	363.6	503.2	578.4	18.2	38.4	14.9
New Orleans	287.8	343.2	373.8	419.3	19.2	8.9	12.2

(cont'd.)

TABLE 4.5 (cont'd.)

	Number of jobs (in thousands)				Percentage of change		
	1960	1965	1970	1975	1960–1965	1965–1970	1970–1975
Tampa–	198.2	233.6	318.1	412.8	17.9	36.2	29.8
San Antonio	NA	205.1	269.9	310.8	NA	31.6	15.2
Louisville	242.0	270.7	335.1	348.7	11.9	23.8	4.1
Memphis	190.7	223.9	278.6	317.8	17.4	24.4	14.1
Fort Worth							
Birmingham	200.1	214.3	263.4	307.6	7.1	22.9	16.8
Norfolk–	150.3	169.4	212.9	241.4	12.7	25.7	13.4
Oklahoma City	175.6	210.3	269.1	310.6	19.8	28.0	15.4
Fort Lauderdale–	NA	106.3	176.5	233.7	NA	66.0	32.4
Nashville–	141.4	187.8	255.1	291.6	32.8	35.8	14.3
Richmond	166.5	198.9	241.5	271.9	19.5	21.4	12.6
West	8,090.7	9,477.4	11,399.6	13,252.4	17.1	20.3	16.4
Los Angeles–	2,189.3	2,480.4	2,863.9	3,046.9	13.3	15.5	6.4
San Francisco–	958.2	1,083.4	1,254.7	1,322.8	13.1	15.8	5.4
Seattle–	369.0	416.9	516.2	568.5	13.0	23.8	10.1
Anaheim–	165.8	293.1	418.9	571.7	76.8	42.9	36.5
San Diego	260.1	272.1	387.1	469.4	4.6	42.3	21.3
Denver	330.9	376.0	483.0	603.9	13.6	28.5	25.0
San Bernardino–	188.9	244.2	293.7	334.4	29.3	20.3	13.9
San Jose	191.8	274.6	377.8	469.1	43.2	37.6	24.2
Portland	266.1	313.1	380.6	437.3	17.7	21.6	14.9
Phoenix	181.7	233.5	327.2	427.4	28.5	40.1	31.2
Sacramento	194.1	230.3	263.4	313.0	18.7	14.4	18.8
Salt Lake City	139.8	163.6	190.8	319.3	17.0	16.6	67.3

Source: U.S. Department of Labor, Bureau of Labor Statistics (1977), *Employment and Earnings, States and Areas, 1937–1957.*

Columbus, Omaha, and Grand Rapids) grew at a higher rate. On the contrary, just 2 of 18 Southern SMSAs (Baltimore and Louisville) failed to grow at a rate higher than the national rate, and likewise only 2 Western SMSAs (Los Angeles–Long Beach and San Francisco–Oakland) failed to grow at a rate better than 8.5%. Among the nation's major metropolitan areas, at least, the locus of urban employment growth clearly remained in the South and the West during the early 1970s.

We previously saw that the period from roughly 1965 to 1970 was one of exceptional employment growth at the national level. This observation is also evident in Table 4.5. Only 2 of the 62 SMSAs (Sacramento and Salt Lake City) experienced higher rates of employment growth between 1970 and 1975 than between 1965 and 1970, and, as we have seen, one of these was due primarily to the changed geographic area covered by the SMSA.

In Chapters 2 and 3 the point was made that the recessionary conditions of the early 1970s had particularly severe consequences in the Northeast, especially in light of the relative prosperity experienced there during the late 1960s. In Table 4.5 these consequences are evident at the level of the individual metropolitan area. Between 1965 and 1970 every sample Northeastern SMSA enjoyed positive nonagricultural employment growth. Other than Jersey City, whose rate of growth was 1.6%, the range was from 5.8% (New York) to 19.1% (Hartford). Like the majority of the nation's major metropolitan areas, every sample Northeastern SMSA experienced a sizeable decrease in its rate of growth during the period from 1970 to 1975. New York suffered a 16.8 percentage point drop in its rate of growth, which was the largest among Northeastern SMSAs. Perhaps the most distinguishing feature of the early 1970s was that seven Northeastern SMSAs (New York, Philadelphia, Boston, Newark, Paterson–Clifton–Passaic, Buffalo, and Jersey City) experienced absolute employment decreases. In the remainder of the country only three sample SMSAs (St. Louis, Cleveland, and Dayton) had similar decreases in employment between 1970 and 1975.

One of the most striking features of Table 4.5 is the extent of the employment decline in the New York SMSA during the 1970–1975 period. Nonagricultural employment in the Northeast declined by 82,500 jobs, or by 0.4%, while nonagricultural employment in the New York SMSA declined by 454,200 jobs, or by 11.0%. Excluding New York, the remainder of the Northeast experienced a job increase of 2.6%.

Growth of Urban Manufacturing Employment, 1950–1970

Both because the manufacturing sector accounts for such a high fraction of urban employment and because much urban nonmanufacturing employment is tied to manufacturing employment, the urban manufacturing sector requires separate attention. Table 4.6 reports rates of growth of manufacturing employment in each of the sample SMSAs for both the 1950–1960 and 1960–1970 periods. The type of information presented in this table is identical to that in Table 4.3, except that rather than relating to total employment it relates to manufacturing employment.

The manufacturing employment growth experience of the nation's metropolitan areas is highly varied. For example, among the sample SMSAs Anaheim–Santa Ana–Garden Grove had the highest rate of growth (121.8%) over the decade of the 1960s, while Sacramento had the lowest rate of growth (−22.6%). Even within the Northeast the rates vary over a considerable range. During the 1960s Rochester experienced the highest rate of growth (20.9%), whereas New York had the lowest (−15.0%).

The ranking of SMSAs by rate of total employment growth and by rate of

TABLE 4.6
Rates of Manufacturing Employment Growth and Regional and National Rankings of SMSAs by Rates of Manufacturing Employment Growth, 1950–1960 and 1960–1970

	1950–1960				1960–1970			
	Growth rate (%)	Relative performance[a]	Rank region	Rank U.S.	Growth rate (%)	Relative performance[a]	Rank region	Rank U.S.
Northeast	7.8				−6.0			
New York	6.0	BB	11	55	−15.0	BB	15	61
Philadelphia	11.8	AB	6	47	−0.8	AB	7	52
Boston	10.5	AB	8	50	−13.0	BB	14	60
Pittsburgh	0.5	BB	12	57	−9.5	BB	12	58
Newark	27.8	AA	3	27	3.5	AB	6	45
Paterson–	59.5	AA	1	15	6.7	AB	3	35
Buffalo	6.1	BB	10	54	−5.1	AB	9	55
Providence–	−6.6	BB	14	61	6.6	AB	4	37
Rochester	14.3	AB	5	43	20.9	AA	1	22
Albany–	−9.6	BB	15	62	−10.1	BB	13	59
Hartford	31.8	AA	2	24	6.0	AB	5	41
Syracuse	11.7	AB	7	48	−6.4	BB	10	56
Jersey City	14.6	AB	4	40	−7.2	BB	11	57
Allentown–	6.4	BB	9	54	9.3	AA	2	33
Springfield–	−3.6	BB	13	59	−1.3	AB	8	54
North Central	13.9				7.6			
Chicago	6.5	BB	14	52	5.8	BB	12	42
Detroit	−3.3	BB	16	58	9.9	AA	7	31
St. Louis	8.0	BB	13	51	0.7	BB	15	49
Cleveland	12.3	BB	11	46	2.1	BB	14	47
Minneapolis–	25.4	AA	5	31	26.8	AA	1	16
Milwaukee	13.2	BB	9	44	−0.0	BB	17	51
Cincinnati	18.8	AB	8	38	9.2	AA	9	34
Kansas City	25.6	AA	4	29	14.4	AA	4	28
Indianapolis	23.3	AA	6	32	13.3	AA	5	29
Columbus	36.9	AA	1	20	18.7	AA	3	23
Dayton	30.2	AA	3	25	23.8	AA	2	21
Toledo	4.4	BB	15	56	11.6	AA	6	30
Akron	13.2	BB	10	45	6.5	BB	11	38
Gary–	19.5	AB	7	37	5.0	BB	13	44
Omaha	32.1	AA	2	23	0.6	BB	16	50
Grand Rapids	11.7	BB	12	49	9.6	AA	8	32
Youngstown–	−6.3	BB	17	60	6.6	BB	10	36
South	31.2				26.2			
Washington, D.C.	32.5	AA	9	22	30.6	AA	11	15
Baltimore	19.6	BB	15	36	3.0	BB	17	46
Houston	39.7	AA	8	19	43.8	AA	6	10
Dallas	74.2	AA	4	13	58.2	AA	5	8
Atlanta	49.4	AA	5	16	33.3	AA	10	14

(cont'd.)

TABLE 4.6 (cont'd.)

	1950–1960				1960–1970			
	Growth rate (%)	Relative performance[a]	Rank region	Rank U.S.	Growth rate (%)	Relative performance[a]	Rank region	Rank U.S.
Miami	165.7	AA	2	7	83.7	AA	2	5
New Orleans	20.7	BA	12	33	5.3	BB	16	43
Tampa–	85.5	AA	3	9	38.5	AA	7	11
San Antonio	25.5	BA	11	30	38.3	AA	8	12
Louisville	15.7	BB	16	39	35.8	AA	9	13
Memphis	20.5	BA	13	34	25.0	BA	12	18
Fort Worth	45.7	AA	6	17	73.1	AA	3	6
Birmingham	14.5	BB	17	41	1.3	BB	18	48
Norfolk–	14.4	BB	18	42	16.9	BA	14	26
Oklahoma City	43.9	AA	7	18	62.0	AA	4	7
Ft. Lauderdale–	508.6	AA	1	1	118.7	AA	1	2
Nashville–	29.6	BA	10	26	24.8	BA	13	19
Richmond	20.4	BA	14	35	15.1	BA	15	27
West	77.1				11.0			
Los Angeles–	77.9	AA	8	11	6.4	BB	10	40
San Francisco–	32.8	BA	11	21	– 1.1	BB	11	53
Seattle–	72.6	BA	10	14	17.3	AA	8	25
Anaheim–	473.2	AA	1	2	121.8	AA	1	1
San Diego	202.1	AA	4	5	6.5	BB	9	39
Denver	80.6	AA	7	10	26.5	AA	5	17
San Bernardino–	136.6	AA	6	8	50.4	AA	4	9
San Jose	258.3	AA	3	4	87.3	AA	3	4
Portland	25.9	BA	12	28	24.1	AA	6	20
Phoenix	256.4	AA	2	3	104.4	AA	2	3
Sacramento	179.7	AA	5	6	–22.6	BB	12	62
Salt Lake City	77.7	AA	9	12	18.1	AA	7	24

Sources: U.S. Bureau of the Census (1952), tables 35 and 43; (1963a), tables 75 and 85; and (1973b), tables 87 and 123.

[a] "A" refers to above average and "B" to below average. The first letter relates to the region and the second to the nation.

manufacturing employment growth is highly correlated. The rank correlation coefficient between the two variables for the 1960–1970 period is 0.84. A number of factors are responsible for this high correlation, and the one that is perhaps most important is definitional—that is, manufacturing employment constitutes a sizeable fraction of total urban employment and is therefore an important component of the total growth experience. Moreover, to the extent that manufacturing employment contributes to the urban "base," total employment presumably grows by some multiple of the growth of manufacturing employment. Many of the same factors that attract nonmanufacturing firms to specific urban areas, or encourage their growth in such areas, may also attract manufacturing firms. Among these factors are growth of regional markets, availability of labor, and regional amenities, as well as others such as discussed in the section entitled "The Behavior of Regional Employment and Population Changes, 1947–1977: The Historical Record" in Chapter 3.

A few exceptions to the high rank correlation between growth of total employment and growth of manufacturing employment are apparent, and the reasons for these deviations are fairly obvious. For example, while during the 1960–1970 period Sacramento ranked 62nd in its rate of manufacturing employment growth, it ranked 22nd in its rate of total employment growth. During the same period San Diego and San Francisco–Oakland ranked 39th and 53rd, respectively, in manufacturing but 13th and 32nd in total employment growth.

As a consequence of persistently lower rates of manufacturing employment growth than rates of total employment growth in the sample SMSAs, the typical metropolitan area has undergone a decrease in the fraction of its employment accounted for by manufacturing. Table 4.7 reports the share of total SMSA employment in manufacturing in 1950, 1960, and 1970. Between 1950 and 1970 only three Northeastern SMSAs (Newark, Paterson–Clifton–Passaic, and Jersey City) experienced an increase in the fraction of their employment in manufacturing, and two North Central SMSAs (Minneapolis–St. Paul and Dayton) experienced similar increases. Even in the South eight SMSAs had a decrease in their share of manufacturing employment, and in those SMSAs where the share increased, the increase was typically modest. In the West only the San Francisco–Oakland SMSA had a decrease in its share of manufacturing employment between 1950 and 1970, but between 1960 and 1970 all but three Western SMSAs (San Bernardino–Riverside–Ontario, San Jose, and Phoenix) experienced such decreases.

Clearly, as has frequently been noted by others, the urban manufacturing employment base is gradually being eroded and replaced by other sources of employment, principally by service employment. Because the advantages of urban locations are not what they once were for manufacturing firms, public policy directed at encouraging growth of urban manufacturing employment should be subjected to careful scrutiny.

Metropolitan Unemployment Rates, 1950–1975

Table 4.8 presents data on metropolitan unemployment rates in 1950, 1960, 1970, and 1975. Data for 1950, 1960, and 1970 are from the census and have been corrected to correspond to 1970 SMSA boundaries. Alternative unemployment rates have also been presented for 1970 and comparable rates are reported for 1975. These alternative rates for 1970, as well as the rates for 1975, are from various state employment security agencies that cooperate with the U.S. Depart-

TABLE 4.7
Manufacturing Employment as a Percentage of Total Employment 1950, 1960, and 1970

	1950	1960	1970		1950	1960	1970
United States	25.9	27.1	25.9	Grand Rapids	40.0	37.5	33.2
Northeast	34.3	33.4	29.5	Youngstown–	48.8	45.4	42.7
New York	27.1	25.8	20.7	South	18.4	21.4	23.1
Philadelphia	36.6	35.8	30.9	Washington, D.C.	7.2	7.5	6.7
Boston	28.7	28.8	22.4	Baltimore	29.2	30.1	25.2
Pittsburgh	37.9	37.0	31.9	Houston	22.1	21.7	20.4
Newark	31.2	35.6	32.7	Dallas	17.5	21.9	23.4
Paterson–	30.5	38.3	33.2	Atlanta	20.0	22.1	19.7
Buffalo	40.4	38.1	33.6	Miami	7.8	11.6	14.8
Providence–	46.8	42.1	37.7	New Orleans	15.7	15.8	14.1
Rochester	41.0	40.9	39.2	Tampa–	14.7	15.4	15.6
Albany–	33.5	29.0	22.4	San Antonio	11.3	11.1	11.9
Hartford	32.8	34.5	29.1	Louisville	30.8	31.3	33.6
Syracuse	35.2	34.0	27.5	Memphis	18.7	19.6	20.6
Jersey City	30.7	37.9	34.7	Fort Worth	24.4	26.1	30.9
Allentown–	49.4	48.5	45.2	Birmingham	25.1	27.1	24.5
Springfield–	41.6	40.0	34.2	Norfolk–	16.5	15.9	14.9
				Oklahoma City	10.2	11.4	13.8
North Central	29.0	30.2	29.7	Fort Lauderdale–	6.4	10.7	11.9
Chicago	36.1	34.2	31.6	Nashville–	21.8	23.7	23.6
Detroit	46.9	40.7	37.5	Richmond	22.6	14.3	21.1
St. Louis	33.9	33.1	28.7	West	17.5	21.2	19.2
Cleveland	40.3	39.4	35.5	Los Angeles–	25.3	30.7	27.3
Minneapolis–	6.8	7.3	24.7	San Francisco–	19.6	21.0	16.8
Milwaukee	41.7	40.6	35.2	Seattle–	21.2	27.8	24.4
Cincinnati	33.2	34.0	32.6	Anaheim–	16.9	29.4	28.4
Kansas City	23.5	24.5	22.7	San Diego	14.2	23.2	17.7
Indianapolis	31.2	31.3	29.3	Denver	16.0	19.1	17.1
Columbus	24.4	26.1	23.5	San Bernardino–	13.0	16.7	17.8
Dayton	36.4	37.7	37.4	San Jose	18.7	30.0	30.6
Toledo	37.9	35.8	33.8	Portland	19.9	22.0	21.1
Akron	47.1	43.9	39.5	Phoenix	9.2	15.6	20.4
Gary–	51.8	48.5	30.0	Sacramento	9.4	15.5	9.4
Omaha	18.3	20.5	17.1	Salt Lake City	13.6	16.7	15.0

Sources: See Tables 4.3 and 4.6.

ment of Labor and are not available for every sample SMSA. Rates for 1970 from this source are presumably not corrected for changes in SMSA boundaries that occurred between 1970 and 1975.

Unemployment rates prevailing in the major metropolitan areas of the West have typically averaged somewhat higher than those prevailing in the major urban centers of other regions. For example, the mean unemployment rate among

TABLE 4.8
Unemployment Rates in Major Metropolitan Areas, 1950, 1960, 1970, and 1975

	Census			Employment security	
	1950[a]	1960[a]	1970	1970	1975
Northeast					
New York	6.8	4.9	3.8	4.4	10.2
Philadelphia	5.8	5.2	3.6	4.5	8.5
Boston	6.0	3.9	3.5	3.9	10.6
Pittsburgh	6.5	7.6	4.3	5.2	7.5
Newark	5.5	4.7	3.6	4.1	10.1
Paterson–	4.1	4.4	3.6	5.5	12.8
Buffalo	6.0	7.1	4.8	4.7	11.9
Providence–	7.7	5.5	3.9	5.3	10.9
Rochester	5.4	5.4	3.6	NA	7.8
Albany–	4.7	5.9	3.2	NA	7.4
Hartford	5.3	4.1	2.8	4.5	7.6
Syracuse	5.6	5.4	4.5	NA	9.4
Jersey City	7.4	5.9	4.6	6.0	13.2
Allentown–	4.3	4.3	2.3	2.7	7.5
Springfield–	4.7	5.5	4.5	5.6	11.2
North Central					
Chicago	4.4	4.5	3.4	4.0	7.2
Detroit	6.5	8.3	5.6	7.0	13.1
St. Louis	4.1	4.7	4.8	4.6	7.9
Cleveland	4.6	5.6	3.5	4.6	7.8
Minneapolis–	3.7	4.0	3.2	4.2	6.8
Milwaukee	2.7	4.0	3.5	4.4	7.4
Cincinnati	4.8	4.9	3.3	4.6	8.7
Kansas City	3.3	4.5	3.3	3.8	7.7
Indianapolis	3.3	3.9	3.9	5.5	6.4
Columbus	5.1	4.8	3.3	3.3	7.2
Dayton	3.1	4.6	3.8	3.6	8.2
Toledo	6.4	6.9	4.1	4.6	9.8
Akron	6.6	5.6	4.3	4.0	9.3
Gary–	4.2	3.5	4.0	4.0	7.9
Omaha	2.7	3.1	2.8	3.3	5.5
Grand Rapids	3.6	5.3	5.7	6.6	10.1
Youngstown–	5.2	6.9	5.5	4.9	11.2
South					
Washington, D.C.	3.2	2.9	2.4	3.1	5.5
Baltimore	5.2	5.6	3.5	4.2	8.1
Houston	3.7	4.4	3.0	4.0	5.2
Dallas	3.1	3.3	2.9	3.6[c]	5.3[b]
Atlanta	3.1	3.6	3.1	3.4	9.0
Miami	6.3	6.1	3.7	4.1	11.3
New Orleans	6.3	5.7	5.1	6.0	7.5

(cont'd.)

TABLE 4.8 (cont'd.)

	Census			Employment security	
	1950[a]	1960[a]	1970	1970	1975
Tampa–	5.3	5.3	4.2	NA	10.3
San Antonio	4.1	5.2	4.1	5.4	7.4
Louisville	4.3	6.0	4.0	4.1	7.6
Memphis	5.0	4.8	4.9	4.0	7.4
Fort Worth	2.9	4.0	3.5	NA	NA
Birmingham	5.8	6.7	4.2	4.1	6.7
Norfolk–	6.6	5.4	3.6	3.4	6.4
Oklahoma City	3.1	3.2	3.2	3.8	7.3
Fort Lauderdale–	6.9	5.8	3.4	NA	NA
Nashville–	3.1	3.8	3.3	2.9	6.5
Richmond	4.4	3.3	2.1	2.0	4.2
West					
Los Angeles–	7.9	6.1	6.2	7.4	9.7
San Francisco–	8.4	6.0	5.7	6.9	11.0
Seattle–	8.0	6.1	8.2	9.7	9.1
Anaheim–	7.1	5.0	5.4	6.6	7.7
San Diego	7.7	6.9	6.4	8.8	11.6
Denver	4.1	3.5	3.7	4.8	7.3
San Bernardino–	7.9	7.0	5.9	7.3	9.8
San Jose	9.4	5.7	5.8	6.3	9.2
Portland	8.0	5.5	6.2	5.5	NA
Phoenix	8.8	4.5	4.0	4.3	13.1
Sacramento	8.0	6.6	7.2	6.6	8.9
Salt Lake City	5.2	3.5	4.6	6.2	6.6[c]

Sources: U.S. Bureau of the Census (1952), Table 35; (1963a), Table 83; (1973b), Table 121; and U.S. Department of Labor (1978). *1978 Employment and Training Report of the President,* Table D-8.
[a]Corrected to correspond to 1970 SMSA boundaries.
[b]Includes both Dallas and Forth Worth, which were combined into a single SMSA.
[c]Includes both Salt Lake City and Ogden, which were combined into a single SMSA.

sample SMSAs in the West was 7.5% in 1950, compared to 5.7% in the Northeast, 4.6% in the South, and 4.4% in the North Central region. In 1970 the corresponding mean unemployment rates among sample SMSAs in the various regions were 5.8% in the West, 4.0% in the North Central region, 3.8% in the Northeast, and 3.6% in the South. These rates have all been derived from census data.

The pattern in 1975 was, however, somewhat different. The mean unemployment rate among Northeastern sample SMSAs was considerably higher than

the corresponding rates for other regions. In the Northeast the mean rate was
10.2%, compared to 9.5% in the West, 8.4% in the North Central region, and
7.0% in the South.[4] The position of the major metropolitan areas of the Northeast
is consistent with the previous observation that the Northeast as a region was
particularly affected by the recessionary conditions of 1974 and 1975. Whereas
the West had high unemployment rates in 1970, the Northeast experienced relatively sizeable increases in such rates between 1970 and 1975. Unemployment
rates among Western SMSAs remained relatively high in 1975, though not as
high as those prevailing in Northeastern metropolitan areas.

A number of metropolitan areas have had unemployment rates that have
remained persistently above the regional average rates for major metropolitan
areas. The following SMSAs had an unemployment rate above the regional
average rate in 1950, 1960, 1970, and 1975:

Northeast	North Central	South	West
1. Buffalo	1. Detroit	1. Miami	1. Los Angeles–
2. Providence–	2. Toledo	2. New Orleans	2. San Diego
3. Jersey City	3. Akron	3. Tampa–	3. San Bernardino–
	4. Youngstown–	4. Memphis	

Growth of Income and Earnings

Table 4.9 reports rates of growth of family median income in the various
SMSAs over both the 1950–1960 and the 1960–1970 periods. Again, all data
have been corrected to reflect 1970 SMSA boundaries. The procedure that was
used to calculate 1950 and 1960 family median income for those SMSAs whose
boundaries changed between 1950 and 1970 is explained in the section entitled
"The Data" in Chapter 5.[5] Each SMSA has again been ranked both within its
region and within the entire national sample of SMSAs.

Recall that, within the national system of sample SMSAs, the rank correlation coefficient between the rate of employment growth during the 1950s and the
rate during the 1960s is positive and quite high (0.84). Hence, SMSAs whose
employment grew relatively rapidly during one decade tended to experience
relatively rapid rates of employment growth during the next. No such tendency is
evident regarding rates of growth of family median income. At the national level
a significant (at 5%) negative rank correlation (-0.22) exists between growth of
family median income during the 1950s and growth during the 1960s.

A number of SMSAs either rose or fell appreciably in the national ranking.

[4]Where mean rates have been calculated for 1970 and 1975 from employment security data, the
means are for those SMSAs for which data exist for both years.

[5]Census income data actually refer to 1949, 1959, and 1969 and relate to persons residing in
the area in 1950, 1960, and 1970, respectively.

TABLE 4.9
Rates of Growth of Family Income and Regional and National Rankings of SMSAs by Rates of Income Growth, 1950-1960 and 1960-1970

	1950-1960[a]				1960-1970[a]			
	Growth rate (%)	Relative performance[b]	Rank region	Rank U.S.	Growth rate (%)	Relative performance[b]	Rank region	Rank U.S.
Northeast	84.0				68.9			
New York	79.9	BB	10	36	66.0	BB	10	42
Philadelphia	85.6	AA	5	23	67.6	BB	8	35
Boston	90.2	AA	3	13	71.2	AA	5	17
Pittsburgh	78.1	BB	12	44	63.5	BB	12	51
Newark	82.5	BB	8	31	65.7	BB	11	44
Paterson–	83.8	BB	7	29	˙70.0	AA	7	24
Buffalo	84.7	AA	6	25	61.6	BB	14	56
Providence–	78.7	BB	11	43	75.2	AA	1	9
Rochester	92.0	AA	2	9	71.6	AA	4	16
Albany–	73.5	BB	15	55	74.8	AA	2	10
Hartford	87.7	AA	4	15	70.9	AA	6	20
Syracuse	94.0	AA	1	6	63.2	BB	13	53
Jersey City	76.6	BB	13	48	57.7	BB	15	58
Allentown–	74.0	BB	14	53	74.0	AA	3	11
Springfield–	80.8	BB	9	35	66.3	BB	9	41
North Central	79.8				71.7			
Chicago	93.0	AA	1	7	62.5	BB	17	55
Detroit	71.7	BB	15	58	77.5	AA	1	7
St. Louis	85.9	AA	5	22	68.2	BB	7	32
Cleveland	79.1	BB	11	41	64.3	BB	13	49
Minneapolis–	81.9	AB	7	32	70.8	BA	3	21
Milwaukee	79.2	BB	10	39	62.6	BB	16	54
Cincinnati	90.7	AA	3	12	63.4	BB	15	52
Kansas City	85.9	AA	4	21	68.8	BB	6	29
Indianapolis	81.8	AB	8	33	67.1	BB	10	38
Columbus	71.7	BB	14	57	65.7	BB	11	43
Dayton	80.8	AB	9	34	69.6	BA	5	26
Toledo	65.9	BB	17	61	71.0	BA	2	18
Akron	91.5	AA	2	10	65.7	BB	12	45
Gary–	69.6	BB	16	60	68.2	BB	8	33
Omaha	84.4	AA	6	27	64.0	BB	14	50
Grand Rapids	76.1	BB	13	51	70.3	BA	4	23
Youngstown–	79.1	BB	12	42	67.3	BB	9	36
South	98.6				80.9			
Washington, D.C.	77.8	BB	11	45	72.6	BA	10	14
Baltimore	86.3	BA	5	19	71.0	BA	12	19
Houston	73.8	BB	16	54	73.0	BA	8	12
Dallas	84.2	BB	8	28	77.7	BA	6	6
Atlanta	99.5	AA	1	4	85.7	AA	2	2

(cont'd.)

TABLE 4.9 (cont'd.)

	1950–1960[a]				1960–1970[a]			
	Growth rate (%)	Relative performance[b]	Rank region	Rank U.S.	Growth rate (%)	Relative performance[b]	Rank region	Rank U.S.
Miami	70.9	BB	17	59	72.9	BA	9	13
New Orleans	86.3	BA	4	18	68.6	BB	15	30
Tampa–	86.7	BA	3	17	75.6	BA	7	8
San Antonio	75.0	BB	15	52	69.2	BB	14	28
Louisville	79.7	BB	9	37	70.4	BA	13	22
Memphis	77.5	BB	13	47	79.7	BA	5	5
Fort Worth	76.1	BB	14	50	79.8	BA	4	4
Birmingham	87.5	BA	2	16	68.5	BB	16	31
Norfolk–	65.0	BB	18	62	71.7	BA	11	15
Oklahoma City	77.5	BB	12	46	66.8	BB	18	40
Ft. Lauderdale–	86.3	BA	6	20	90.9	AA	1	1
Nashville–	84.7	BA	7	26	81.4	BA	3	3
Richmond	79.5	BB	10	38	67.0	BB	17	39
West	85.1				61.6			
Los Angeles–	92.0	AA	5	8	55.7	BB	10	60
San Francisco–	79.2	BB	10	40	65.3	AB	5	46
Seattle–	83.6	BB	9	30	69.3	AB	2	27
Anaheim–	117.5	AA	1	1	69.6	AA	1	25
San Diego	89.4	AA	7	14	54.8	BB	11	61
Denver	91.1	AA	6	11	64.5	AB	7	48
San Bernardino–	97.9	AA	4	5	57.4	BB	9	59
San Jose	99.6	AA	3	3	67.9	AB	3	34
Portland	72.9	BB	12	56	65.0	AB	6	47
Phoenix	103.9	AA	2	2	67.2	AB	4	37
Sacramento	85.0	BA	8	24	49.8	BB	12	62
Salt Lake City	76.2	BB	11	49	57.9	BB	8	57

Sources: U.S. Bureau of the Census (1952), Table 37; (1963a), Table 76; and (1973b), Table 89.

[a] All data have been corrected to correspond to 1970 definitions of the geographic area covered by the various SMSAs.

[b] "A" refers to above average and "B" refers to below average. The first letter relates to the region and the second, to the nation.

For example, in the Northeast Providence–Pawtucket–Warwick (up from 43rd to 9th), Albany–Schenectady–Troy (up from 55th to 19th), and Allentown–Bethlehem–Easton (up from 53rd to 11th) climbed appreciably, while Buffalo (down from 25th to 56th) and Syracuse (down from 6th to 53rd) fell considerably. In the North Central region Detroit rose from 58th to 7th and Toledo from 61st to 18th, whereas Chicago slipped from 7th to 55th, Cincinnati from 12th to

52nd, and Akron from 10th to 45th. In the South no SMSA declined substantially in the ranking, but several rose considerably, including Washington, D.C. (45th to 10th), Houston (54th to 12th), Miami (59th to 13th), Memphis (47th to 5th), Fort Worth (50th to 4th), and Norfolk-Portsmouth (62nd to 15th). On the contrary, with few exceptions, Western SMSAs slipped in the national rankings, with Los Angeles-Long Beach (8th to 60th), San Diego (14th to 61st), Denver (11th to 48th), San Bernardino-Riverside-Ontario (5th to 59th), San Jose (3rd to 34th), Phoenix (2nd to 37th), and Sacramento (24th to 62nd) particularly standing out.

During the 1960s a positive rank correlation of 0.33 exists between the rate of employment growth and the rate of income growth. This correlation is significant at better than 1%. However, although Western SMSAs generally had relatively high rates of employment growth, they had relatively low rates of income growth. For example, whereas Anaheim-Santa Ana-Garden Grove ranked first in the sample in terms of employment growth, it ranked 25th in terms of income growth. San Diego was 13th in employment growth and 61st in income growth; Denver had respective ranks of 11 and 48; SanBernardino-Riverside-Ontario ranked 12th and 59th; San Jose, 3rd and 34th; Phoenix, 4th and 37th; Sacramento, 22nd and 62nd; and Salt Lake City, 19th and 57th. In only one Western SMSA (Anaheim-Santa Ana-Garden Grove) was the rate of income growth during the 1960s above the national average rate.

Clearly, relatively rapid rates of employment growth do not guarantee relatively rapid rates of income growth. A number of factors are responsible for this situation. One of these is that the employment growth may be concentrated in industries or occupations with relatively low rates of earnings growth. Another is that the labor supply effects of in-migration and increased labor force participation may dominate the increase in labor demand that is occurring in the locality, with a consequent tendency for wages to rise less rapidly than they otherwise would.

The argument is frequently voiced that areas experiencing relatively rapid rates of employment growth are doing so because of relatively low prevailing local wage levels. With growth, it is argued, wage levels will rise relatively and counteract the initial advantages of the area. Although this is one possible consequence of growth, other consequences are also possible, and no reason appears to exist for the inevitable faster growth of (average) wages, earnings, or income in areas experiencing faster employment growth. In Chapter 7 it will be shown that whereas in-migration encourages higher rates of employment growth, in-migration does not appear to have encouraged correspondingly higher rates of (average) income growth during the 1960s, although some tendency did exist during the 1950s for in-migration to encourage income growth.

One observation that can be made from the information presented in Table 4.9 is that during the 1960s the locus of growth in the South was in the major

TABLE 4.10
Family Median Income, by Region, 1950, 1960, and 1970

	1950	1960	1970
United States	$3,073	$5,660	$ 9,590
Northeast	3,365	6,191	10,454
North Central	3,277	5,892	10,115
South	2,248	4,465	8,079
West	3,430	6,348	10,228

Source: U.S. Bureau of the Census (1953a), Table 37; (1964), Table 76; and (1973a), Table 89.

metropolitan areas. Only five Southern SMSAs failed to experience income growth greater than the national rate, but only two (Atlanta and Fort Lauderdale–Hollywood) had rates above the regional rate of 80.9%. This observation suggests that in the South income growth was most rapid in either nonmetropolitan areas or in smaller metropolitan areas than those examined in this study, or both. As shown in Table 4.10, although 1970 median family income in the South was low relative to the national level, relative income gains in the South were substantial between 1950 and 1970. Whereas in 1950 family median income in the South was 73.2% of the national family median income, in 1970 income in the South was 84.2% of the national level.

At the national level a mild negative relation exists between 1970 rank size and rate of income growth during the decade of the 1960s. The rank corelation coefficient of −0.20 is significant at 10% but fails significance at 5%.

Data on family median income in the various SMSAs are not available for 1975, and therefore an alternative source of data must be employed to examine rates of income or earnings growth over the 1970–1975 period. *Employment and Earnings* does report on an annual basis average weekly earnings in a number of nonagricultural pursuits. Table 4.11 indicates rates of growth of average weekly earnings in the manufacturing sector over the 1970–1975 period. For comparative purposes similar information is reported for the 1960–1965 and 1965–1970 periods. Data are not available for every sample SMSA, and thus for the 1970–1975 period rates of earnings growth are indicated for only 55 SMSAs.

The data of Table 4.11 suggest that no clear tendency exists for SMSAs in the South to experience more rapid rates of growth of manufacturing earnings than SMSAs located in other regions of the country. Three Southern SMSAs (Memphis–4th, Richmond–8th, and Louisville–10th) rank among the top 10 in terms of rate of 1970–1975 earnings growth, but a number of Southern SMSAs ranked among the lowest of the sample metropolitan areas. Four Northeastern

TABLE 4.11

Rates of Growth of Average Weekly Earnings in Manufacturing, 1960–1965, 1965–1970, and 1970–1975, and 1975 Average Weekly Earnings Levels in Manufacturing

	1960–1965 (%)	1965–1970 (%)	1970–1975 (%)	1975 average weekly earnings
Northeast				
New York	NA	NA	NA	$175.03
Philadelphia	19.7	25.6	40.9	198.00
Boston	20.8	30.3	40.0	193.16
Pittsburgh	16.9	19.0	52.3	232.06
Newark	17.7	22.6	50.5	208.37
Paterson–	21.3	19.1	41.0	191.24
Buffalo	21.5	21.0	48.5	236.40
Providence–	20.4	27.0	32.2	148.92
Rochester	24.1	31.2	44.3	228.98
Albany–	21.8	26.8	34.6	199.40
Hartford	21.4	26.1	44.0	216.84
Syracuse	19.8	24.1	43.3	204.93
Jersey City	17.2	30.4	32.8	191.00
Allentown–	19.9	22.0	50.6	190.46
Springfield–	16.9	24.9	36.6	175.82
North Central				
Chicago	19.6	24.6	NA	NA
Detroit	27.4	19.6	47.2	$266.66
St. Louis	19.6	27.8	42.5	215.56
Cleveland	22.2	18.0	68.3	227.29
Minneapolis–	20.6	25.6	43.9	214.38
Milwaukee	19.7	25.0	47.5	231.92
Cincinnati	20.7	23.2	43.2	210.94
Kansas City	19.4	13.2	61.5	211.33
Indianapolis	22.8	22.4	46.7	221.10
Columbus	15.1	24.2	45.8	206.98
Dayton	25.6	23.0	37.3	236.90
Toledo	21.2	22.1	45.8	233.69
Akron	25.7	18.9	41.7	236.49
Gary–	NA	NA	NA	NA
Omaha	18.7	23.4	46.8	202.11
Grand Rapids	16.7	25.1	38.3	206.28
Youngstown–	20.8	18.8	54.2	246.65
South				
Washington, D.C.	16.3	30.2	43.8	$212.52
Baltimore	18.9	24.4	45.8	206.33
Houston	17.5	26.3	45.7	225.78
Dallas	NA	NA	NA	NA
Atlanta	28.3	25.5	37.4	180.03
Miami	14.3	31.2	27.7	143.13

(cont'd.)

TABLE 4.11 (cont'd.)

	1960–1965 (%)	1965–1970 (%)	1970–1975 (%)	1975 average weekly earnings
New Orleans	24.6	23.9	42.4	$193.19
Tampa–	26.3	29.3	40.4	173.66
San Antonio	13.0	34.0	37.5	143.91
Louisville	24.1	20.5	47.6	214.58
Memphis	18.7	26.0	52.9	186.99
Fort Worth	NA	NA	NA	NA
Birmingham	19.3	13.5	NA	NA
Norfolk–	22.7	27.7	32.7	159.20
Oklahoma City	19.4	27.8	41.6	175.82
Fort Lauderdale–	NA	NA	22.6	156.35
Nashville–	18.0	26.4	37.1	160.63
Richmond	19.4	28.9	49.7	183.35
West				
Los Angeles–	18.1	19.1	33.8	$194.44
San Francisco–	20.7	25.3	46.3	241.96
Seattle–	22.9	34.0	39.4	233.05
Anaheim–	20.4	22.0	27.8	193.68
San Diego	19.3	25.0	18.9	195.97
Denver	19.4	24.4	NA	NA
San Bernardino–	13.7	22.3	40.2	208.15
San Jose	16.5	24.9	37.7	219.29
Portland	19.8	25.1	45.8	212.74
Phoenix	15.2	15.9	43.0	190.81
Sacramento	19.0	20.3	38.8	221.31
Salt Lake City	17.6	12.3	24.7	156.00

Source: U.S. Department of Labor, Bureau of Labor Statistics, (1977). *Employment and Earnings, States and Areas, 1937–1975.*

SMSAs (Pittsburgh–5th, Allentown–Bethlehem–Easton–6th, Newark–7th, and Buffalo–9th) were also included among the top 10 in earnings growth, in spite of the fact that Northeastern SMSAs in general experienced declines in manufacturing employment over the period.

Metropolitan Migration and Economic Growth

In recent years a number of studies have focused on the determinants of migration from or to metropolitan areas.[6] A few studies have also examined the

[6]See, for example, Fields (1979), Greenwood and Sweetland (1972), and Lowry (1966).

impacts that migration has had on employment and/or income growth in sending and receiving localities.[7] These latter studies have typically considered the interaction between the causes and effects of migration. Generally, the findings have been that metropolitan areas with high income levels are attractive to migrants, but those with high rates of income growth do not appear to be differentially attractive. Moreover, some tendency appears to exist for areas with high income levels to experience lower rates of out-migration. Localities with relatively high rates of employment growth are also quite attractive to migrants, but areas with high unemployment rates have frequently been shown to be no less attractive than other localities, *ceteris paribus*. These issues will be considered in greater analytical detail in subsequent chapters.

Not only is the number of migrants to or from a locality likely to influence the growth of that locality, but also the characteristics of the migrants are important. In the following discussion, three characteristics have been identified— employment status, age, and income. These characteristics are critical both for the future economic prospects of an area and for the immediate demands placed on the local public sector. Table 4.12 presents information on the migration of employed and of unemployed persons. Table 4.13 distinguishes two age groups, the 5 to 19 group and the group 65 and over. Migration of the younger group has important implications for the local public sector due to the demand for education to which it gives rise. Migration of the older group is expected to be induced by retirement and also has important consequences for both sending and receiving areas, as discussed in the section entitled "The Conceptual Underpinnings" in Chapter 3. Table 4.14 distinguishes two income classes, $0–5,999 and $15,000– and over, which are intended to reflect the migration of low-income and of high-income persons. Let us in turn consider the migratory behavior of each of these three groups.

MIGRANT EMPLOYMENT STATUS

The data of Table 4.3 indicate that during the 1950s only one sample SMSA (Jersey City) suffered an absolute decline in employed residents and that during the 1960s none did. The data of Table 4.5, which refer to growth of nonagricultural jobs by 5-year increments starting in 1960 and running to 1975, corroborate these findings for the 1960s but indicate the possible beginnings of a new pattern—one of absolute decline—in the 1970s. Whereas no sample SMSA experienced an absolute loss of jobs during the 1965–1970 period, 10 (7 in the Northeast and 3 in the North Central region) experienced such a loss during the 1970–1975 period.

Table 4.12 reports net in-migration rates of employed and of unemployed

---

[7]Included among these studies are Greenwood (1975a, 1976) and Muth (1971).

persons for the sample SMSAs over both the 1955–1960 and the 1965–1970 periods. Employment status is determined at the end of the period, and each rate is defined as the number of in-migrants minus the number of out-migrants divided by the end-of-period level of SMSA employment or unemployment.[8] Negative rates thus indicate SMSAs that experienced net out-migration of the respective group.

During the 1955–1960 period 18 of the 61 sample SMSAs on which an observation is available experienced net out-migration of employed persons. Of these 18, 9 were in the Northeast; 5 in the North Central region; and 4 in the South. Over the 1965–1970 period 20 of the 62 sample SMSAs had net out-migration of the employed. Of these 20, 8 were in the Northeast; 5 in the North Central region; 4 in the South; and 3 in the West. Clearly, then, the typical SMSA experiencing net out-migration of employed persons must have more than offset these losses through "natural increase," which in this context refers to an excess of employed labor force entrants over exits and/or the transition from unemployed to employed status.

We previously saw that, especially in the late 1960s, labor force entry was high due both to the aging of the war baby cohort and to increased labor force participation rates of women. As these sources of new labor force members become less important during the 1980s, SMSAs experiencing net out-migration are likely to also experience absolute declines in their numbers of employed residents. This tendency may be particularly likely due to the recently observed net migration from metropolitan to nonmetropolitan areas, which will be discussed in more detail at a later point in this study.

In spite of the fact that between 1950 and 1960 the number of employed residents increased in every Northeastern SMSA except Jersey City, nine Northeastern SMSAs had net out-migration of employed persons between 1955 and 1960. In six of these nine net in-migration of unemployed persons occurred. However, between 1965 and 1970, when eight Northeastern SMSAs were experiencing net out-migration of employed persons, only one of these (Springfield–Chicopee–Holyoke) had net in-migration of unemployed persons. Moreover, during the period from 1965 to 1970 the rate of net out-migration of unemployed persons exceeded the rate of net out-migration of employed persons in nine Northeastern SMSAs. Thus, while during the 1950s the *direct* effect of the migration mechanism was to decrease the number of employed and increase the number of unemployed in several Northeastern SMSAs, during the 1960s the direct effect of migration was to relieve unemployment more than in proportion to the reduction in employment.

In the North Central region 5 SMSAs experienced net out-migration of

---

[8] It should be recognized that if the migrants had not moved, their employment status and income may have been different than what was reported.

TABLE 4.12
Net In-Migration Rates of Civilian Labor Force Members, by Employment Status,
1955–1960 and 1965–1970 (in percentages)

	Employed migrants		Unemployed migrants	
	1955–1960	1965–1970	1955–1960	1965–1970
Northeast				
New York	−1.7	−2.9	−2.8	−6.1
Philadelphia	0.3	0.0	0.7	−1.5
Boston	−1.3	−0.2	−0.4	−1.6
Pittsburgh	−2.5	−2.6	1.5	−1.8
Newark	−0.4	−1.2	1.0	−5.5
Paterson–	4.0	0.7	3.0	−3.9
Buffalo	−1.0	−2.4	1.0	−1.7
Providence–	−2.2	2.1	0.9	0.1
Rochester	2.5	3.8	0.4	−1.6
Albany–	−2.5	1.3	−1.9	−3.5
Hartford	4.0	6.2	1.0	−3.0
Syracuse	1.7	−0.3	4.8	−0.9
Jersey City	−7.9	−5.7	0.8	−4.6
Allentown–	0.1	1.5	3.1	0.8
Springfield–	−0.8	−0.2	2.5	1.2
North Central				
Chicago	1.0	−0.6	−0.7	−8.1
Detroit	−3.0	0.3	−1.9	0.9
St. Louis	0.2	0.5	−0.4	−1.2
Cleveland	−0.4	−0.4	2.1	−2.7
Minneapolis–	6.4	5.9	9.2	−1.7
Milwaukee	2.9	−0.5	6.4	−2.7
Cincinnati	−0.3	0.5	3.5	−2.1
Kansas City	1.9	2.6	3.3	−2.4
Indianapolis	1.0	1.9	−0.6	−2.4
Columbus	4.7	2.0	3.5	−1.1
Dayton	2.0	1.9	5.4	−2.1
Toledo	−0.5	1.1	−4.0	0.3
Akron	1.6	0.6	3.8	1.4
Gary–	3.5	−1.4	−2.9	−4.0
Omaha	3.4	3.3	−2.2	1.6
Grand Rapids	0.4	2.1	4.1	3.8
Youngstown–	−0.0	−0.2	5.1	7.4
South				
Washington, D.C.	5.9	5.7	2.5	−3.1
Baltimore	0.5	0.3	0.5	−2.8
Houston	6.3	9.4	4.8	5.4
Dallas	7.3	9.9	4.9	3.7
Atlanta	5.6	9.0	7.5	6.0

(cont'd.)

TABLE 4.12 (cont'd.)

	Employed migrants		Unemployed migrants	
	1955–1960	1965–1970	1955–1960	1965–1970
Miami	10.6	2.8	24.8	2.7
New Orleans	1.3	−0.5	−0.8	−2.7
Tampa–	19.6	8.2	39.5	37.2
San Antonio	−4.6	−2.8	−5.2	−2.3
Louisville	−0.2	1.9	1.0	−0.4
Memphis	0.9	0.4	−2.9	−1.7
Fort Worth	4.7	9.7	8.1	9.0
Birmingham	−0.0	−1.1	0.4	−1.5
Norfolk–	−9.9	−10.5	−4.3	−11.8
Oklahoma	4.2	2.8	5.8	1.7
Fort Lauderdale–	37.7	20.8	65.0	20.7
Nashville–	4.6	0.8	4.4	−2.0
Richmond	5.0	4.9	0.9	0.8
West				
Los Angeles–	10.1	−0.2	16.6	0.1
San Francisco–	2.9	2.1	8.0	2.9
Seattle–	7.3	9.7	10.4	13.2
Anaheim–	NA	13.3	NA	11.6
San Diego	7.5	0.8	27.4	9.5
Denver	10.2	6.8	11.7	3.2
San Bernardino–	12.3	2.6	37.2	5.5
San Jose	28.8	9.6	27.7	6.4
Portland	2.4	6.7	11.1	8.4
Phoenix	27.5	7.8	19.6	7.1
Sacramento	16.5	−1.4	33.9	2.8
Salt Lake City	4.2	−0.4	10.5	−1.8

Source: U.S. Bureau of the Census (1963b), Tables 4 and 5; and (1973d), Tables 15 and 16.

employed persons during each period. However, during the 1965–1970 period 11 SMSAs had net out-migration of the unemployed. Chicago's net out-migration rate of the unemployed, which was 8.1%, was particularly high compared to other SMSAs in the North Central region, and nationally only 1 sample SMSA (Norfolk–Portsmouth) had a higher net out-migration rate of this group.

The typical SMSA in the South experienced net in-migration of employed persons during each period. Of the 18 Southern sample SMSAs, in each period only 4 had net out-migration of the employed. All but 4 of the Southern SMSAs also experienced net in-migration of the unemployed during the 1955–1960 period. Net in-migration rates were especially high in Miami (24.8%), Tampa–

St. Petersburg (39.5%), and Fort Lauderdale–Hollywood (65.0%), all of which are retirement centers. During the 1965–1970 period 9 Southern SMSAs had net out-migration of unemployed persons, but net in-migration rates of such persons remained high in Tampa–St. Petersburg (37.2%) and Fort Lauderdale–Hollywood (20.7%).

In the West the typical sample SMSA had net in-migration of both employed and unemployed persons during each period. However, during the period from 1965 to 1970 three SMSAs (Los Angeles–Long Beach, Sacramento, and Salt Lake City) did experience net out-migration of the employed.

AGE-SPECIFIC MIGRATION

The information presented in Table 4.13 is age-specific net in-migration rates for the sample SMSAs. Each rate is defined as the number of in-migrants minus the number of out-migrants divided by the end-of-period SMSA population of the age class. Migration has been measured over both the 1955–1960 and 1965–1970 periods.

Most SMSAs that experienced net in-migration of employed persons from 1965 to 1970 also experienced net in-migration of persons in the 5–19 age class. However, a number of SMSAs that had net in-migration of employed persons had net out-migration of persons of school age. From the perspective of the local public sector, the incremental effects of this latter condition are probably most desirable because the local tax base is rising while the demand for the largest locally financed public service (education) is falling due to migration. The following SMSAs fall into this category: Northeast—Philadelphia and Paterson–Clifton–Passaic; North Central—Detroit, St. Louis, Cincinnati, Kansas City, Indianapolis, Dayton, Akron, and Omaha; South—Baltimore, Louisville, and Oklahoma City; and West—San Francisco–Oakland. In the present context, perhaps the least desirable situation for a metropolitan area is to lose employed persons while gaining school–aged population, and three SMSAs fell into this catagory during the 1965–70 period—Syracuse, Springfield–Chicopee–Holyoke, and San Antonio.

During the period from 1955 to 1960 every Northeastern and North Central SMSA experienced net out-migration of persons 65 and over, and during the period from 1965 to 1970 every North Central SMSA also experienced such out-migration. However, during the later period four Northeastern SMSAs had a reversal of net retirement migration and actually experienced net in-migration of the elderly. These SMSAs are Providence–Pawtucket–Warwick, Hartford, Allentown–Bethlehem–Easton, and Springfield–Chicopee–Holyoke. In the Northeast the New York, Newark, and Jersey City SMSAs had especially high rates of net out-migration of older persons, whereas in the North Central region the Chicago, Detroit, and Gary–Hammond–East Chicago SMSAs had high net out-migration rates of these persons.

TABLE 4.13
Net In-Migration Rates of Persons Five to Nineteen Years Old and Sixty-Five and Over,
1955-1960 and 1965-1970 (in percentages)

	1955-1960		1965-1970	
	Persons 5-19	Persons 65+	Persons 5-19	Persons 65+
Northeast				
New York	-4.6	-4.2	-5.2	-5.9
Philadelphia	0.5	-1.5	-0.4	-1.5
Boston	-2.1	-2.9	-1.2	-3.4
Pittsburgh	-3.3	-2.9	-3.1	-2.8
Newark	-2.7	-4.7	-2.5	-6.4
Paterson-	0.4	-0.5	-2.6	-3.3
Buffalo	-2.7	-2.7	-3.4	-2.5
Providence-	-1.2	-1.5	2.2	0.7
Rochester	0.3	-3.0	1.8	-2.5
Albany-	-3.3	-1.6	1.5	-2.0
Hartford	0.5	-1.8	1.9	1.7
Syracuse	1.4	-2.4	1.0	-2.8
Jersey City	-12.7	-7.3	-9.1	-6.7
Allentown-	0.2	-0.2	1.5	0.4
Springfield-	4.9	-0.1	0.7	1.0
North Central				
Chicago	-0.8	-5.6	-3.2	-6.2
Detroit	-4.4	-4.6	-2.3	-5.6
St. Louis	-2.1	-2.0	-1.6	-1.7
Cleveland	-4.1	-5.2	-3.1	-4.0
Minneapolis-	2.7	-2.0	0.0	-3.8
Milwaukee	1.2	-1.9	-3.1	-2.4
Cincinnati	-3.0	-2.9	-1.1	-1.5
Kansas City	-2.6	-2.0	-2.0	-2.2
Indianapolis	-2.5	-3.7	-1.1	-1.7
Columbus	3.3	-2.1	1.3	-1.2
Dayton	-0.5	-1.1	-0.1	-1.7
Toledo	1.1	-1.4	1.2	-1.5
Akron	-0.9	-4.2	-0.5	-4.1
Gary-	1.9	-3.1	-3.0	-4.8
Omaha	2.9	-3.3	-2.7	-2.8
Grand Rapids	-2.0	-0.0	1.5	-0.9
Youngstown-	-0.8	-1.3	-0.6	-1.3
South				
Washington, D.C.	3.1	-0.8	2.7	-2.0
Baltimore	-0.3	-0.6	-0.8	-0.9
Houston	1.8	1.4	5.4	1.2
Dallas	4.4	1.4	5.7	0.7
Atlanta	4.9	-0.2	5.3	-1.0
Miami	9.7	16.1	0.7	9.9

(cont'd.)

TABLE 4.13 (cont'd.)

	1955–1960		1965–1970	
	Persons 5–19	Persons 65+	Persons 5–19	Persons 65+
New Orleans	−1.6	−0.7	−2.9	−0.9
Tampa–	20.7	27.7	8.7	15.7
San Antonio	4.3	1.5	3.4	0.3
Louisville	−2.6	−0.2	−1.2	−0.8
Memphis	7.5	1.0	1.5	0.4
Fort Worth	1.9	2.3	8.5	1.7
Birmingham	−3.9	−0.4	−3.1	−0.2
Norfolk–	3.8	−0.9	−2.3	0.5
Oklahoma City	16.6	0.5	−0.2	0.2
Fort Lauderdale–	36.3	48.5	16.6	26.4
Nashville–	3.8	0.9	1.5	0.0
Richmond	2.6	1.0	2.3	0.1
West				
Los Angeles–	7.2	2.6	−4.0	−3.4
San Francisco–	3.2	−0.7	−1.8	−2.5
Seattle–	4.5	−0.1	8.0	−1.4
Anaheim–	NA	NA	9.3	14.7
San Diego	23.4	11.2	10.6	10.1
Denver	10.8	2.4	4.0	0.8
San Bernardino–	15.0	14.1	5.1	9.5
San Jose	23.7	7.8	6.0	4.1
Portland	1.1	0.1	5.2	1.1
Phoenix	20.3	20.7	6.2	12.9
Sacramento	16.5	4.8	−0.1	1.2
Salt Lake City	1.5	1.0	−1.6	−0.5

Sources: U.S. Bureau of the Census (1963b), Tables 4 and 5; and (1973d), Tables 15 and 16.

Among the sample SMSAs retirement in-migration is largely concentrated in the states of Florida, California, and Arizona. During each period the Fort Lauderdale–Hollywood SMSA had a considerably higher rate of net in-migration of persons 65 and over than any other SMSA in the sample. The Tampa–St. Petersburg and Miami SMSAs were the only others in the South to experience high rates of net in-migration of the elderly. In the West Anaheim–Santa Ana–Garden Grove, San Diego, San Bernardino–Riverside–Ontario, and Phoenix had high rates.

MIGRANT INCOME

Income and wealth of the in- and out-migrants of any given locality contribute importantly to the manner in which the migration affects the local economy.

Income and wealth are crucial determinants of family consumption expenditures, which tend to be greater for higher income families. Since in large metropolitan areas a substantial fraction of family consumption expenditures is for locally produced goods and services, areas receiving relatively more high-income net in-migrants should experience relatively large positive impacts of migration on local employment and income.

Moreover, the mix of publicly provided services demanded by high-income families is different from that demanded by low-income families. Whereas high-income families may demand more of certain types of public services, like perhaps education or police and fire protection, low-income families may demand more of other types, such as welfare or health and hospital facilities. Furthermore, families with higher income and wealth are likely to provide greater tax revenues to the local government. Hence, migrant income characteristics have profound implications for both the private and the public sector impacts of population redistribution.

Because of generally rising incomes over time, the comparison of 1955–1960 and 1965–1970 migrants within given income classes makes little sense. Table 4.14 therefore presents data for the later period only. Two income classes are distinguished in this table, a "low-income" class of $0-5,999 and a "high-income" class of $15,000 and over, and net in-migrants in each class are reported.[9] Actually, the data refer to the number of persons in families whose income fell in the given ranges, and hence differences in family size by income could distort the results. Nevertheless, these are the only data on SMSA migrant income reported in the census, and therefore little alternative exists to the use of these data. The census reports data on migrant family members for six income classes, and these data were employed to calculate in- and out-migrant median income for each SMSA, which is also indicated in Table 4.14.

Migration is generally viewed as contributing importantly to the low-income population of the metropolitan areas of the Northeast and North Central regions. At least for the low-income class as defined in this study, this view is clearly incorrect. Of the 15 Northeastern SMSAs, 11 experienced net out-migration of the low-income population, and 16 of the 17 SMSAs in the North Central region experienced such out-migration. For certain of the SMSAs the net out-migration rate was quite substantial: For Paterson–Clifton–Passaic the rate was 9.4%; for Chicago, 8.8%; for Detroit, 7.4%; and for New York, 4.7%. If sizeable numbers of low-income in-migrants fail to be counted in the census, then the figures reported in Table 4.14 could understate the actual rate of net in-migration. Such could be the case if, for example, illegal aliens are undercounted in the census. The undercount of central city minorities is a well-known phenomenon.

---

[9]Such definitions of low- and high-income classes are somewhat arbitrary, but have largely been dictated by available data. The two lowest income classes for which data are reported form the low-income group, while the two highest form the high-income group.

TABLE 4.14
Net In-Migration Rates by Income Class, 1965–1970

	Net migration rates of family members[a]		Median family income[b]	
	Under $6000 (%)	Over $15,000 (%)	In- migrants ($)	Out- migrants ($)
Northeast				
New York	−4.7	−3.9	13,326	12,003
Philadelphia	−1.1	0.4	12,304	11,756
Boston	−2.8	−1.4	13,040	12,237
Pittsburgh	−2.8	−2.3	11,812	11,602
Newark	−5.9	1.0	14,275	12,546
Paterson–	−9.4	3.7	14,658	12,478
Buffalo	−3.2	−4.0	11,394	11,689
Providence–	2.8	1.7	10,690	11,145
Rochester	−4.2	3.0	12,834	11,505
Albany–	−2.6	0.0	12,489	12,097
Hartford	0.6	4.8	12,888	12,093
Syracuse	−0.2	−2.6	11,496	12,071
Jersey City	−3.9	−10.9	10,262	11,818
Allentown–	0.2	0.2	11,040	11,703
Springfield–	2.8	−2.3	10,183	11,219
North Central				
Chicago	−8.8	−0.0	13,214	10,842
Detroit	−7.4	0.8	12,526	10,631
St. Louis	−4.3	0.4	11,579	10.564
Cleveland	−4.3	−0.6	12,387	11,740
Minneapolis–	−4.3	0.8	12,154	11,502
Milwaukee	−5.6	−1.6	11.873	11,388
Cincinnati	−2.8	−0.4	11,528	11,110
Kansas City	−5.2	0.2	11,310	10,562
Indianapolis	−3.7	0.1	11,341	10,817
Columbus	0.3	−4.0	10,640	11,293
Dayton	−6.2	1.1	11,641	10,990
Toledo	−3.6	0.0	11,770	11,378
Akron	−3.7	0.1	11,689	11,474
Gary–	−8.5	−1.3	10,534	9,743
Omaha	−4.1	−3.2	10,917	10,824
Grand Rapids	−1.4	0.6	10,912	10,566
Youngstown–	−1.5	−0.3	10,706	11,191
South				
Washington, D.C.	−2.4	6.0	13,765	12,187
Baltimore	−1.9	0.7	12,030	12,378
Houston	2.1	8.9	11,461	10,328
Dallas	1.6	8.4	11,497	10,560

(*cont'd.*)

TABLE 4.14 (cont'd.)

	Net migration rates of famiy members[a]		Median family income[b]	
	Under $6000 (%)	Over $15,000 (%)	In-migrants ($)	Out-migrants ($)
Atlanta	0.1	8.2	12,318	11,041
Miami	2.7	4.1	10,150	9,980
New Orleans	−2.0	−3.5	10,946	10,968
Tampa−	13.5	9.9	8,697	9,421
San Antonio	2.9	−0.9	9,070	9,629
Louisville	−1.4	1.3	10,419	10,005
Memphis	0.3	1.3	9,567	9,495
Fort Worth	4.2	8.8	10,789	9,948
Birmingham	−2.0	−0.6	9,601	9,521
Norfolk−	1.3	−8.9	8,615	9,647
Oklahoma City	0.4	−2.9	9,840	10,112
Fort Lauderdale−	19.4	25.9	10,450	9,554
Nashville−	−1.8	−1.1	10,346	10,271
Richmond	1.6	0.8	11,100	11,239
West				
Los Angeles−	−3.5	−2.7	10,929	11,050
San Francisco−	−4.3	1.0	12,133	11,172
Seattle−	0.6	7.9	12,056	10,998
Anaheim−	1.3	16.0	12,945	11,123
San Diego	10.5	3.4	9,528	9,787
Denver	2.2	3.0	11,262	11,083
San Bernardino−	9.0	2.9	9,432	9,952
San Jose	0.2	7.5	12,853	12,082
Portland	4.0	3.2	10,600	10,354
Phoenix	6.3	8.2	10,255	9,950
Sacramento	3.9	−2.8	9,990	10,859
Salt Lake City	0.0	−3.4	9,958	10,891

Source: U.S. Bureau of the Census, (1973d), Tables 15 and 16.

A number of Northeastern SMSAs experienced net out-migration of low-income persons while simultaneously experiencing net in-migration of high-income persons. Philadelphia, Newark, Paterson–Clifton–Passaic, Rochester, and Albany–Schenectady–Troy were included in this group. Among Northeastern SMSAs only Springfield–Chicopee–Holyoke had net in-migration of low-income persons and net out-migration of high-income persons. New York, Boston, and Pittsburgh had net out-migration of each group but higher out-migration rates of the low-income than of the high-income group. Jersey City also had net out-migration of each group, but the rate of out-migration of the high-income group was considerably greater than that of the low-income group.

In the North Central states Detroit, St. Louis, Minneapolis–St. Paul, Kansas City, Indianapolis, Dayton, Toledo, Akron, and Grand Rapids all experienced net out-migration of low-income persons and net in-migration of high-income persons. Chicago, Cleveland, Milwaukee, Cincinnati, Gary–Hammond–East Chicago, Omaha, and Youngstown–Warren had net out-migration of both groups but higher out-migration rates of the low-income than of the high-income group. For Chicago and for Gary–Hammond–East Chicago the difference between the two rates was particularly sizeable. The only North Central SMSA to experience both net in-migration of low-income persons and net out-migration of high income persons was Columbus, and this phenomenon was probably due to the presence of a major state university there.

If low-income persons are migrating out of the major metropolitan areas of the Northeast and North Central regions, then to where are they moving? Among the sample SMSAs, 12 of 18 in the South and 10 of 12 in the West had net in-migration of low-income persons. However, the retirement centers stand out as having considerably higher rates of net in-migration of low-income persons than the other metropolitan areas in the sample. In the South Fort Lauderdale–Hollywood and Tampa–St. Petersburg have particularly high rates, and in the West San Diego and San Bernardino–Riverside–Ontario, and to a lesser degree, Phoenix, have high rates. In many instances the net in-migration of low-income retired persons may have considerably different impacts on the receiving community than the net in-migration of other low-income persons. The reason is that while retirement income may be relatively low for many elderly persons, wealth may be substantial and the consequences of the in-migration may be similar to those that result from the in-migration of high-income persons.

The net out-migration of low-income persons from the large metropolitan areas of the Northeast and North Central states is of such a magnitude as to make it unlikely that the retirement centers of the South and the West are absorbing the bulk of the migrants. It is more likely that many of these persons are moving to smaller metropolitan areas than those contained in this sample and to nonmetropolitan areas. A number of factors that could motivate such movements are discussed in the following section.

The Rural to Urban Migration Turnaround

After many decades of the reverse, a strong tendency has recently been observed for migrants to move from metropolitan to nonmetropolitan areas of the country. Berry and Dahmann (1977) have described the phenomenon in the following way:

While the nation's total population increased 13.3 percent during the 1960s, the number of individuals residing in metropolitan areas increased 16.6 percent, a rate of metropolitan increase that was 8.5 times the rate of nonmetropolitan areas. Since 1970, however, a reversal has occurred; as a result, the growth rates for nonmetropolitan areas have exceeded those of metropolitan areas. Nationwide statistics for the first half of the 1970s indicate that population has increased 6.3 percent in nonmetropolitan areas and only 3.6 percent in metropolitan areas [p.7].

Table 4.15 shows the 1970–1977 population growth experience of metropolitan and nonmetropolitan areas in the nation's four regions as well as in the country as a whole. National nonmetropolitan population growth over the period amounted to 10.7%, while national metropolitan growth amounted to only 4.4%. Each region of the country experienced a somewhat higher rate of nonmetropolitan than of metropolitan population growth, but the Northeast especially stands out in this respect because its nonmetropolitan population increased by 12.0% and its metropolitan population decreased by 2.4%. Together the Northeast and North Central regions had approximately 600,000 fewer residents in 1977 than in 1970. A question that naturally arises regarding such observations is, "What are the underlying causes of the recently observed phenomena?" Some possible causes are discussed below.

TABLE 4.15
Regional Population Growth, 1970–1977, by Metropolitan and Nonmetropolitan Status

	Population (in thousands)		Absolute change	Percentage change
	1970	1977		
Northeast				
Metropolitan	38,675	37,742	−933	−2.4
Nonmetropolitan	9,655	10,817	1,162	12.0
North Central				
Metropolitan	37,173	37,503	330	0.9
Nonmetropolitan	18,620	19,711	1,091	5.9
South				
Metropolitan	34,416	37,846	3,430	10.0
Nonmetropolitan	27,187	30,475	3,288	12.1
West				
Metropolitan	26,795	30,015	3,220	12.0
Nonmetropolitan	7,299	8,456	1,157	15.9
United States				
Metropolitan	137,059	143,106	6,047	4.4
Nonmetropolitan	62,761	69,459	6,698	10.7

Source: U.S. Bureau of the Census, *Current Population Reports,* Special Studies, P-23, No. 75, "Social and Economic Characteristics of the Metropolitan and Nonmetropolitan Population: 1977 and 1970" (Washington, D.C.: U.S. Government Printing Office, 1978), Table 3.

For many decades, the urbanization of economic opportunities coupled with farm mechanization led simultaneously to an increasing concentration of population in urban areas and a decreasing concentration in rural areas.[10] The movement off the farm and into the cities that was inherent in this process was sustainable because of the decided advantage of firm location in large urban centers where geographic concentration allowed firms to take advantage of scale and agglomeration economies and where improved access to markets and to suppliers also allowed them to earn higher profits.

During the 1960s, however subtle changes began to occur in long-term historical patterns of population concentration. Certain nonmetropolitan counties that were previously not distinctive in their behavior showed evidence of relatively rapid population growth. These countries were typically characterized by the growth of college towns, by the presence of recreational amenities, or by concentrations of retired persons. Such areas were commonly regarded as anomalies. Coincident with these changes in rural America, certain of the older industrial areas of the Northeast and North Central states began to show serious signs of long-term economic decay, as described previously. Several central cities actually suffered absolute population decline, with the more affluent families and persons moving to the suburbs.

As documented by Beale (1977) and by McCarthy and Morrison (1977), the isolated cases of the previous decade have become commonplace during the first half of the 1970s. Central city urban decay has become more pervasive, and changing incomes and preferences have encouraged previous urban dwellers to seek nonmetropolitan residences. The reversal of net migration flows between metropolitan and nonmetropolitan areas has been one of the most conspicuous changes. When combined with the more rapid decline of fertility rates in metropolitan areas, nonmetropolitan net in-migration has resulted in a striking new phenomenon—nonmetropolitan areas of the U.S. now have more rapidly growing populations than metropolitan areas. Employment is also growing more rapidly in nonmetropolitan America.

The underlying causes of these trends can be conveniently grouped into four broad and somewhat interrelated classes. Certain of the causes are associated with the social costs (i.e., externalities) of transacting business in extremely densely populated urban centers; some, with rising income and wealth; others, with more or less exogenous changes in demand and/or supply conditions for primary inputs; and still others, with the changing demographic structure of the population and the labor force. Let us consider each underlying cause in more detail.

First, the cumulative causation that has characterized the process of urban growth in the past seems increasingly less applicable for the future. Historically,

---

[10]The remainder of this section is drawn from Chalmers and Greenwood (1977).

increased size and density have been associated with high levels of labor productivity and of wages. Higher urban productivity and wages have been attributable partly to technological advantages and to agglomeration economies connected with size and partly to the quality and skill of the urban labor force. The resulting differentially high wages and profits have attracted labor and capital, which have caused more growth, which in turn has allowed even more efficiency gains.

What seems to have happened recently, however, is that diseconomies associated with dense urban locations, in combination with the declining relative economic importance of distance, have improved the competitive position of dispersed spatial arrangements. The result is that relative productivity differentials between the urban and rural labor forces have diminished, and the social costs of urban disamenities have in some localities begun to exceed urban-rural wage differentials. Moreover, as Berry (1977) points out, regional hierarchical structures are less relevant in a system in which transport, communication, and technology have combined to lessen the importance of distance.

Second, as suggested by McCarthy and Morrison (1977), much nonmetropolitan growth is tied directly to increased population density in the more distant areas of urban commuting fields. This phenomenon is a natural result of increased urban incomes and perhaps of changed preferences that have led to increased demands for land. These increased demands can best be exercised in places more distant from urban centers because of the availability of larger parcels of less expensive land. The development of second-home and weekend recreational sites, which are also largely functions of increased urban incomes, is an example of a closely related phenomenon.

The growth of college towns in rural areas reflects the demand for education, which is also related to income. Since the institutions of higher learning that are located in rural areas provide education for large numbers of urban young persons, at least a large fraction of the income that underlies this demand for education is generated in urban areas. Moreover, a growing and increasingly affluent retirement-age population has responded to the environmental amenities associated with warmer climates by moving in large numbers to retirement communities in Florida, in other Southern areas, and in the Southwest. Each of the examples given here, although not closely tied in any direct sense, is in large part a function of increasing affluence that can be traced to urban sources.

Third, increased demands for domestic sources of energy have had the result of stimulating rapid growth in several parts of rural America. Areas impacted by coal extraction are obvious examples. Changing market conditions for primary inputs, such as iron and copper, have also had important local effects in rural communities, although these effects have not always been in the direction of increased population.

Fourth, the coincidence and interaction between economic and demographic forces have probably also contributed importantly to the net migration from metropolitan to nonmetropolitan areas. The recessions of 1969 and 1974 had particularly serious consequences for manufacturing employment, which fell nationally by 1,820,000 jobs between 1969 and 1975. Since manufacturing employment is concentrated in urban areas, urban areas were particularly impacted by these recessions. At the same time, the aging of the war baby cohort, in combination with sharply rising labor force participation rates of young women, especially young married women, brought an extremely large number of young persons into the labor force. Decreasing fertility rates of young women, of course, also interacted with, and jointly reinforced, the increasing labor force participation rates of these women.

As pointed out in Chapter 2, young persons are known to be quite mobile geographically. For example, the 22–24-year-old age group has an intercounty migration rate roughly twice that of the 30–34-year-old group. Since, as previously discussed, absolutely and relatively large numbers of persons were concentrated in the most mobile age classes after about 1965 and since these persons had the added incentive of lagging employment opportunities in urban areas, especially in urban areas of the Northeast and North Central regions, large numbers of persons who were predisposed to migrating were induced to actually seek alternative locations, some of which have been in nonmetropolitan areas.

As suggested earlier, the increased labor force participation of young married women has meant that many young families now have two wage earners. Location in areas with historically low wages but desirable amenities, such as sunshine, mountains, and seashore, has been made possible at reasonably high levels of family income, when with a single wage earner such location decisions would have been unlikely at these early stages of the family life cycle.[11]

Recent migration to nonmetropolitan areas could be self-reinforcing in much the same way that the earlier migration to metropolitan areas was self-reinforcing. Given the increased economic viability of nonmetropolitan places, sustained growth in such places could be induced by the recent migration, especially if the migrants tend to be relatively young and relatively well-educated and tend to have relatively high incomes.

To confirm many of the hypotheses suggested in this section, we will need considerably more research on the phenomenon of nonmetropolitan net in-migration. The socioeconomic characteristics of the migrants need to be better described, the metropolitan places that serve as source localities need to be better identified, the attractions of nonmetropolitan destinations need to be better un-

---

[11]The metropolitan to nonmetropolitan migration rate of 25 to 34-year-old males with wife present and no own children under 18 was somewhat higher over the 1970–1975 period (17.0%) than that of otherwise comparable males with own children under 18 (13.2%), which is consistent with the above contention. See U.S. Bureau of the Census, *Current Population Reports,* Series P-25, No. 285, "Mobility of the Population of the United States: March 1970 to March 1975" (Washington, D.C.: U.S. Government Printing Office, 1975).

derstood, and the consequences of the migration for both origin and destination localities need to be better explained.

Finally, care must be exercised in jumping too soon to conclusions about changed motivations in the decision to migrate. There is nothing in the evidence to date that is inconsistent with traditional analyses of the role of economic opportunity in population redistribution. What is clear, however, is that economic opportunities in the nonmetropolitan areas of the U.S. have enjoyed an unprecedented reversal at the very time that a large proportion of the U.S. population is both mobile and underutilized in metropolitan labor markets.

Summary and Conclusions

A number of aspects of urban growth have been discussed in this chapter. We have seen that a wide variety of employment and income growth rates characterize the sample metropolitan areas. During the post-World-War-II years the urban areas of the Northeast generally experienced somewhat lower rates of employment growth than urban areas located in other regions of the country. In the North Central region the growth record was more mixed, and in the South and West most metropolitan areas grew at rates above the national average rate of employment growth. A high correlation does not exist between size and rate of growth, primarily because metropolitan areas of intermediate size have been the most rapidly growing. SMSAs whose employment growth rate was high during the 1950s also tended to have relatively high rates during the 1960s, but the relationship between the two periods was far from perfect. Several metropolitan areas that grew rapidly during one period experienced moderate growth during the next, and a number of areas improved their ranking considerably.

Four metropolitan areas have the most persistent relatively poor employment growth performance:

1. Jersey City
2. Pittsburgh
3. Birmingham
4. Youngstown–Warren

During each decade each of these SMSAs had the same national ranking: Jersey City, 62nd; Pittsburgh, 61st; Birmingham, 58th; and Youngstown–Warren, 55th. The New York, Boston, and Springfield–Chicopee–Holyoke SMSAs also had quite poor performances in the sense that none ranked better than 50th during either decade.

Unlike the behavior of employment growth over the decades of the 1950s and the 1960s, growth of family median income is not positively correlated for the two periods. Actually, a significant negative relationship exists between growth rates during the two decades. A number of SMSAs either rose or fell appreciably in the national ranking. Certain SMSAs can, however, be distinguished as having somewhat more persistent low rates of income growth than others. In terms of income growth rates, the following SMSAs ranked no better than 40th during either decade:

1. Pittsburgh (44,51)
2. Jersey City (48,58)
3. Cleveland (41,49)
4. Columbus (57,43)
5. Oklahoma City (46,40)
6. San Francisco–Oakland (40,46)
7. Portland (56,47)
8. Salt Lake City (49,57)

During the 1960s a positive and significant rank correlation exists between rate of employment growth and rate of income growth, but this relationship is not particularly high, which suggests that rapid rates of employment growth do not guarantee rapid rates of income growth.

At the descriptive level, at least, little empirical support appears to exist for the position that areas with low average earnings levels in manufacturing enjoy relatively rapid rates of growth of such earnings, with the consequence that the initial alleged advantages of the areas are eroded over time. A number of Northeastern SMSAs that experienced recent absolute declines in manufacturing have ranked high nationally in terms of growth of manufacturing earnings.

Clearly, migration from and to the nation's major metropolitan areas has interacted with the reinforced trends in employment and income growth. In general, migration appears to have had the direct effect of relieving a number of metropolitan-wide problems. For example, during the 1960s a number of Northeastern SMSAs experienced net out-migration rates of the unemployed that were more than in proportion to the net out-migration rates of the employed. Moreover, net out-migration of the school-aged population should have had the effect of reducing the local fiscal sector's burden of financing education.

The view that migration contributes to the low-income population of the metropolitan areas of the Northeast and North Central regions appears to be incorrect. During the 1960s, 11 of 15 Northeastern SMSAs and 16 of 17 North Central SMSAs experienced net out-migration of low-income persons, and in many instances the rates were quite high.

Appendix

STANDARD METROPOLITAN STATISTICAL AREA COUNTY COMPONENTS, 1970 AND 1960

Akron, Ohio
    Portage County (1970 only)
    Summit County

Albany-Schenectady-Troy, New York
   Albany County
   Rensselaer County
   Saratoga County
   Schenectady County

Allentown-Bethlehem-Easton, Pennsylvania-New Jersey
   Lehigh County, Pa.
   Northampton County, Pa.
   Warren County, N.J.

Anaheim-Santa Ana-Garden Grove, California
   Orange County

Atlanta, Georgia
   Clayton County
   Cobb County
   DeKalb County
   Fulton County
   Gwinnett County

Baltimore, Maryland
   Anne Arundel County
   Baltimore City
   Baltimore County
   Carroll County
   Harford County (1970 only)
   Howard County

Birmingham, Alabama
   Jefferson County
   Shelby County (1970 only)
   Walker County (1970 only)

Boston, Massachusetts
   Essex County (part)
   Middlesex County (part)
   Norfolk County (part)
   Plymouth County (part)
   Suffolk County

Buffalo, New York
   Erie County
   Niagara County

Chicago, Illinois
   Cook County
   Du Page County
   Kane County
   Lake County
   McHenry County
   Will County

Cincinnati, Ohio–Kentucky–Indiana
  Clermont County, Ohio (1970 only)
  Hamilton County, Ohio
  Warren County, Ohio (1970 only)
  Boone County, Ky. (1970 only)
  Campbell County, Ky.
  Kenton County, Ky.
  Dearborn County, Ind. (1970 only)

Cleveland, Ohio
  Cuyahoga County
  Geauga County (1970 only)
  Lake County
  Medina County (1970 only)

Columbus, Ohio
  Delaware County (1970 only)
  Franklin County
  Pickaway County (1970 only)

Dallas, Texas
  Collin County
  Dallas County
  Denton County
  Ellis County
  Kaufman County (1970 only)
  Rockwall County (1970 only)

Dayton, Ohio
  Greene County
  Miami County
  Montgomery County
  Preble County (1970 only)

Denver, Colorado
  Adams County
  Arapahoe County
  Boulder County
  Denver County
  Jefferson County

Detroit, Michigan
  Macomb County
  Oakland County
  Wayne County

Fort Lauderdale–Hollywood, Florida
  Broward County

Fort Worth, Texas
  Johnson County
  Tarrant County

Gary-Hammond-East Chicago, Indiana
　　Lake County
　　Porter County
Grand Rapids, Michigan
　　Kent County
　　Ottawa County (1970 only)
Hartford, Connecticut
　　Hartford County (part)
　　Middlesex County (part)
　　Tolland County (part)
Houston, Texas
　　Brazoria County (1970 only)
　　Fort Bend County (1970 only)
　　Harris County
　　Liberty County (1970 only)
　　Montgomery County (1970 only)
Indianapolis,[12] Indiana
　　Boone County (1970 only)
　　Hamilton County (1970 only)
　　Hancock County (1970 only)
　　Hendricks County (1970 only)
　　Johnson County (1970 only)
　　Marion County
　　Morgan County (1970 only)
　　Shelby County (1970 only)
Jersey City, New Jersey
　　Hudson County
Kansas City, Missouri-Kansas
　　Cass County, Mo. (1970 only)
　　Clay County, Mo.
　　Jackson County, Mo.
　　Platte County, Mo. (1970 only)
　　Johnson County, Kan.
　　Wyandotte County, Kan.
Los Angeles-Long Beach, California
　　Los Angeles County
　　Orange County (1960 only)
Louisville, Kentucky-Indiana
　　Jefferson County, Ky.
　　Clark County, Ind.
　　Floyd County, Ind.

---

[12]The governments of Indianapolis and all places in Marion County except Beech Grove and Southport Cities and Lawrence and Speedway Towns consolidated on January 1, 1970.

Memphis, Tennessee–Arkansas
  Shelby County, Tenn.
  Crittenden County, Ark. (1970 only)

Miami, Florida
  Dade County

Milwaukee, Wisconsin
  Milwaukee County
  Ozaukee County (1970 only)
  Washington County (1970 only)
  Waukesha County

Minneapolis–St. Paul, Minnesota
  Anoka County
  Dakota County
  Hennepin County
  Ramsey County
  Washington County

Nashville, Tennessee
  Davidson County
  Sumner County (1970 only)
  Wilson County (1970 only)

New Orleans, Louisiana
  Jefferson Parish
  Orleans Parish
  St. Bernard Parish
  St. Tammany Parish (1970 only)

New York New York
  New York City
  Nassau County
  Rockland County
  Suffolk County
  Westchester County

Newark, New Jersey
  Essex County
  Morris County
  Union County

Norfolk–Portsmouth, Virginia
  Chesapeake City
  Norfolk City
  Portsmouth City
  Virginia Beach City

Oklahoma City, Oklahoma
  Canadian County
  Cleveland County
  Oklahoma County

Omaha, Nebraska-Iowa
    Douglas County, Nebr.
    Sarpy County, Nebr.
    Pottawattamie County, Iowa

Paterson-Clifton-Passaic, New Jersey
    Bergen County
    Passaic County

Philadelphia, Pennsylvania-New Jersey
    Bucks County, Pa.
    Chester County, Pa.
    Delaware County, Pa.
    Montgomery County, Pa.
    Philadelphia County, Pa.
    Burlington County, N.J.
    Camden County, N.J.
    Gloucester County, N.J.

Phoenix, Arizona
    Maricopa County

Pittsburgh, Pennsylvania
    Allegheny County
    Beaver County
    Washington County
    Westmoreland County

Portland, Oregon-Washington
    Clackamas County, Oreg.
    Multanomah County, Oreg.
    Washington County, Oreg.
    Clark County, Wash.

Providence-Pawtucket-Warwick (1970 only), Rhode Island-Massachusetts
    Bristol County, R.I.
    Kent County, R.I. (part)
    Newport County, R.I. (part)
    Providence County, R.I. (part)
    Washington County, R.I. (part)
    Bristol County, Mass. (part)
    Norfolk County, Mass. (part)
    Worcester County, Mass. (part)

Richmond, Virginia
    Chesterfield County
    Hanover County (1970 only)
    Henrico County
    Richmond City

Rochester, New York
    Livingston County (1970 only)
    Monroe County

  Orleans County (1970 only)
  Wayne County (1970 only)

Sacramento, California
  Placer County (1970 only)
  Sacramento County
  Yolo County (1970 only)

St. Louis, Missouri–Illinois
  Franklin County, Mo. (1970 only)
  Jefferson County, Mo.
  St. Charles County, Mo.
  St. Louis County, Mo.
  St. Louis City, Mo.
  Madison County, Ill.
  St. Clair County, Ill.

Salt Lake City, Utah
  Davis County (1970 only)
  Salt Lake County

San Antonio, Texas
  Bexar County
  Guadalupe County (1970 only)

San Bernardino–Riverside–Ontario, California
  Riverside County
  San Bernadino County

San Diego, California
  San Diego County

San Francisco–Oakland, California
  Alameda County
  Contra Costa County
  Marin County
  San Francisco County
  San Mateo County
  Solano County (1960 only)

San Jose, California
  Santa Clara County

Seattle–Everett (1970 only), Washington
  King County
  Snohomish County

Springfield–Chocopee–Holyoke, Massachusetts–Connecticut
  Hampden County, Mass. (part)
  Hampshire County, Mass. (part)
  Worcester County, Mass. (part)
  Tolland County, Conn. (1970 only) (part)

Syracuse, New York
    Madison County
    Onondaga County
    Oswego County

Tampa-St. Petersburg, Florida
    Hillsborough County
    Pinellas County

Toledo, Ohio-Michigan
    Lucas County, Ohio
    Wood County, Ohio (1970 only)
    Monroe County, Mich. (1970 only)

Washington, D.C.-Maryland-Virginia
    Washington, D.C.
    Montgomery County, MD.
    Princes Georges County, Md.
    Arlington County, Va.
    Fairfax County, Va.
    Loudoun County, Va. (1970 only)
    Prince William County, Va. (1970 only)
    Alexandria City, Va.
    Fairfax City, Va.
    Falls Church City, Va.

Youngstown-Warren, Ohio
    Mahoning County
    Trumbull County

5

Changing Intrametropolitan Location Patterns of Labor Force and Economic Activity

Central city decay in the major metropolitan areas of the country is a well-known phenomenon. One prominent explanation for the plight of central cities is that both workers and jobs have been involved in self-reinforcing movement to the suburbs. Moreover, by eroding the central city tax base and thus shifting the burden of local taxes to employers and to relatively high-income residents remaining behind, this movement is thought to have encouraged further flight from the central city.

A number of studies dealing with the cumulative flight phenomenon have focused specifically on the causal relationships between the movement of jobs and the movement of workers.[1] Do jobs follow workers to the suburbs, or do workers follow jobs? Partially because manufacturing has historically been the single most important source of urban employment and partially because more and better data are available on manufacturing, the manufacturing sector has

---

[1]See, for example, Bradford and Kelejian (1973), Brown (1975), Harrison (1974b), Kain (1962, 1968b), Mills (1970), Steinnes (1977), and Steinnes and Fisher (1974). A number of these and of related studies have focused on the location of minority residences in relationship to the location of minority employment opportunities or housing availability and/or central city fiscal conditions. This second group includes Bradford and Kelejian (1973), Cohen (1971), Harrison (1974a), Kain (1968a), Mooney (1969), Noll (1970), and Siegel (1975).

received particular attention. Kain (1968b), for example, argues that "manufacturing determines the locational decisions of urban households, not vice versa [p.17]." Mills (1970), on the other hand, tentatively concludes that "the movement of people to the suburbs has attracted manufacturing employment rather than vice versa [p.12]." In a more recent study Steinnes (1977) concludes that "people do not follow manufacturing and services, but retail trade [p.78]." He argues further that while manufacturing jobs follow people, people may actually be moving away from manufacturing jobs.

Other studies, such as those of Muth (1969), place more emphasis on the role of housing services in determining the optimal location of an urban household's place of residence. These models and supporting empirical work suggest that a high-income elasticity of demand for high-quality, low-density housing could also be responsible for the movement of many households to the suburbs. Rather than taking a suburban job, many workers may opt for a suburban residence and commute a longer distance to the same job.

In a study of the San Francisco–Oakland and San Jose metropolitan areas, Brown (1975) found that when the land is divided into 300 traffic zones, 28% of those households with a job change to a new zone also moved to a new zone (during any year from 1955 to 1965), with an average time-saving of 6.2 minutes to their new place of work from their new residence relative to the trip to their new place of work from their old residence. Of those households that either changed jobs within a zone or did not make a job change, 11% moved to a new zone. Households that made a job change within a zone or did not make a job change, but did move to a new zone, outnumbered households that both made a job change to a new zone and a move to a new zone by better than three to one. Clearly, then, not only suburban employment opportunities but also suburban housing may attract many central city residents to the suburbs.

From his work on urban density functions Mills (1972) concludes that an urban area whose population and income are not growing is likely to become more centralized. Metropolitan areas with different growth characteristics may thus exhibit different intraurban location patterns. In a growing urban area new suburban residents need not have been attracted from the central city. Because of the availability of suburban housing and suburban employment, in-migrants to the metropolitan area may select suburban locations. Actual and anticipated location decisions of in-migrants, and relocation decisions of prior residents, could encourage suburban employment and housing growth, and in turn other in-migrants and central city residents could be attracted to the suburbs.

In the present chapter the behavior of a number of important central city phenomena are contrasted with their suburban counterparts. The relative growth of employment opportunities is examined, along with the relative growth of civilian labor force residents. Intrametropolitan location patterns are discussed.

Moreover, changes over time in family median income of central city and suburban residents are explored. In Chapter 8 a model is specified and estimated for the purpose of explaining these and other changes.

The Data

The set of metropolitan areas examined in this chapter is identical to that defined in Chapter 4. Each SMSA has been divided into two components—its central city or cities and its suburban ring. Geographically, the central city or cities are defined by the political boundaries of the city or cities included in the SMSA title. The suburban ring is the remainder of the SMSA. For many of the purposes of this chapter, two periods are distinguished—1950–1960 and 1960–1970. For the 1950–1960 period *all* data are adjusted to correspond to the 1960 SMSA boundaries, and for the 1960–1970 period all data are adjusted to correspond to the 1970 SMSA boundaries. Moreover, beginning-of-period central city and suburban values for employment and civilian labor force have been adjusted for intercensal annexation of outlying areas by the various central cities. These adjustments will be discussed in more detail at a later point in this section.

Data on CLF residents and on family median income, disaggregated by central city and suburbs, have been calculated from the *1950, 1960,* and *1970 Censuses of Population.* Data on actual central city and suburban employment, as distinct from data on the residence of employed persons, are interpolated from various *Censuses of Manufactures* and *Censuses of Business.* Four types of employment are distinguished in these latter two census sources—manufacturing, retail, wholesale, and selected services. Since the timing of the *Censuses of Manufactures* and *Business* differs from that of the *Census of Population,* linear interpolations were performed to obtain estimates of actual 1950 employment (from 1947 and 1954 data on manufacturing and from 1948 and 1954 data on retail, wholesale, and service), 1960 employment (from 1958 and 1963 data), and 1970 employment (from 1967 and 1972 data).

The census does not provide data on earlier (prior census) levels of population or employment in areas subsequently annexed by central cities. The only information available on annexed areas is 1960 (1970) population and land area in places annexed since 1950 (1960). Hence, estimates of employment and labor force in the annexed areas at the time of the previous census must be based on population or on density estimates, which have led to a number of criticisms of various adjustment techniques. For example, Kain (1968b), following Meyer, Kain, and Wohl (1965), based his adjustment estimates on the assumption that the percentage of employment annexed in each catagory was the same as the percentage of annexed population. He essentially attempted to hold central city boundaries constant at their earlier locations by adding his adjustments to the suburbs and subtracting them from the central cities. For one reason or another, various urban scholars, such as Cohen and Noll (1968) and Harrison (1974b), have criticized Kain's adjustments. Steinnes (1977) goes to the extent of making no annexation adjustments whatsoever, which, given his sample of cities, is clearly inappropriate for analytical purposes.

In the present study annexation adjustments are based on the assumption that annexed areas are represented by average suburban per capita values of the relevant variables. The adjustments themselves were calculated as follows:

1. Per capita suburban values for the earlier year (1950 or 1960) and for the earlier suburban boundaries were calculated for CLF, manufacturing employment, retail employment, service employment, and wholesale employment.
2. The 1950–1960 and 1960–1970 rates of population growth within the respective 1950 and 1960 suburban boundaries were computed, and population of the annexed areas, which is known for the end of each period, was assumed to have grown at the same rate as the suburban population. Hence, an estimate of the respective 1950 and 1960 populations of the annexed areas was obtained. These estimates are reported in Table 5.1.
3. The population estimates, in combination with the per capita values of the variables previously mentioned, yield 1950 and 1960 estimates of the values of each of the five variables for areas annexed, respectively, between 1950 and 1960 and between 1960 and 1970. The adjustments were then added to the respective 1950 and 1960 central city values and were deducted from the respective suburban values.

The procedure thus attempts to hold central city boundaries constant at their end-of-period definition. In addition to having intuitive appeal, the end-of-period boundaries require fewer adjustments than would have been required if beginning-of-period boundaries had been utilized. The migration and intrametropolitan relocation data are defined for the end of the respective periods, and adjustments to these data would have involved far greater problems than those otherwise encountered.

Computation of SMSA, central city, and suburban family median income was accomplished as follows:

1. End-of-period (i.e., 1960 and 1970) SMSA median income is routinely reported in the 1960 and 1970 Censuses, as is median income of the various central cities. Where SMSAs contained multiple central cities, central city family median income was calculated as the weighted average median income of the component central cities, with the weights being the specific central city's share of total central city families.

TABLE 5.1
1950-1960 and 1960-1970 Adjustments for Central City Annexations

Central cities	1950–1960 Annexations			1960–1970 Annexations		
	1960 Population in 1950 area	1960 Population in annexed area	Estimated 1950 population in annexed area	1970 Population in 1960 area	1970 Population in annexed area	Estimated 1960 population in annexed area
Akron	289,822	529	320	275,425	707	574
Albany–	278,900			255,851		
Allentown–	215,174	436	361	210,949	1,520	1,263
Anaheim–	288,772	171,467	96,754	405,470	40,356	16,503
Atlanta	315,988			493,542	3,431	2,027
Baltimore	939,014			905,759		
Birmingham	328,173	12,714	9,654	298,440	2,470	1,647
Boston	697,197			641,071		
Buffalo	532,759			462,768		
Chicago	3,543,428	6,976	2,559	3,362,220	4,737	3,498
Cincinnati	495,165	7,385	5,130	451,467	1,057	644
Cleveland	876,050			750,903		
Columbus	395,681	75,635	33,571	513,384	26,293	13,814
Dallas	486,977	192,707	99,817	833,065	11,336	6,334
Dayton	229,560	32,772	19,362	240,579	3,022	2,143
Denver	455,604	38,283	15,865	457,806	56,872	32,177
Detroit	1,670,144			1,511,482		
Fort Lauderdale–	111,043	7,842	1,675	191,805	54,658	27,446
Fort Worth	299,469	56,799	23,626	382,431	11,045	6,311
Gary–	346,962	725	424	327,722	2,465	1,822
Grand Rapids	176,658	655	392	158,694	38,955	1,822
Hartford	162,178			158,017		19,027

(cont'd.)

TABLE 5.1 (cont'd.)

Central cities	1950–1960 Annexations			1970 Population in 1960 area	1960–1970 Annexations	
	1960 Population in 1950 area	1960 Population in annexed area	Estimated 1950 population in annexed area		1970 Population in annexed area	Estimated 1960 population in annexed area
Houston	687,026	251,193	95,095	1,197,278	35,524	13,751
Indianapolis	428,809	47,449	21,999	744,624		
Jersey City	276,101			260,545		
Kansas City	433,521	42,018	24,805	437,143	69,944	48,294
Los Angeles–	2,756,467	66,716	35,931	3,156,595	18,099	15,017
Louisville	328,410	62,229	32,589	348,752	12,720	8,905
Memphis	428,429	69,095	30,058	486,968	136,562	62,443
Miami	291,680	8		334,859		
Milwaukee	617,454	123,870	68,622	710,176	6,923	4,522
Minneapolis–	796,283			744,380		
Nashville–	163,597	7,277	4,544	448,003		
New Orleans	627,525			593,471		
New York	7,781,984			7,894,862		
Newark	405,220			382,417		
Norfolk–	295,605	125,040	67,469	406,553	12,361	7,120
Oklahoma City	254,077	70,176	40,546	356,919	9,562	6,316
Omaha	261,382	40,216	23,594	275,460	71,868	42,433
Paterson–	179,710			282,385		

Philadelphia	2,002,512	332,398	134,308	1,948,609	64,478	32,114
Phoenix	106,772	91	78	517,084	15,262	10,683
Pittsburgh	604,241	11,013	7,925	520,117	47,262	28,201
Portland	361,663			367,357		
Providence[a]	288,499			339,891		
Richmond	219,958	18		202,359	63,882	32,578
Rochester	318,593			296,233		
Sacramento	138,995	52,672	20,208	190,531	488	247
St. Louis	750,026			622,236		
Salt Lake City	185,989	3,465	1,631	175,397	14,466	6,412
San Antonio	448,226	139,492	53,723	639,687	53,247	35,195
San Bernardino-	205,404	17,467	4,966	255,211	9,945	6,814
San Diego	507,381	65,843	27,862	686,824	719	593
San Francisco-	1,107,864			1,076,516		
San Jose	104,816	99,380	36,104	365,798	79,981	50,135
Seattle[b]	471,008	86,079	51,007	571,424	13,029	8,428
Springfield-	288,705		155	280,693		
Syracuse	215,817	221	57,881	197,208	15,437	9,140
Tampa-	315,321	140,947	11,148	478,562	85,020	29,996
Toledo	298,832	19,171		298,798	1,771	1,505
Washington, D.C.	763,956			756,510		
Youngstown-	226,337			201,511		

Sources: U.S. Bureau of the Census (1963a), Table 9; and U.S. Bureau of the Census (1972a), Table 40.
[a] Includes Providence, Pawtucket in 1960 and Providence, Pawtucket, Warwick in 1970.
[b] Includes Seattle in 1960 and Seattle, Everett in 1970.

2. Suburban income was computed as the weighted suburban component necessary for weighted suburban income and weighted central city income to sum to SMSA income, where the weights were the respective SMSA shares of suburban and central city families.
3. The same type of procedure was followed to calculate beginning-of-period (i.e., 1950 and 1960) incomes, except that SMSAs were adjusted to correspond to end-of-period boundaries. This adjustment was accomplished by weighting added counties in proportion to their contribution to adjusted total SMSA families.

For both central cities and suburban rings Table 5.2 reports 1950–1960 and 1960–1970 sample mean rates of growth for a number of relevant variables. During each period the various suburban variables grew at considerably more rapid rates than their central city counterparts. The 1960–1970 differential rate of growth of CLF residents especially stands out. Whereas the suburbs grew by 71.5%, the central cities grew by only .2%. Also noteworthy is the fact that the rate of central city CLF growth declined substantially between the 1950–1960 and the 1960–1970 periods, whereas the rate of growth of actual central city employment declined very little, from 11.2 to 10.8%.

The rates of growth of suburban manufacturing and suburban retail employment declined somewhat, but the rate of growth of suburban wholesale employment increased appreciably. Both the rates of suburban in-migration and movement from central city to suburbs fell between the two periods. The ratio of suburban in-migration relative to suburban in-movement from the central city was about 3 to 2 in 1960 and about 2 to 1 in 1970.

Changes in the Location of Urban Labor Force and Employment

AGGREGATE DATA FOR SAMPLE METROPOLITAN AREAS

A number of studies have documented the behavior of central city relative to suburban population and employment trends.[2] The general conclusion of these studies is that for the largest metropolitan areas in the country, the relative decline of the central city has been occurring since 1920 and in several instances since at least 1900. That is, the central city's share of total metropolitan population has been declining for some time. Although comprehensive historical data are not available on employment, what data do exist for certain cities suggest roughly the same conclusion regarding the decentralization of employment.[3] In recent years, however, relative central city decline has been replaced by absolute decline in many major urban centers.

[2]Among these studies are Birch (1970), Kain (1968b), Meyer, Kain, and Wohl (1965), Noll (1970), and Vernon (1966).
[3]See Moses and Williamson (1967).

Table 5.3 reports central city and suburban levels of civilian labor force, manufacturing employment, and other measurable sources of employment for various years. These data are regional aggregates for the sample SMSAs and are not corrected for central city annexations of outlying territory. All data are, however, corrected to correspond to 1970 SMSA geographic definitions. Note that if the data were adjusted for central city annexations, based on 1970 central city definitions, central city data entries back through time would generally have higher values while suburban entries would have lower values.

Central city manufacturing employment has declined in the Northeast during each year for which data are presented. The decline between 1963 and 1967 was, however, by far the smallest recorded. Similar declines in the central cities of the major metropolitan areas of the North Central region are also evident, except that an increase occurred between 1963 and 1967. Probably due mainly to Vietnam, 1967 was an unusually good year for the manufacturing sector and again served to mask the longer term plight of the sector in the central cities of the older industrial areas. By 1975 the long term trend had reestablished itself, with the added effects of a serious recession superimposed. Even the central

TABLE 5.2
Sample Mean Percentage Change for Central Cities and Suburbs, 1950–1960 and 1960–1970

Variables	1950–1960[a]		1960–1970[b]	
	Central city	Suburbs	Central city	Suburbs
CLF	13.5	76.0	.2	71.5
Total employment	11.2	106.2	10.8	80.7
Manufacturing employment	13.8	109.9	7.0	58.2
Retail employment	4.8	129.1	6.5	97.8
Service employment	34.6	151.8	43.4	146.8
Wholesale employment	17.9	108.0	9.9	154.0
Income	71.9	92.7	60.1	72.7
IM[c]	16.0	37.0	13.3	27.8
MCS[d]		25.3		15.9
MSC[e]	4.3		4.9	

Source: See Tables 5.3, 5.10, and 5.11.

[a]Based on 61 observations.

[b]Based on 62 observations, with prior Los Angeles–Long Beach SMSA split into two components, Los Angeles–Long Beach and Anaheim–Garden Grove–Santa Ana.

[c]In-migration of CLF members (1955–1960 and 1965–1970) expressed as rates relative to respective central city and suburban beginning-of-period (1950 and 1960) CLF.

[d]Movement of CLF members from central cities to suburbs expressed as rates relative to beginning-of-period suburban CLF.

[e]Movement of CLF members from suburbs to central cities expressed as rates relative to beginning-of-period central city CLF.

TABLE 5.3
Central City and Suburban Civilian Labor Force and Employment for Various Years (in thousands)[a]

Year	Civilian labor force		Manufacturing employment[b]		Other measured employment[b]	
	CC[c]	R[d]	CC	R	CC	R
Northeast						
1947			2,162.9	1,343.8		
1948					1,900.7	567.3
1950	6,547.6		2,129.4*		1,856.8*	
1954			2,084.7	1,539.2	1,769.1	697.5
1958			1,964.4	1,594.7	1,896.9	870.0
1960	6,287.9	5,728.1	1,941.4*	1,623.9*	1,873.8*	959.1*
1963			1,907.0	1,667.6	1,839.1	1,092.7
1967			1,906.2	1,871.6	1,902.8	1,299.0
1970	5,903.4	7,227.9	1,699.0*	1,817.4*	1,863.7*	1,532.9*
1972			1,560.8	1,781.2	1,837.7	1,688.9
North Central						
1947			2,326.9	975.6		
1948					1,647.5	372.0
1950	5,502.2		2,272.7*		1,629.3*	
1954			2,200.5	1,115.9	1,592.8	495.6
1958			2,009.2	1,255.1	1,652.5	610.9
1960	5,412.0	4,487.5	1,974.3*	1,325.8*	1,604.1*	698.5*
1963			1,922.0	1,431.8	1,531.4	830.0
1967			1,937.0	1,503.2	1,639.6	1,061.5
1970	4,996.3	6,611.3	1,799.7*	1,721.8*	1,619.0*	1,357.0*
1972			1,708.1	1,867.6	1,605.3	1,554.0

(cont'd.)

cities of the major metropolitan areas of the South suffered manufacturing employment declines between 1967 and 1972. Moreover, suburban manufacturing employment declined in the Northeast and in the West.

The argument has been made that during recessions the least productive capital is first removed from the production process. The least productive capital is typically the oldest capital, which consequently embodies the least recent technology. Since the oldest vintages of plant and equipment are found in central cities, especially in the central cities of the older industrial areas of the Northeast and North Central regions, central cities tend to be most seriously affected by national recessions. If this argument is valid, the central cities of the Northeast and North Central regions are particularly susceptible to recessions such as that of 1974–1975.

Other measurable sources of central city employment have performed somewhat better than manufacturing. In both the Northeast and North Central regions modest declines have occurred in retail, wholesale, and selected service

TABLE 5.3 (cont'd.)

Year	Civilian labor force		Manufacturing employment[b]		Other measured employment[b]	
	CC[c]	R[d]	CC	R	CC	R
South						
1947			588.5	210.7		
1948					976.4	166.3
1950	3,277.1		640.5*		996.0*	
1954			709.9	294.4	1,035.2	216.5
1958			775.0	359.3	1,209.4	319.3
1960	4,047.2	2,581.6	785.3*	381.0*	1,219.3*	369.7*
1963			800.7	413.5	1,234.1	445.2
1967			889.7	561.6	1,402.4	667.0
1970	4,363.1	4,617.6	879.9*	650.8*	1,545.0*	927.6*
1972			873.3	710.2	1,640.0	1,101.3
West						
1947			438.5	318.0		
1948					756.4	271.3
1950	2,261.6		513.5*		775.0*	
1954			613.4	549.7	812.3	367.6
1958			722.8	648.7	932.5	510.0
1960	3,058.7	3,103.1	733.8*	725.5*	967.7*	596.8*
1963			750.3	845.7	1,020.5	727.1
1967			761.7	1,077.3	1,135.8	861.2
1970	3,446.1	4,779.1	770.1*	1,024.5*	1,230.2*	1,072.6*
1972			775.7	990.0	1,293.2	1,213.5

Sources: Civilian labor force data are from U.S. Bureau of the Census (1952), Tables 35 and 43; U.S. Bureau of the Census (1963a), Tables 73 and 83; and U.S. Bureau of the Census (1973b), Tables 85 and 121. Sources of manufacturing employment data are reported in Table 5.7. Sources of data on other measured employment are reported in Tables 6.8 and 6.9. These latter two sources relate to retail and service employment, respectively. The remaining component of other measured employment is wholesale employment, whose sources are U.S. Bureau of the Census (1951c), Tables 102 and 103; (1956c), Tables 102 and 103; (1961c), Tables 102 and 103; (1966c), Tables 4 and 5; (1970c), Tables 4 and 5; and (1976d), Tables 2 and 4.

[a]Asterisk indicates that value has been interpolated.

[b]All data are based on 1970 SMSA definitions. No adjustments have been made for central city annexations of outlying areas.

[c]CC refers to central cities.

[d]R refers to suburban rings.

employment between 1948 and 1972 (3.3 and 2.6%, respectively), but these declines have not been steady. Over both the 1950–1960 and 1960–1970 decades central city manufacturing employment declined somewhat more rapidly than central city civilian labor force, but CLF declined more rapidly than other sources of employment. These changes suggest that, as far as employment is concerned, the decline of the manufacturing sector is a critical component of central city problems. Not only are absolutely fewer jobs available, but the central city tax base has correspondingly been diminished.

During the decade of the 1960s suburban CLF grew rapidly. As calculated from Table 5.3, the suburban CLF of the major metropolitan areas of the Northeast grew by 26.2%, or about one-third the rate of 78.9% for the major Southern metropolitan areas. Whereas suburban manufacturing employment did not grow as rapidly as either suburban CLF or other measurable sources of suburban employment, manufacturing employment grew quite rapidly in the suburbs and certainly grew far more rapidly than in the central cities. In the South suburban manufacturing grew by 70.8%, whereas in the West it grew by 41.2%. Suburban retail, wholesale, and selected service employment grew at roughly twice the rate of suburban CLF in the Northeast, the North Central region, and the South.

CHANGES IN THE LOCATION OF LABOR FORCE MEMBERS IN SAMPLE METROPOLITAN AREAS

Table 5.4 reports central city and suburban rates of CLF growth for each sample SMSA. Changes over two periods, 1950-1960 and 1960-1970, are indicated. The data reported in this table are corrected for central city annexations of outlying territory.

During the 1960s, 37 of the 62 sample metropolitan areas (12 in the Northeast, 14 in the North Central region, 7 in the South, and 4 in the West) suffered absolute declines in their number of CLF residents. In relative terms the declines were particularly great in St. Louis (20.6%), Sacramento (20.0%), Cleveland (17.4%), Newark (17.3%), Grand Rapids (17.0%), Richmond (16.5%), Pittsburgh (16.0%), Buffalo (15.9%), Kansas City (15.2%), and Toledo (15%), although fairly sizeable declines occurred in several other central cities. Not a single sample metropolitan area had a more rapid rate of central city than suburban CLF growth.

The behavior of central city CLF during the 1950s was similar to that during the 1960s. During the earlier period 29 of the 61 central cities experienced absolute labor force decline.

A number of factors are, of course, responsible for the suburbanization of the metropolitan labor force. As will be demonstrated in the following section, suburban employment opportunities have been growing at considerably higher rates than central city employment opportunities, and thus the location decisions of labor force members and of business firms have jointly reinforced one another. The availability of newer and better housing in less densely populated surroundings has also influenced and mutually reinforced the household location decisions of labor force members. Moreover, in terms of a number of "quality of life" factors, suburban living has proved more attractive than central city living for

TABLE 5.4
1950-1960 and 1960-1970 Rates of Central City and Suburban Civilian Labor Force
Growth (in percentages)

	1950-1960		1960-1970	
	Central city	Suburbs	Central city	Suburbs
Northeast				
New York	-0.9	65.9	-4.8	34.4
Philadelphia	-4.6	39.1	-5.5	31.0
Boston	-9.9	17.0	-8.4	19.5
Pittsburgh	-13.7	12.4	-16.0	8.7
Newark	-11.9	21.7	-17.3	21.0
Paterson-	-2.2	41.8	2.1	28.7
Buffalo	-13.2	47.1	-15.9	21.3
Providence-	11.4	-3.2	0.4	30.3
Rochester	-8.7	70.2	-7.9	51.7
Albany-	-10.4	23.2	-7.8	30.7
Hartford	-11.1	232.0	-9.0	40.4
Syracuse	-6.4	37.8	-10.3	32.7
Jersey City	-11.1	-6.4	-7.8	6.6
Allentown-	-0.7	16.9	0.3	26.8
Springfield-	19.4	-8.5	-0.7	31.6
North Central				
Chicago	-6.4	62.4	-9.1	48.5
Detroit	-17.0	67.8	-11.2	41.8
St. Louis	-19.0	45.5	-20.6	39.1
Cleveland	-11.5	60.3	-17.4	37.1
Minneapolis-	-5.6	110.4	-4.3	86.0
Milwaukee	0.3	70.0	-3.0	43.6
Cincinnati	-6.6	35.9	-9.1	28.0
Kansas City	10.1	40.0	-15.2	75.9
Indianapolis	-1.6	142.8	8.4	58.2
Columbus	15.8	86.7	8.8	83.0
Dayton	-5.8	69.3	-7.8	44.7
Toledo	22.9		-15.0	114.0
Akron	-1.3	62.7	-6.1	41.0
Gary-	12.1	61.4	-4.2	51.5
Omaha	28.5	-17.3	4.8	76.1
Grand Rapids	15.8	22.3	-17.0	76.7
Youngstown-	22.4	2.7	-9.4	30.3
South				
Washington, D.C.	-8.3	81.8	-2.5	81.8
Baltimore	-6.8	74.9	-4.9	51.7
Houston	32.7	136.5	32.6	98.4
Dallas	23.8	94.6	26.6	85.5
Atlanta	9.4	80.5	5.0	94.4
Miami	17.2	155.1	14.5	54.8

(cont'd.)

TABLE 5.4 (cont'd.)

	1950–1960		1960–1970	
	Central city	Suburbs	Central city	Suburbs
New Orleans	3.1	101.8	−7.0	78.5
Tampa–	57.6	125.0	4.3	88.0
San Antonio	27.6	68.6	14.6	143.8
Louisville	−7.8	77.4	−7.5	70.2
Memphis	6.3	121.5	5.2	
Fort Worth	13.6	133.7	11.2	115.3
Birmingham	−2.0	28.2	−11.0	31.3
Norfolk–	4.4	90.3	−1.6	100.7
Oklahoma City	16.2	116.9	9.2	01.4
Fort Lauderdale–	182.8	393.4	39.0	160.3
Nashville–	−10.1	66.1	16.3	79.4
Richmond	9.7	36.4	−16.5	119.2
West				
Los Angeles–	24.4	84.8	12.1	28.2
San Francisco–	−3.7	54.8	−3.8	46.5
Seattle–	8.8	68.4	6.6	77.5
Anaheim–			52.4	198.9
San Diego	59.2	135.1	22.0	65.0
Denver	24.8	120.5	14.7	126.8
San Bernardino–	106.7	279.2	1.9	64.0
San Jose	112.0	124.8	37.6	129.8
Portland	−4.2	32.5	−1.2	64.7
Phoenix	112.5	92.7	22.8	181.7
Sacramento	60.7	88.1	−20.0	82.2
Salt Lake City	5.9	107.8	−2.5	65.9

Sources U.S. Bureau of the Census (1952), Tables 35 and 43; (1963a), Tables 73 and 83; and (1973b), Tables 85 and 121.

many who can afford to reside in either type of area. Higher central city crime rates and antiquated physical infrastructure, such as schools and streets, have contributed to CLF suburbanization. Some evidence also suggests that the net fiscal deficit that accrues to higher income families living in the central city has added further to the attractiveness of the suburbs.[4] A number of other factors could be listed.

CHANGES IN THE LOCATION OF URBAN EMPLOYMENT

Table 5.5 reports central city and suburban rates of employment growth for each sample SMSA. Recall that employment consists of manufacturing, retail,

[4]See Bradford and Kelejian (1973).

service, and wholesale and is defined at the place of work. Changes over two periods, 1950-1960 and 1960-1970, are indicated. The data of Table 5.5 are corrected for annexations. On the basis of the information reported in this table, a number of observations can be made.

Absolute employment declines in the central cities of the nation's major metropolitan areas is not a new phenomenon. During the decade of the 1950s, 29 of 61 central cities experienced such declines, while during the 1960s, 25 of 62 had absolute employment decreases. The urban centers of the Northeast and North Central regions have been particularly affected. Of the central cities of the 15 Northeastern SMSAs, only New York avoided an absolute employment decline during the 1950s, and during the 1960s Rochester, Syracuse, and Allentown-Bethlehem-Easton avoided such a decline. In the North Central region 4 of 17 sample SMSAs (Minneapolis-St. Paul, Columbus, Gary-Hammond-East Chicago, and Omaha) failed to suffer a decrease in central city employment during the 1950s. Of the 17, 8 did so during the 1960s.

Particularly in the Northeast, the behavior of central city employment growth during the 1960s was quantitatively somewhat different than during the 1950s. The rate of central city employment decline decreased substantially in three areas (Buffalo, Providence-Pawtucket-Warwick, and Springfield-Chicopee-Holyoke) and actually reversed in three other areas (Rochester, Syracuse, and Allentown-Bethlehem-Easton). However, the central city of the New York SMSA switched from employment increase to employment decrease, and three other central cities (Pittsburgh, Newark, and Albany-Schenectady-Troy) experienced a substantial increase in their rate of decline.

In the North Central region the central cities of most of the major metropolitan areas fared somewhat better in terms of employment growth during the 1960s than during the 1950s. In the South the pattern was mixed, with certain central cities growing more rapidly during the 1960s while others grew less rapidly. The central cities of two Southern SMSAs (Baltimore and Richmond) suffered absolute employment decreases during the 1960s. In the West most central cities experienced somewhat lower rates of employment growth during the 1960s after having very high rates during the 1950s. Employment actually declined absolutely in the central cities of both the San Francisco-Oakland and Seattle-Everett SMSAs.

The argument is frequently made that the cause of central city employment decline is that central city firms are seeking and finding suburban locations. If this were the case, however, suburban relative to central city employment growth in the Northeast should be high compared to other regions. In fact, just the opposite is true. Suburban relative to central city employment growth tends to be comparatively low in the Northeast and high in the South. This observation is consistent with Mills' conclusion that urban areas that are not growing tend to become more centralized. The present observation is probably more accurate if the term "relatively more centralized" is used.

TABLE 5.5
1950-1960 and 1960-1970 Rates of Central City and Suburban Employment Growth
(in percentages)

	1950-1960		1960-1970	
	Central city	Suburbs	Central city	Suburbs
Northeast				
New York	4.6	47.3	−4.3	32.3
Philadelphia	−8.1	27.5	−12.7	38.8
Boston	−10.3	26.0	−9.3	25.5
Pittsburgh	−0.6	−9.9	−15.3	14.6
Newark	−10.1	31.3	−23.6	28.9
Paterson−	−2.6	62.4	−3.5	47.6
Buffalo	−19.7	14.2	−8.6	16.4
Providence−	−15.9	6.5	−1.8	33.7
Rochester	−13.1	229.0	13.2	44.4
Albany−	−12.6	11.5	−24.5	47.3
Hartford	−9.3	85.9	−16.9	46.2
Syracuse	−18.9	43.2	2.8	10.8
Jersey City	−7.8	−9.9	−11.0	−6.1
Allentown−	−2.4	21.0	10.8	22.0
Springfield−	−12.6	15.6	−2.3	34.5
North Central				
Chicago	−10.1	43.0	−7.4	63.3
Detroit	−25.8	31.9	−9.9	53.8
St. Louis	−13.3	44.7	−17.5	52.4
Cleveland	−14.1	64.8	−14.1	56.9
Minneapolis−	3.7	108.2	2.4	141.3
Milwaukee	−7.9	59.6	−6.2	53.6
Cincinnati	−12.0	42.6	−1.1	33.8
Kansas City	−5.7	58.9	−2.0	73.2
Indianapolis	−1.8	103.1	14.7	61.8
Columbus	10.2	59.1	17.2	87.9
Dayton	−1.3	19.7	−2.9	112.4
Toledo	−8.6	19.2	10.9	61.1
Akron	−15.6	66.5	1.3	44.6
Gary−	6.1	14.5	−1.7	71.5
Omaha	3.1	84.6	18.2	78.6
Grand Rapids	−10.9	59.9	2.7	89.6
Youngstown−	−9.9	−17.9	6.3	38.2
South				
Washington, D.C.	4.4	162.6	3.2	124.6
Baltimore	−2.8	55.3	−24.3	68.6
Houston	33.0	200.9	53.8	48.5
Dallas	42.8	162.6	36.5	227.4
Atlanta	15.3	131.2	21.3	132.7
Miami	44.5	174.4	12.0	125.6

(*cont'd.*)

TABLE 5.5 (cont'd.)

	1950–1960		1960–1970	
	Central city	Suburbs	Central city	Suburbs
New Orleans	2.3	58.8	7.1	97.9
Tampa–	45.8	233.5	38.1	157.4
San Antonio	22.4	288.7	35.1	118.6
Louisville	−3.4	80.4	6.2	89.8
Memphis	12.6	103.4	32.4	90.7
Fort Worth	20.7	163.7	17.3	157.1
Birmingham	11.6	9.3	5.3	36.3
Norfolk–	3.6	166.0	28.7	106.2
Oklahoma City	31.3	54.5	41.6	76.2
Fort Lauderdale–	185.7	578.9	94.3	295.5
Nashville–	23.0	28.1	36.4	70.7
Richmond	12.7	68.5	−3.1	183.9
West				
Los Angeles–	32.1	90.6	9.4	34.1
San Francisco–	1.6	57.0	−5.0	48.9
Seattle–	24.8	120.9	−1.6	114.7
Anaheim–			67.9	212.9
San Diego	65.3	173.7	14.7	81.9
Denver	16.3	229.6	17.6	143.2
San Bernardino–	72.5	62.8	36.7	74.7
San Jose	64.7	341.9	31.1	136.6
Portland	6.8	40.3	18.1	94.0
Phoenix	91.7	367.0	80.1	122.2
Sacramento	21.7	390.4	36.4	9.2
Salt Lake City	31.4	130.8	19.3	113.0

Sources: See Tables 5.3, 5.7, 5.8, and 5.9.

One fact that is evident in Tables 5.4 and 5.5 is that certain SMSAs that maintained relatively rapid rates of employment growth had central cities that had fairly substantial employment and labor force losses. In the Northeast Hartford especially stands out in this respect. Additionally, Kansas City and Grand Rapids, and perhaps Dayton, had similar experiences in the North Central region. Baltimore and Richmond in the South and San Francisco–Oakland in the West can also be included in this group.

As regards the decade of the 1960s, the data of Tables 5.4 and 5.5 are summarized in Table 5.6, where central cities are categorized with respect to employment and CLF growth or decline. The various central cities are placed in one of four cells according to their combination of employment growth (negative

TABLE 5.6
Central City Patterns of Employment and Civilian Labor Force Growth and Decline, 1960-1970[a]

	Employment growth negative	Employment growth positive

CLF growth negative	Employment falls faster than CLF
	1. Philadelphia 8. Milwaukee
	2. Boston 9. Baltimore
	3. Newark 10. San Francisco-
	4. Albany-
	5. Hartford
	6. Jersey City
	7. Springfield-
	
	CLF falls faster than employment
	1. New York 5. Chicago
	2. Pittsburgh 6. Detroit
	3. Buffalo 7. St. Louis
	4. Richmond 8. Cleveland
	   9. Cincinnati
	   10. Kansas City
	   11. Dayton
	   12. Gary-
		1. Rochester 5. Minneapolis-
		2. Syracuse 6. Toledo
		3. Sacramento 7. Akron
		4. Salt Lake City 8. Grand Rapids
		   9. Youngstown-
		   10. Washington, D.C.
		   11. New Orleans
		   12. Louisville
		   13. Birmingham
		   14. Norfolk-

CLF growth positive	1. Paterson- 3. Seattle-
	2. Providence- 4. Portland
		Employment rises faster than CLF
		1. Allentown- 9. Houston
		2. Indianapolis 10. Dallas
		3. Columbus 11. Atlanta
		4. Omaha 12. Tampa-
		5. Anaheim- 13. San Antonio
		6. Denver 14. Memphis
		7. San Bernardino- 15. Fort Worth
		8. Phoenix 16. Oklahoma City
		   17. Fort Lauderdale-
		   18. Nashville-
		
		CLF rises faster than employment
		1. Miami 2. Los Angeles-
		   3. San Diego
		   4. San Jose

[a]*Sources:* Compiled from data reported in Tables 5.4 and 5.5.

or positive) and of CLF growth (negative or positive). The central cities of SMSAs within a given region tend to fall into fairly distinct cells. The typical pattern in the Northeast and North Central regions was for both employment and CLF to decline. However, in the Northeast central city employment tended to decline more rapidly than central city CLF (7 SMSAs), while in the North

Central region CLF tended to decline more rapidly than employment (8 SMSAs). The most typical pattern of change in the South and the West was for both central city employment and labor force to rise. For most Southern SMSAs (10) that experienced such a pattern, central city employment grew more rapidly than central city CLF. Finally, five North Central and five Southern central cities had a combination of employment increase and CLF decline.

CHANGES IN THE LOCATION OF URBAN MANUFACTURING EMPLOYMENT

We saw previously that the absolute decline of central city manufacturing employment is not a recent phenomenon. Table 5.7 documents this position for the metropolitan areas included in the sample. Data for three periods are reported, 1950-1960, 1960-1970, and 1967-1972. Data on the former two periods have been estimated as previously indicated and are corrected for central city annexations of outlying territory. Data on the latter period are actual rather than estimated and are not corrected for annexations.

As the data of Table 5.7 indicate, manufacturing employment declined in the central cities of almost every Northeastern SMSA during each period. Only New York avoided a decline during the 1950s, whereas Rochester, Syracuse, and Allentown-Bethlehem-Easton avoided one during the 1960s. Syracuse was the only Northeastern central city to experience an increase in manufacturing employment between 1967 and 1972, but Syracuse's suburban areas had by far the largest drop (24.3%) in the Northeast during this period. During the 1950s and 1960s certain of the Northeastern metropolitan areas had decreased suburban manufacturing employment, but between 1967 and 1972 such decreases became rather commonplace, with 10 of the 15 Northeastern suburban areas experiencing one. Thus, the decline of the manufacturing sector in the Northeast was pervasive after 1967. The post-Vietnam adjustments in combination with the reallocation brought on by sharply rising oil prices and the recessionary conditions of the early 1970s had severe impacts on the manufacturing sector of both Northeastern central cities and suburban areas.

The pattern of manufacturing employment decline in the North Central region has been similar to that in the Northeast, except that such employment has generally increased in suburban areas. Between 1967 and 1972 manufacturing employment in the suburban areas of the North Central region behaved somewhat differently than in the suburban areas of the Northeast. Manufacturing employment increased in the suburbs of all but four North Central SMSAs (Detroit, St. Louis, Milwaukee, and Kansas City). Manufacturing employment declined in three Southern suburban areas, but declined in 10 Southern central cities. In the West the five largest metropolitan areas had decreases in suburban manufacturing employment, and 5 of the 12 Western central cities also had such decreases. Moreover, of the six largest metropolitan areas in the country, only the suburban

TABLE 5.7
Central City and Suburban Rates of Manufacturing Employment Growth, 1950-1960, 1960-1970, and 1967-1972 (in percentages)

	1950-1960		1960-1970		1967-1972	
	Central city	Suburbs	Central city	Suburbs	Central city	Suburbs
Northeast						
New York	2.8	-5.7	-10.6	11.2	-15.4	-7.7
Philadelphia	-11.1	15.2	-20.2	19.7	-23.1	-4.8
Boston	-11.9	19.6	-22.6	5.7	-25.4	-9.7
Pittsburgh	18.9	-18.5	-22.3	2.6	-27.0	-6.9
Newark	-16.0	22.0	-27.3	15.4	-30.9	1.5
Paterson-	-8.4	41.6	-9.2	26.7	-13.5	3.2
Buffalo	-27.3	1.8	-7.9	-2.4	-20.2	-10.0
Providence-	-20.2	-3.6	-7.0	20.2	-10.7	1.2
Rochester	-18.3	300.8	19.6	17.4	-21.2	52.1
Albany-	-21.2	-4.7	-40.6	29.7	-16.8	-4.7
Hartford	-21.3	73.9	-33.6	24.0	-45.1	-16.2
Syracuse	-33.1	34.7	10.3	-15.6	15.8	-24.3
Jersey City	-14.6	-14.9	-21.2	-13.8	-12.9	-11.0
Allentown-	-3.8	19.2	12.3	7.1	-6.3	12.1
Springfield-	-16.8	5.4	-15.5	17.3	-22.6	-2.6
North Central						
Chicago	-15.6	25.6	-12.6	47.7	-21.3	9.8
Detroit	-35.0	18.4	-7.8	37.6	-14.0	-1.6
St. Louis	-16.1	36.7	-20.3	31.7	-26.0	-3.4
Cleveland	-18.3	49.0	-16.4	36.3	-23.5	1.5
Minneapolis-	7.1	71.9	2.3	101.6	-11.8	5.0
Milwaukee	-12.4	43.4	-10.6	31.1	-10.4	-4.2
Cincinnati	-18.9	43.9	-2.4	9.3	-19.3	8.0
Kansas City	-7.3	64.6	-10.9	61.5	-12.9	-3.6
Indianapolis	-12.5	81.1	10.6	46.0	-11.3	7.6
Columbus	13.2	15.7	4.4	52.1	-5.2	52.3
Dayton	-4.1	-8.4	-0.9	109.2	-18.0	22.2
Toledo	-10.9	-19.2	2.9	52.5	-5.6	42.5
Akron	-23.4	58.7	-2.0	26.5	-18.5	12.3
Gary-	3.0	-9.0	-2.8	44.3	-8.2	13.5
Omaha	4.7	152.5	7.8	28.7	4.2	1.7
Grand Rapids	-19.4	40.3	-2.0	66.9	-23.5	24.7
Youngstown-	-13.1	-28.8	12.6	18.8	-9.6	19.3
South						
Washington, D.C.	14.3	177.3	-3.5	72.0	-16.0	8.3
Baltimore	-8.3	34.0	-43.9	46.2	-16.7	-13.2
Houston	28.7	212.9	38.2	12.6	7.3	36.1
Dallas	60.5	201.1	32.3	133.5	-5.5	47.8
Atlanta	8.7	121.4	-1.2	75.6	-11.5	7.0
Miami	69.0	374.4	21.8	155.4	24.9	59.5

(*cont'd.*)

TABLE 5.7 (cont'd.)

	1950–1960		1960–1970		1967–1972	
	Central city	Suburbs	Central city	Suburbs	Central city	Suburbs
New Orleans	−14.7	22.4	0.8	40.2	−15.1	19.4
Tampa–	33.1	340.7	29.9	120.2	44.7	−0.9
San Antonio	24.3	186.3	32.6	79.8	14.1	30.8
Louisville	−6.4	70.2	7.5	68.9	−5.9	15.7
Memphis	11.0	90.6	30.2	116.9	4.4	35.7
Fort Worth	22.4	142.5	20.5	114.0	−25.4	53.4
Birmingham	19.0	2.6	−6.6	11.3	−3.0	−6.7
Norfolk–	−4.3	166.3	51.4	39.7	29.0	82.1
Oklahoma City	61.8	14.7	70.8	12.7	28.5	103.3
Fort Lauderdale–	271.9	592.2	94.4	320.6	18.6	105.6
Nashville–	31.2	3.0	23.9	74.2	−1.9	42.5
Richmond	18.8	30.0	−12.0	130.7	−21.7	44.0
West						
Los Angeles–	38.0	83.5	−0.9	24.3	2.3	−15.2
San Francisco–	5.3	28.8	−23.8	19.0	−14.5	−4.1
Seattle–	37.7	142.3	−17.2	86.8	−8.9	−53.9
Anaheim–			52.6	102.3	40.4	−11.2
San Diego	91.2	209.4	−18.1	52.9	4.4	−3.4
Denver	13.5	316.3	6.6	113.4	2.5	59.9
San Bernardino–	97.3	30.8	34.0	80.2	0.5	34.6
San Jose	70.5	400.8	11.6	130.3	−1.6	16.9
Portland	1.4	36.0	12.8	70.5	−1.7	17.3
Phoenix	140.4	366.4	117.1	93.0	24.2	14.0
Sacramento	15.7	484.3	88.7	−70.6	−28.3	29.8
Salt Lake City	69.9	148.5	26.4	18.9	24.6	18.8

Sources: U.S. Bureau of the Census (1950), Tables 2 and 5; (1957), Tables 3 and 5; (1961d), Table 3; (1966d), Table 4; (1971a), Table 4; and (1976a), Table 4.

area of Chicago experienced an increase in manufacturing employment between 1967 and 1972.

Vernon (1966) details a number of factors that have been responsible for the decreasing concentration of manufacturing establishments in central cities. The following are perhaps the most prominent:

1. The advent of horizontal manufacturing technology made older manufacturing structures obsolete and fostered the demand for one-story structures placed on large sites with expansion possible in any direction.
2. The development of trucking allowed manufacturers to seek sites away from rail or waterside locations.

3. After the 1920s zoning probably played some role in discouraging the expansion of central city manufacturing.
4. Site assembly also became a formidable task as cities became covered with durable structures.

Others feel that tighter central city labor markets encouraged the dispersal of manufacturing firms to the suburbs. Certain researchers think that high central city crime rates have not only motivated the outward movement of families but also of business firms. In Chapter 8 of the present study, however, no support is found for the position that central city crime rates encourage the movement of business firms to the suburbs.

CHANGES IN THE LOCATION OF URBAN RETAIL EMPLOYMENT

Just as central city manufacturing employment has declined absolutely in most major metropolitan areas in the Northeast and North Central regions since at least 1950, central city retail employment has declined absolutely in most of the same SMSAs. Typically, the rate of decrease of manufacturing employment has been sharper than the rate of decrease of retail employment, but in each case the relative employment declines have been substantial. These trends in retail employment growth are documented in Table 5.8. The data presented in this table also indicate that, especially since 1960, suburban retail employment has grown somewhat more rapidly than suburban manufacturing employment in most metropolitan areas in each region of the country.

During the 1950s only one Northeastern central city (Paterson–Clifton–Passaic) failed to suffer a decrease in central city retail employment. The declines in Pittsburgh and Providence–Pawtucket were particularly high. During the 1960s both Providence–Pawtucket–Warwick and Springfield–Chicopee–Holyoke experienced increases in central city retail employment. These same two central cities plus Jersey City were the only ones in the Northeast to sustain retail employment increases between 1967 and 1972. The magnitudes of the reversals in the Providence and Springfield areas between the 1950s and the 1960s is fairly remarkable. In Providence–Pawtucket–Warwick the rate of change of retail employment increased 22.1 percentage points and in Springfield–Chicopee–Holyoke the increase was 38.3 percentage points. After 1960 the central cities of Newark and Hartford had especially severe relative decreases in retail employment.

In the North Central region Detroit stands out as having had the most persistently high rate of decrease in central city retail employment, though St. Louis and Cleveland are not far behind. Between the 1950s and 1960s Toledo experienced the largest percentage point reversal in its rate of retail employment change, from a decline of 14.2% to an increase of 16.6%. Indianapolis, Columbus, and Omaha experienced an increase in retail employment over each period that is reported in Table 5.8.

TABLE 5.8
Central City and Suburban Rates of Retail Employment Growth, 1950–1960, 1960–1970,
and 1967–1972 (in percentages)

	1950–1960		1960–1970		1967–1972	
	Central city	Suburbs	Central city	Suburbs	Central city	Suburbs
Northeast						
New York	−1.0	90.5	−5.8	42.3	−2.9	20.2
Philadelphia	−12.0	46.5	−8.5	55.7	−6.6	25.4
Boston	−14.5	32.6	−12.9	37.9	−7.5	24.2
Pittsburgh	−23.4	10.7	−15.4	28.9	−17.9	28.2
Newark	−7.1	37.7	−31.2	31.4	−18.5	22.5
Paterson–	1.9	82.6	−8.5	57.3	−18.0	29.7
Buffalo	−17.0	56.8	−18.9	53.8	−5.0	29.9
Providence–	−18.3	42.3	3.8	65.1	2.5	36.5
Rochester	−5.7	123.8	−10.2	81.3	−13.7	45.5
Albany–	−7.6	30.7	−17.8	58.8	−9.6	30.9
Hartford	−10.7	130.6	−20.3	91.7	−17.4	46.4
Syracuse	−12.0	52.5	−14.1	59.3	−11.3	29.6
Jersey City	−6.3	0.7	−3.8	6.3	0.9	5.2
Allentown–	−5.5	37.9	−0.5	73.6	−3.9	43.4
Springfield–	−12.2	37.7	26.1	58.7	14.6	24.0
North Central						
Chicago	−8.8	68.3	−7.7	75.4	−11.2	37.4
Detroit	−23.7	70.2	−20.7	68.7	−16.6	29.4
St. Louis	−12.3	52.0	−26.7	66.0	−14.4	33.6
Cleveland	−14.5	88.2	−21.8	77.2	−12.3	27.1
Minneapolis–	−11.6	189.5	−3.9	161.0	−4.5	59.0
Milwaukee	−6.5	124.8	−4.3	90.2	−7.5	48.5
Cincinnati	−8.4	35.3	−10.6	71.1	−4.8	41.2
Kansas City	−10.8	65.1	−4.4	72.7	0.3	33.7
Indianapolis	3.8	347.1	13.9	67.8	3.7	32.5
Columbus	0.8	208.7	16.7	117.3	26.9	45.7
Dayton	−6.0	74.4	−16.8	95.9	−10.3	42.3
Toledo	−14.2	128.7	16.6	70.5	19.6	42.3
Akron	−5.7	79.9	−0.3	72.8	−3.8	42.9
Gary–	15.6	69.8	0.4	89.6	−2.1	59.2
Omaha	2.9	51.8	22.5	127.7	23.7	27.3
Grand Rapids	−9.7	111.1	4.2	116.2	−6.2	51.2
Youngstown–	−9.7	74.9	−6.9	109.3	−10.7	80.4
South						
Washington, D.C.	−8.4	131.8	−9.8	102.4	−8.6	42.3
Baltimore	−4.9	131.1	−15.7	90.4	−7.1	45.4
Houston	20.3	203.4	50.5	86.1	29.3	64.4
Dallas	19.2	141.4	30.0	109.7	10.7	66.2
Atlanta	11.3	141.3	18.0	178.9	8.8	84.5
Miami	17.0	127.4	0.7	97.9	4.1	48.1
New Orleans	5.1	143.6	−1.2	156.7	−8.4	67.6

(cont'd.)

TABLE 5.8 (cont'd.)

	1950–1960		1960–1970		1967–1972	
	Central city	Suburbs	Central city	Suburbs	Central city	Suburbs
Tampa–	46.3	223.6	28.5	146.6	20.4	76.8
San Antonio	14.4	383.7	32.2	126.9	25.2	80.1
Louisville	−2.7	118.4	−2.3	112.4	−4.2	55.1
Memphis	5.4	198.1	27.3	68.2	33.1	−5.2
Fort Worth	13.1	216.4	6.0	160.9	−1.9	99.6
Birmingham	1.3	33.1	4.9	77.8	−3.5	64.1
Norfolk–	7.3	182.3	9.5	131.3	11.8	61.8
Oklahoma City	7.7	111.8	23.7	108.3	21.5	60.8
Fort Lauderdale–	137.5	540.0	82.8	269.0	30.9	128.5
Nashville–	9.3	90.1	45.3	61.1	28.5	32.2
Richmond	4.4	228.7	−5.2	211.5	6.8	98.5
West						
Los Angeles–	14.5	81.8	10.4	33.9	8.8	15.6
San Francisco–	−4.9	76.6	−3.7	62.5	−2.9	26.7
Seattle–	5.9	109.9	8.3	125.3	−7.5	50.3
Anaheim–			47.9	215.4	11.7	71.2
San Diego	32.2	158.3	32.7	100.6	32.9	53.3
Denver	10.4	159.8	3.9	155.3	6.2	72.8
San Bernardino–	54.2	101.2	46.6	67.5	32.6	29.8
San Jose	39.0	226.5	51.7	109.9	27.7	41.2
Portland	0.2	62.5	8.2	105.5	3.0	65.6
Phoenix	66.7	386.4	42.5	152.6	31.7	102.7
Sacramento	18.0	383.2	6.7	84.7	−8.8	49.4
Salt Lake City	12.5	123.3	10.2	201.9	8.1	149.2

Sources: U.S. Bureau of the Census (1951a), Tables 102 and 103; (1956a), Tables 102 and 103; (1961a), Tables 102 and 103; (1966a), Tables 3 and 4; (1970a), Tables 3 and 4; and (1976b), Tables 2 and 6.

In the South and the West, Washington, D.C., Baltimore, Louisville, and San Francisco–Oakland had a decrease in central city retail employment during each period. However, the magnitude of the relative declines in these areas did not approach those of the Northeastern and North Central areas that were especially affected by retail employment decrease. Note that, during each period, retail employment grew dramatically in the suburban areas of almost every Southern and Western metropolitan area.

Vernon (1966) mentions three factors that have been especially important in the erosion of the central city's retail trade function:

1. Population has either grown slowly or declined absolutely in the older sections of the central city, which has meant that retail market potential has shifted strongly to the suburbs.

2. The slower rate of central city employment growth, or the absolute decline, has meant that relatively or absolutely fewer prospective shoppers come into the central city, with the result that central city retail market potential is further impaired.

3. The preference for shoppers to use the automobile rather than mass transit facilities in traveling from home to retail markets has placed central city retailers at a severe competitive disadvantage relative to suburban retailers. Access to suburban shopping centers and parking facilities around them are two important factors contributing to shopper preference for suburban retail centers.

Vernon feels that this third factor is probably the most important.

CHANGES IN THE LOCATION OF URBAN SERVICE EMPLOYMENT

Of the measured sources of central city employment, selected services is clearly the most rapidly growing. Moreover, even in the central cities of the Northeast and North Central regions, selected service employment has risen absolutely while manufacturing, retail, and wholesale employment have declined in the typical metropolitan center. Table 5.9 shows rates of growth of selected service employment for the sample metropolitan area central cities and suburban rings. The claims made above are verified by the data presented in the table.

Over the decades of the 1950s and 1960s selected service employment grew in every sample central city. During the 1967–1972 period two central cities, Newark and Detroit, experienced a decline in service employment, as did the suburban area of New York. On the whole, however, service employment in the sample central cities grew at a somewhat higher annual rate between 1967 and 1972 than during the 1960s. During this same 5-year interval central city manufacturing employment in the Northeast and North Central regions declined at a considerably higher rate than during the 1960s. Hence, the continuing tendency for service employment to consitute the central city employment base appears to have accelerated during recent years. Note also that in most sample metropolitan areas the rate of growth of suburban service employment was considerably higher than the rate of growth of suburban retail employment.

A number of urban scholars have discussed the central city as a service center. Financial institutions—including banking, insurance, and securities dealers—have long been known to concentrate in the central city, where face-to-face communication can occur with relative ease. Moreover, large manufacturing, utility, and transportation concerns have found distinct advantages of having central city offices through which they keep informed regarding market and technological developments. Such concerns also have frequent need to negotiate over credit, terms of sales and purchases, and other matters that require close

TABLE 5.9
Central City and Suburban Rates of Growth of Selected Service Employment, 1950–1960,
1960–1970, and 1967–1972 (in percentages).

	1950–1960		1960–1970		1967–1972	
	Central city	Suburbs	Central city	Suburbs	Central city	Suburbs
Northeast						
New York	27.0	106.2	17.1	37.4	5.8	−8.2
Philadelphia	22.9	65.7	20.8	112.2	16.5	70.6
Boston	23.1	39.4	47.1	98.4	30.5	62.3
Pittsburgh	8.5	25.0	19.3	69.6	16.8	71.1
Newark	26.5	46.7	7.9	76.3	−7.4	57.3
Paterson–	35.9	127.8	37.6	103.0	45.0	64.5
Buffalo	3.7	79.3	22.8	72.2	25.3	67.3
Providence–	11.5	40.5	22.2	67.8	20.4	11.1
Rochester	2.5	207.0	23.1	130.3	19.5	86.0
Albany–	7.4	165.4	13.6	93.0	18.2	34.6
Hartford	39.1	113.1	55.2	148.3	30.4	85.8
Syracuse	16.4	81.5	29.9	117.8	36.5	106.4
Jersey City	20.0	18.8	13.7	36.3	10.0	27.5
Allentown–	17.6	31.1	32.4	81.1	29.0	81.7
Springfield–	12.9	20.0	16.6	122.2	22.5	41.7
North Central						
Chicago	14.5	100.4	20.5	102.6	13.9	70.5
Detroit	8.4	101.4	5.6	153.8	−2.2	79.0
St. Louis	11.1	60.6	14.4	142.6	9.6	67.5
Cleveland	13.7	111.4	19.5	115.1	14.6	46.6
Minneapolis–	37.7	257.5	36.7	249.0	27.1	138.4
Milwaukee	20.0	110.8	31.6	141.5	29.3	79.2
Cincinnati	6.2	57.0	24.1	126.9	21.8	87.3
Kansas City	13.6	66.8	45.8	109.2	36.7	89.5
Indianapolis	21.4	102.3	32.8	111.1	35.9	82.5
Columbus	17.9	341.1	77.7	158.7	61.6	126.3
Dayton	40.6	109.4	9.1	164.2	14.2	57.5
Toledo	11.1	179.1	45.5	113.8	19.3	75.6
Akron	18.6	103.9	29.8	116.0	23.4	62.1
Gary–	19.4	58.7	11.6	145.1	13.2	117.6
Omaha	16.3	73.3	46.0	105.0	47.6	36.3
Grand Rapids	21.8	89.0	21.0	177.9	24.9	74.9
Youngstown–	1.4	78.0	0.8	141.3	6.6	72.1
South						
Washington, D.C.	26.9	232.1	40.4	204.2	23.4	76.1
Baltimore	29.8	154.6	16.6	160.9	24.7	124.6
Houston	67.7	223.5	112.3	244.0	68.5	131.1
Dallas	57.8	155.7	75.0	146.5	37.8	107.6
Atlanta	48.0	117.8	89.8	287.8	50.9	120.0
Miami	74.9	130.6	29.7	107.3	17.0	43.8

(cont'd.)

TABLE 5.9 (cont'd.)

	1950–1960		1960–1970		1967–1972	
	Central city	Suburbs	Central city	Suburbs	Central city	Suburbs
New Orleans	42.7	171.3	45.1	195.8	24.7	106.2
Tampa–	58.9	194.8	86.7	258.2	73.3	97.8
San Antonio	40.0	579.8	49.7	135.1	38.8	65.0
Louisville	7.1	102.1	23.5	184.0	15.0	91.0
Memphis	33.8	25.4	50.2	103.4	45.1	33.5
Fort Worth	34.4	211.4	32.1	290.3	18.9	146.4
Birmingham	7.0	33.9	51.0	87.4	33.3	82.0
Norfolk–	18.3	136.5	48.0	139.1	36.5	99.6
Oklahoma City	32.9	112.9	50.6	99.0	23.8	105.2
Fort Lauderdale–	247.5	827.1	126.3	321.2	35.3	91.6
Nashville–	21.3	54.8	62.3	60.0	45.8	32.7
Richmond	20.3	159.4	31.6	318.2	33.0	115.5
West						
Los Angeles–	68.9	166.3	46.0	60.2	17.7	41.5
San Francisco–	26.9	120.6	44.9	105.6	22.7	56.9
Seattle–	37.8	101.4	40.0	262.0	25.9	92.1
Anaheim–			167.5	223.0	57.4	103.8
San Diego	74.1	150.1	100.4	108.4	59.7	70.6
Denver	45.9	208.8	64.1	220.7	61.7	95.6
San Bernardino–	87.5	121.0	24.0	71.9	48.1	36.9
San Jose	101.7	424.2	66.4	190.0	25.5	84.2
Portland	25.4	59.2	55.5	190.3	32.9	94.1
Phoenix	110.1	464.4	121.5	169.8	73.0	72.1
Sacramento	44.6	540.8	45.5	107.6	33.6	38.4
Salt Lake City	47.9	107.2	41.0	311.0	27.5	108.4

Sources: U.S. Bureau of the Census (1951b), Tables 102 and 103; (1956b), Tables 102 and 103; (1961b), Tables 102 and 103; (1966b), Tables 3 and 4; (1970b), Tables 3 and 4; and (1976c), Tables 2 and 5.

personal contacts. The office space that these types of firms need in the central city is relatively expensive but constitutes only a small fraction of business expenses. For these and other reasons, demand for central city office space to satisfy service requirements has tended to dominate other types of demand for central city space. Historically, central cities also had a relatively abundant supply of articulate and well-trained female labor that could satisfy the demands of firms specializing in service functions.

Vernon argues that two types of changes could erode the central city's advantage as a center for high-level services. One is that central city labor force decline may eliminate the pool of female labor that has historically satisfied the labor requirements of central city firms. An associated point is that the changing racial and ethnic composition of the central city labor force may mean that the labor force that does reside in the central city will have restricted job opportunities. Vernon's second point is that technological developments in communications and data processing could be such as to negate much of the existing labor requirements for information gathering and retrieval and for face-to-face communication. Vernon raised these issues in 1959, and, on the basis of available data, these possibilities do not appear to have unfolded to date.

Suburban and Central City Income Growth

Little comprehensive information exists on suburban and central city income growth. The data of Table 5.10 are therefore of some interest in themselves. The data relate to growth of family median income over two periods, 1950–1960 and 1960–1970. The manner in which the income estimates were made was described in the section entitled "The Data" in this chapter.

Almost every SMSA experienced a more rapid rate of suburban income growth than central city income growth during each period. One question that arises in connection with these comparative rates of growth concerns whether the suburban growth advantage has been widening or narrowing over time. Although a number of exceptions exist, in general suburban compared to central city income growth was poorer during 1960s than during 1950s. Listed below are the number of SMSAs that fall into each growth categoy.

	Suburban income growth rises relative to central city income growth	Suburban income growth falls relative to central city income growth
Northeast	5	9
North Central	4	12
South	5	13
West	4	6

During the 1960s the following SMSAs had a rate of suburban income growth that exceeded the rate of central city income growth by 10 percentage points or more:

1. Northeast: New York, Newark, Syracuse
2. North Central: St. Louis, Minneapolis–St. Paul, Dayton, Akron
3. South: Baltimore, Dallas, Atlanta, New Orleans, San Antonio, Fort Worth, Birmingham, Norfolk–Portsmouth, Nashville–Davidson
4. West: Seattle, Anaheim–Santa Ana–Garden Grove, Denver, Portland, Phoenix, Sacramento, Salt Lake City

TABLE 5.10
Central City and Suburban Rates of Income Growth, 1950–1960 and 1960–1970[a]

	1950–1960[b]			1960–1970[c]		
	Central city (%)	Suburbs (%)	$\dfrac{S^d}{CC}$	Central city (%)	Suburbs (%)	$\dfrac{S^d}{CC}$
Northeast						
New York	72.7	86.7	1.08	57.7	74.7	1.11
Philadelphia	74.1	91.1	1.10	62.0	67.8	1.04
Boston	77.1	92.1	1.09	58.7	72.3	1.09
Pittsburgh	69.1	80.7	1.07	57.0	64.4	1.05
Newark	65.9	83.2	1.10	41.8	67.2	1.18
Paterson–	67.8	86.0	1.11	59.3	70.7	1.07
Buffalo	68.0	93.5	1.15	54.1	61.4	1.05
Providence–	76.3	80.4	1.02	71.2	76.0	1.03
Rochester	78.6	98.0	1.11	57.2	71.8	1.09
Albany–	69.6	75.8	1.04	61.6	80.2	1.12
Hartford	57.8	91.8	1.22	52.1	70.8	1.12
Syracuse	80.0	106.6	1.15	48.0	68.8	1.14
Jersey City	73.8	78.5	1.03	56.5	57.9	1.01
Allentown–	69.9	78.0	1.05	65.1	79.5	1.09
Springfield–	76.4	88.4	1.07	59.9	70.1	1.06
North Central						
Chicago	70.3	86.7	1.10	52.0	65.1	1.09
Detroit	53.5	85.5	1.21	65.5	78.2	1.08
St. Louis	67.1	91.3	1.15	52.8	67.6	1.10
Cleveland	68.1	70.9	1.02	53.4	63.0	1.06
Minneapolis–	70.7	97.2	1.16	58.0	73.9	1.10
Milwaukee	75.4	83.0	1.04	54.0	68.3	1.09
Cincinnati	78.9	97.1	1.10	56.0	63.8	1.05
Kansas City	73.7·	96.2	1.13	67.2	68.4	1.01
Indianapolis	71.8	95.4	1.14	76.1	59.1	0.90
Columbus	63.4	85.6	1.14	62.7	66.9	1.03
Dayton	67.4	89.7	1.13	53.2	73.6	1.13
Toledo	58.7	83.9	1.16	66.3	77.5	1.07
Akron	85.3	98.4	1.07	55.4	71.1	1.10
Gary–	61.9	81.7	1.12	61.3	71.6	1.06
Omaha	83.1	88.2	1.03	61.6	68.8	1.04
Grand Rapids	65.8	88.7	1.14	64.9	72.9	1.05
Youngstown–	70.9	85.5	1.09	59.1	70.6	1.07
South						
Washington, D.C.	57.7	76.8	1.12	59.9	68.3	1.05
Baltimore	72.8	98.5	1.15	55.8	75.7	1.13
Houston	74.2	73.0	0.99	67.3	82.1	1.09
Dallas	69.5	104.1	1.20	67.7	91.7	1.14
Atlanta	88.1	108.6	1.11	67.9	84.6	1.10
Miami	48.1	76.6	1.19	64.1	72.1	1.05

(cont'd.)

TABLE 5.10 (cont'd.)

	1950–1960[b]			1960–1970[c]		
	Central city (%)	Suburbs (%)	$\frac{S^d}{CC}$	Central city (%)	Suburbs (%)	$\frac{S^d}{CC}$
New Orleans	73.7	114.4	1.23	54.9	73.7	1.12
Tampa–	84.8	89.2	1.02	68.0	82.1	1.08
San Antonio	74.7	80.7	1.03	64.9	81.4	1.10
Louisville	66.8	92.8	1.16	62.2	70.2	1.05
Memphis	71.9	118.7	1.27	75.9	90.3	1.08
Fort Worth	65.8	102.2	1.22	69.1	88.0	1.11
Birmingham	75.1	106.0	1.18	56.4	76.8	1.13
Norfolk–	62.2	74.0	1.07	62.3	78.9	1.10
Oklahoma City	72.4	89.8	1.10	62.4	72.7	1.06
Fort Lauderdale–	73.1	130.3	1.33	86.1	93.5	1.04
Nashville–	56.0	86.9	1.20	77.7	125.1	1.27
Richmond	57.1	95.0	1.24	68.2	64.0	0.98
West						
Los Angeles–	91.5	93.7	1.01	53.2	57.3	1.03
San Francisco–	69.1	83.4	1.09	55.1	66.9	1.08
Seattle–	75.9	94.2	1.10	59.5	75.7	1.10
Anaheim–				57.9	74.1	1.10
San Diego	86.1	95.6	1.05	53.7	56.2	1.02
Denver	79.0	114.8	1.20	51.8	71.1	1.13
San Bernardino–	93.2	101.3	1.04	51.5	60.2	1.06
San Jôse	87.4	105.1	1.09	71.6	67.8	0.98
Portland	70.3	80.1	1.06	54.7	71.0	1.11
Phoenix	91.5	98.1	1.03	62.8	78.9	1.10
Sacramento	69.1	102.9	1.20	39.9	54.5	1.10
Salt Lake City	67.1	93.8	1.16	43.7	63.4	1.14

Source: U.S. Bureau of the Census (1952), Table 37; (1963a), Table 76; and (1973b), Table 89.
[a]Income refers to family median income.
[b]Based on 1960 SMSA definitions.
[c]Based on 1970 SMSA definitions.
[d]1.0 was added to both central city and suburban percentage changes before this ratio was calculated.

Since higher suburban relative to central city income growth could be due to a high suburban rate of growth, a low central city rate of growth, or some combination of the two, the relative growth rates mean little in themselves. However, where the central city rate is exceptionally low and the suburban relative to central city rate is exceptionally high, some indication may exist that central city residents are ill-equipped to share in the metropolitan growth experience. Four SMSAs stand out in this regard, two in the Northeast and two in the West. Each experienced income growth of less than 50% during the 1960s. SMSAs so characterized are Newark, Syracuse, Sacramento, and Salt Lake City.

At the opposite extreme, a number of central cities had income growth in excess of 70% during the 1960s. Included in this group are Providence–Pawtucket–Warwick, Indianapolis, Fort Lauderdale–Hollywood, Memphis, Nashville–Davidson, and San Jose. Fort Lauderdale–Hollywood's rate of 86.1% was easily the highest among sample central cities.

Some differences do exist between mean central city rates of income growth across regions. Similar differences exist between mean suburban rates. The mean central city and suburban rates of income growth over the 1960–1970 period are given below for each region.

	Central cities	Suburbs
Northeast	57.5%	70.2%
North Central	60.0	69.4
South	66.2	81.7
West	54.6	66.4

The mean rate for both Southern central cities and suburban areas was somewhat higher than for comparable areas in other regions. The West clearly had the lowest rates in each category, whereas the Northeast and North Central areas were roughly the same in each category.

Location Patterns of Intrametropolitan Movers and Metropolitan In-Migrants

As previously indicated, for the sample SMSAs the *1970 Census* reports fairly detailed characteristics of both 1965–1970 in-migrants to central cities as opposed to suburban rings and 1965–1970 movers from central city or cities (suburban ring) to suburban ring (central city or cities). These data contribute to an understanding of why the central cities of the major metropolitan areas of the Northeast and, to a lesser extent, those of the North Central states have experienced critical fiscal and economic problems.

Table 5.11 indicates that relative to their suburbs, the central cities of the major metropolitan areas of the Northeast have difficulty in attracting CLF in-migrants. For every one in-migrant CLF member who locates in the central city, 1.9 locate in the suburbs. In other regions, though the suburbs also attract absolutely more in-migrant CLF members than the central cities, the relative attractiveness of the suburbs is somewhat less. In the South, for example, for every in-migrant CLF member who locates in the central city, only 1.3 locate in the suburbs.

Relative to both the CLF of the central cities and of the suburbs, the movement of CLF members from central cities to suburbs is quite low in the

TABLE 5.11
Suburban Relative to Central City In-Migration and Intraurban Relocation of Civilian Labor
Force Members for Major Metropolitan Areas, 1965–1970[a]

	Northeast	North Central	South	West
IMR / IMCC	1.9	1.6	1.3	1.5
CC → R / R → CC	3.0	2.5	2.6	1.7
CC → R / CLFCC	7.2%	12.0%	10.4%	11.7%
CC → R / CLFR	5.8%	9.1%	9.8%	8.4%
IMCC / CLFCC	5.6%	9.1%	14.5%	16.2%
IMR / CLFR	8.7%	10.8%	18.2%	18.0%

Source: Calculated from data presented in U.S. Bureau of the Census (1973d), Table 15.

[a] All mobility data refer to place of residence in 1965 and place of residence in 1970 of persons defined as civilian labor force members in 1970. Symbols are as follows: IMR = in-migration to suburban ring; IMCC = in-migration to central city; CC → R = movers from central city to ring; R → CC = movers from ring to central city; CLFR = 1970 CLF of ring; CLFCC = 1970 CLF of central city.

Northeast and North Central states compared to the South and the West. However, in the Northeast and North Central regions CLF in-migration to the central cities fails to replace the CLF members who move to the suburbs, whereas in the South and the West CLF in-migration to the central cities is considerably greater than the CLF losses of the central cities to the suburbs. The major impetus for CLF growth in the suburbs of the South and West is from in-migration rather than from movement out of the central cities, although such movement is of some consequence. In the Northeast and North Central regions in-migration and movement from the central cities contribute more equally to suburban CLF growth.

As indicated in Table 5.12, the central cities of the Northeast, relative to their suburbs, have had an especially difficult time attracting and retaining high-income residents. If the $25,000+ income class is considered, between 1965 and 1970 Northeastern central cities attracted one high-income in-migrant for every 5.6 attracted to the suburbs. For every one such high-income mover from suburbs to central city, 5.8 moved in the opposite direction. By contrast, the central cities of the South attracted one high income in-migrant for every 1.9 who located in the suburbs, and for every high-income mover from suburbs to central city, 1.7 such persons moved from central city to suburbs.

When the data of Tables 5.11 and 5.12 are compared, it is apparent that in the South and the West the metropolitan location patterns of both in-migrants and intraurban movers are fairly similar for CLF members as a whole and for high-income persons. High-income persons do have a greater tendency than CLF members as a whole to locate in the suburbs, but this tendency is nowhere near as pronounced as in the Northeast.

Hence, when compared to the central cities of the South and the West, the central cities of the Northeast and, to a slightly lesser extent those of the North Central region, have difficulty in attracting and retaining CLF members and have substantially greater difficulty in attracting and retaining high-income persons. A number of factors influence the intraurban location decisions of households. Among these factors are proximity to job opportunities, housing with the appropriate quality characteristics, and neighborhood amenities such as good schools and perhaps low crime rates. These factors will be discussed and analyzed in more detail in Chapter 8.

Table 5.13 presents data on metropolitan location patterns of CLF in-migrants to the sample SMSAs and on intrametropolitan relocation patterns of CLF residents of the various SMSAs. As reported, the data refer to the ratio of the number of in-migrant CLF members locating in the suburbs relative to the

TABLE 5.12
Suburban Relative to Central City In-Migration and Intraurban Relocation for Major Metropolitan Areas, 1965–1970, by Income Class[a]

	$\dfrac{\text{IMR}}{\text{IMCC}}$	$\dfrac{\text{CC} \rightarrow \text{R}}{\text{R} \rightarrow \text{CC}}$
Northeast (15)		
Income $25,000+	5.6	5.8
Less than $25,000	2.9	4.2
North Central (17)		
Income $25,000+	4.4	2.1
Less than $25,000	5.2	2.9
South (18)		
Income $25,000+	1.9	1.7
Less than $25,000	3.2	3.1
West (12)		
Income $25,000+	2.4	1.9
Less than $25,000	2.0	2.1

Source: Calculated from data presented in U.S. Bureau of the Census, (1973d), Table 15.

[a]All mobility data refer to persons in families with 1969 family income as indicated. See Table 5.11 for the meaning of the symbols.

TABLE 5.13
Location of CLF In-Migrants and Intrametropolitan Movers, 1965–1970

	$\dfrac{\text{IMR}}{\text{IMCC}}$	$\dfrac{\text{CC} \to \text{R}}{\text{R} \to \text{CC}}$		$\dfrac{\text{IMR}}{\text{IMCC}}$	$\dfrac{\text{CC} \to \text{R}}{\text{R} \to \text{CC}}$
Northeast			South		
New York	0.50	3.56	Washington, D.C.	4.11	5.30
Philadelphia	2.69	3.77	Baltimore	2.41	2.97
Boston	2.41	1.46	Houston	0.56	2.44
Pittsburgh	3.59	2.97	Dallas	0.93	1.25
Newark	7.42	4.01	Atlanta	2.42	2.95
Paterson–	7.95	2.06	Miami	4.08	6.97
Buffalo	2.04	3.07	New Orleans	1.01	6.06
Providence–	1.97	2.01	Tampa–	1.40	3.02
Rochester	2.07	5.05	San Antonio	0.42	2.30
Albany–	1.81	2.33	Louisville	1.50	3.86
Hartford	3.22	4.46	Memphis	0.21	0.66
Syracuse	1.90	2.83	Fort Worth	1.33	3.12
Jersey City	2.12	0.85	Birmingham	1.52	1.72
Allentown–	1.59	2.76	Norfolk–	0.84	2.48
Springfield–	1.25	2.28	Oklahoma City	1.04	1.69
North Central			Fort Lauderdale–	1.54	3.37
Chicago	1.81	2.75	Nashville–	0.19	4.79
Detroit	1.99	3.28	Richmond	1.19	1.74
St. Louis	4.60	3.75			
Cleveland	2.48	3.83			
Minneapolis–	1.41	2.84	West		
Milwaukee	0.88	1.76	Los Angeles–	1.14	1.44
Cincinnati	1.70	1.81	San Francisco–	1.86	2.14
Kansas City	1.80	1.59	Seattle–	1.59	2.84
Indianapolis	0.45	0.68	Anaheim–	2.97	1.57
Columbus	0.63	2.43	San Diego	0.83	0.96
Dayton	2.79	4.41	Denver	1.50	2.06
Toledo	1.25	1.34	San Bernardino–	3.04	1.49
Akron	2.32	1.66	San Jose	1.48	1.25
Gary–	1.23	2.87	Portland	1.73	3.05
Omaha	0.50	0.82	Phoenix	0.71	1.24
Grand Rapids	1.52	2.87	Sacramento	3.26	3.75
Youngstown–	1.83	2.55	Salt Lake City	1.56	4.81

Source: Calculated from data presented in U.S. Bureau of the Census (1973d), Table 15.

number of in-migrant CLF members locating in the central city and a similar ratio for the number of CLF movers from central city to suburbs relative to the number of CLF movers from suburbs to central city. In each instance the ratio can be interpreted as the number of CLF members who locate in or relocate to the suburbs for every one CLF member who locates in or relocates to the central city.

In the Northeast, Newark and Paterson–Clifton–Passaic especially stand out as having suburban areas that, relative to the central cities, are extremely attractive to in-migrant CLF members. For every one in-migrant CLF member who located in the respective central cities, 7.42 CLF members located in the suburbs of Newark and 7.95 located in the suburbs of Paterson–Clifton–Passaic. No other metropolitan area in the country has ratios even remotely approaching these values. Movement from central city to suburbs compared to movement in the opposite direction is relatively great in Newark, Rochester, and Hartford, all of which have ratios of over 4 to 1.

The New York SMSA also stands out in the Northeast. For every in-migrant CLF member who moves to the suburbs of New York, two such persons move to the central city. New York is the only Northeastern SMSA with a ratio of in-migration to suburbs relative to central city of less than one.

Among sample SMSAs in the North Central region St. Louis has suburbs that are particularly attractive to CLF in-migrants, and Dayton has relatively heavy movement of such persons from its central city to its suburbs. St. Louis and Cleveland also have moderately high rates of relative intrametropolitan movement to the suburbs. In the South, Washington, D.C. and Miami have relatively heavy location in the suburbs compared to the central city, and in the West, Sacramento is the best example of such a situation.

Since the values reported in Table 5.13 are ratios of absolute numbers of migrants and movers, they must be interpreted with some caution. However, the data do indicate a strong tendency for CLF members to choose suburban rather than central locations, and the tendency appears to be national in scope.

Although much attention is justifiably focused on the movement of CLF members to the suburbs, the fact that considerable movement occurs from suburbs to central city is often neglected. For example, for the SMSAs employed in this study, the mean number of CLF members who moved from suburbs to central city between 1955 and 1960 is 9253. The comparable mean for movement between 1965 and 1970 is 12,581. Corresponding mean values for movement from central city to suburbs are 30,751 for 1955–1960 and 29,945 for 1965–1970. Since many policy-makers feel that an essential ingredient in the solution of central city problems is not only the reduction of central city flight to the suburbs but also reversal of the net movement, relocation from suburbs to central city requires attention. This type of movement is discussed in greater detail in Chapter 8.

Summary and Conclusions

A number of aspects of central city and suburban growth have been examined in this chapter. We have seen that during the 1960s the suburbs of the nation's major metropolitan areas absorbed almost the entire increase in the metropolitan labor force. Among the country's 62 largest SMSAs the mean rate of increase of the suburban labor force was 71.5%, whereas the mean rate of increase of the central city labor force was .2%. Hence, the labor force residing in the average central city in 1970 was only slightly larger than in 1960. The CLF has declined absolutely in certain central cities in each region, but this phenomenon has clearly been most prevalent in the Northeast and North Central regions.

Relative to the decade of the 1950s, the rate of central city employment growth in the average SMSA dropped very little during the 1960s. However, the Northeast and North Central regions were particularly affected by absolute employment decline between 1960 and 1970. In the Northeast central city employment appears to be declining more rapidly than CLF, whereas in the North Central region CLF appears to be declining more rapidly than employment. Because measured sources of central city employment are probably performing less well than unmeasured sources, which include government employment, the actual behavior of central city employment is likely to be better than reported in this study.

The manufacturing sector has contributed importantly to central city employment decline in the Northeast and North Central regions. Each region has experienced a decrease in central city manufacturing employment during the post-World-War-II period. In the Northeast the decline between 1963 and 1967 was by far the smallest recorded, and during this period manufacturing employment actually increased in the central cities of the North Central region. These findings are generally consistent with those discussed in previous chapters, where we saw that the mid-1960s was a relatively prosperous time for the older industrial regions of the country. Since 1967, however, the decline of the manufacturing sector in the Northeast has been severe and pervasive. Moreover, recent recessions have had serious consequences for manufacturing industries in many areas of the country, and among the six largest metropolitan areas such employment declined even in the suburbs. Suburban Chicago, where manufacturing employment increased between 1967 and 1972, was the only exception.

Decreases in central city retail employment have added further to central city employment problems of the Northeast and North Central regions. Although the rate of decrease of manufacturing employment in the central cities of these regions has typically been greater than that of retail employment, each type of employment has sustained relatively sizeable declines. In SMSAs in all regions of the country, suburban retail employment has typically risen at somewhat more rapid rates than suburban manufacturing employment.

Service employment continues to rise in almost all central cities, and in many cities the rate of increase accelerated between 1967 and 1972, when the rate of decrease of manufacturing employment increased in the Northeast. In the typical metropolitan area suburban service employment is growing even more rapidly than suburban retail employment.

Another serious central city problem—one that has particular consequences for the local public sector—is that high-income persons have a strong tendency to opt for suburban locations, and this tendency is especially strong in the Northeast. The rate of movement of CLF members from central cities to suburbs is relatively low in the Northeast and North Central regions compared to the South and the West, but in the former regions in-migration fails to replace the CLF losses to the suburbs.

6

A Model of Metropolitan
Growth and Migration

In the beginning of his well-known paper Sjaastad (1962) clearly makes the point that most earlier migration research has concentrated primarily on examining the causes of migration:

> Migration research has dealt mainly with the factors which affect migration and how strongly they have affected it, but little has been done to determine the influence of migration as an equilibrating mechanism in a changing economy. The movements of migrants clearly are in the appropriate direction, but we do not know whether the numbers are sufficient to be efficient in correcting income disparities as they emerge. There is a strong presumption that they are not [p. 80].

Though a few notable exceptions exist, during the years since the publication of Sjaastad's paper relatively little has been done to rectify this imbalance in research effort.

Although the importance of examining the causes of migration is not questioned, it seems at least as interesting to examine the effects that migration has had on the sending and receiving regions. Surely, a "complete" model of migration would be extremely complex. Migration has important influences on demographic and social factors, as well as on more purely economic variables, and the many variables in turn interact with one another.

One important reason for the lack of comprehensive studies dealing with the effects of migration is that the appropriate data simply do not exist, particularly for the United States. Such studies would require a fairly long time series for a number of variables and for a number of geographic areas. Good time series data on migration within the U.S. are almost nonexistent, and hence even the most basic data requirements cannot be met.

The interaction between the causes and effects of migration suggests that an appropriate specification of an urban growth model would take into account the various interdependent factors involved in the growth process. Hence, a simultaneous-equations model of urban growth and migration is developed in this study. Because the study employs Census data, the period of analysis is 10 years. Two such periods, 1950–1960 and 1960–1970, are studied.

Location decisions of firms and of persons are likely to immediately affect supply and demand curves in both product and factor markets. In-migrants will increase factor supply schedules and product market demand functions. Out-migrants will have opposite effects. The product market effects will in turn shift derived factor demand curves, and any resulting change in factor prices will be reflected in shifting product supply functions. The consequences of industrial relocation are equally pervasive. The general set of interrelationships that characterizes the location decisions of individuals and firms is illustrated in Figure 6.1.

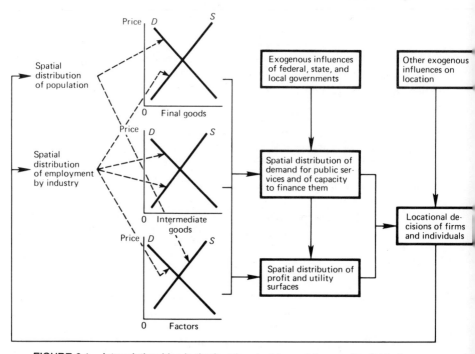

FIGURE 6.1.   Interrelationships in the location decisions of firms and individuals.

The cause and effect relationships that link the variables of interest operate on the supply and demand sides of both the factor market and the product market in a way that makes analytic manipulation of the system difficult.

Most of the remainder of this chapter describes the principal links that exist among the interdependent variables of the system developed here. First, however, the results of other studies that employ a simultaneous-equations model to examine the interrelationships between economic growth and migration are briefly surveyed.

Simultaneous-Equations Models of Migration

In the 1940s and early 1950s the orthodox economic theory of mobility was challenged by proponents of the "job vacancies" thesis, who argued that a high income or wage level means little to a worker if he does not have a job. In its purest form the job vacancies thesis regards workers as being responsive to job openings and not to income differentials. As suggested by Gallaway (1969) and Raimon (1962), however, no necessary conflict exists between the conventional wage differences model and the job vacancies model, and the empirical findings of Gallaway, Raimon, and others strongly confirm this contention.

It is now generally argued that destination population size is a proxy for the size of the labor market, and the larger the size of the labor market, the greater are likely to be both the number and type of available job opportunities. On the other hand, the larger the size of the origin population, the greater the number of persons who are likely to have any given reason to migrate.

The argument that migration is a positive function of the number of job opportunities has naturally led to the hypothesis that migration is a function of increases in such opportunities. Since good measures of changes in job vacancies do not exist, researchers commonly argue that where employment is expanding, vacancies must be expanding also. Hence, migration is expected to be in the direction of localities in which employment is growing most rapidly.

A major problem with this approach is that since migration must be measured over a finite time interval, it is itself influencing the observed growth of employment opportunities during this interval. An assumption that underlies the many single-equation, multiple-regression approaches to migration is that, whereas the various explanatory factors influence migration, migration does not in turn influence these factors. If this assumption does not in fact hold, the parameter estimates of the various models possess a simultaneous-equations bias that may be sufficiently great to vitiate the findings.

Borts and Stein (1964) come full-circle from stating that changes in employment cause migration to the position that migration causes changes in employment. A number of critical assumptions underlie the Borts and Stein argument, and from these flow the implication that the labor demand curve for a given locality is perfectly elastic. Hence, any increase in labor supply that results from migration must result in increased employment. Moreover, migration may induce increased investment expenditures in receiving localities, which causes the demand curve for labor to shift upward, and thus gives rise to higher wages. The higher wages induce increased labor force participation, which results in further increases in employment.

In spite of the data shortcomings referred to earlier, a few studies have been directed at examining the effects of migration within the context of a simultaneous-equations model. These studies have generally, but not always, focused on metropolitan areas, primarily because more and better data are typically available for such areas.

Muth (1968, 1971) attempts to reconcile the opposing views of the causal relationship between migration and employment growth by specifying a simultaneous-equations model of net migration and employment change. He argues that employment growth and migration are mutually dependent. Muth estimates his model by means of appropriate simultaneous-equations techniques and finds some support for each of the opposing hypotheses, although his results tend to favor the Borts and Stein hypothesis. As pointed out by Mazek and Chang (1972), Greenwood (1975b) and Goldstein and Moses (1973), certain problems underlie the Muth model. However, Muth's approach itself constitutes an important contribution to the migration literature.

Olvey (1972) has further developed the simultaneous-equations approach by introducing structural equations for jointly dependent variables other than migration and employment change. In his study of 1955–1960 migration and employment change in 56 large SMSAs, Olvey, like Muth, takes wages as exogenously determined. However, Olvey introduces five structural equations, one each for manufacturing employment growth, service employment growth, gross in-migration from within the state that contains the SMSA or from a contiguous state, gross in-migration from other states, and gross out-migration. By following the approach of many of the single-equation migration models that employ separate relationships for gross out- and gross in-migration, rather than one equation for net migration, Olvey better specifies his migration equations. Perhaps as a consequence, his results concerning migration tend to be stronger in the expected directions than do Muth's. This conclusion is particularly true regarding the effects of income on migration.

In his earlier paper Muth (1968) employs as his wage variable an index of manufacturing wage rates, which never appears significantly in his alternative estimates of the migration equation. In his later paper (1971) he utilizes family median income instead of manufacturing wages and obtains more favorable results. Moreover, in his earlier paper Muth treats manufacturing wage change as endogenous, but he never introduces his migration variable in his wage-change equation. The wage-change variable does have the anticipated (positive) sign in the four alternative migration equations in which it appears, but in two instances the t-value is less than one and in the highest alternative the value is less than 1.7.

Like Muth, Olvey finds that migration and employment growth are mutually dependent. However, whereas Muth's simultaneity runs between employment growth and net migration, Olvey's runs between employment growth and in-migration. Both the two- and three-stage least squares estimates of Olvey's model suggest that the coefficient on the employment-growth variable is over twice as high for in-migration from noncontiguous states as for in-migration from contiguous states. Although a strong case can be made for the inclusion of the employment-growth variable in the out-migration equation, Olvey does not so include the variable.

Perhaps one of the reasons that Olvey did not include his employment growth variable in the equation for out-migration is that his results were perverse when he did. As pointed out by Renshaw (1974), such perverse results are not uncommon. Renshaw argues that such results may be due largely to the fact that areas that experience much in-migration have relatively many persons who are "chronic movers," and thus these same areas tend to have much out-migration. In the framework of a single-equation model Renshaw has used time series data to demonstrate the existence of a negative relationship between employment growth and out-migration.

In a simultaneous-equations model of 1940–1950 net interstate migration, Okun (1968) introduces an endogenous variable for change in service income per capita. He finds that states with high levels of such income were attractive to migrants, whereas states with relatively great (absolute) increases tended to lose migrants. Moreover, he concludes that net in-migration tended to encourage absolute growth in service income per capita. Okun also finds that the racial composition of migrants had no significant effect on per capita service income.

Okun obtains a seemingly impressive R^2 of 0.86 (presumably based on instruments) on his two-stage least squares estimate of his income-change equation while employing just four explanatory variables: (a) service income per capita; (b) migrant racial composition; (c) net migration (1940–1950); and (d) an age-sex migrant selectivity factor. The specification of such an equation is, however, highly questionable. First, it is difficult to imagine how migration itself can be treated as endogenous while migrant characteristics, such as racial composition, are treated as exogenous. Second, Okun's apparently "good" results appear to be due largely to his using the income level to explain the absolute change in income level. (The simple correlation between the two variables is 0.88.) He argues simply that those factors that contribute to a high level are likely to contribute to large absolute changes in the level, but the meaningfulness of such reasoning is questionable. In an alternative model Okun replaces the income level as an explanatory variable with the precentage change in the percent of the state's labor force engaged in agriculture (L). The income level and L are highly correlated, with the simple correlation coefficient between their raw values being 0.81. No justification is presented for this alteration, but at an earlier point in his paper Okun argues that L is a function of the state's income level. The reasoning appears to suggest that the same argument that was used to justify the use of the income level to explain absolute changes in the level can be employed to justify the use of L to explain such absolute changes.

Persky and Kain (1970), in the context of a simultaneous-equations model of race-specific white and nonwhite migration and employment change for 250 nonmetropolitan counties in the Deep South, conclude that expansion or contraction of employment of black labor has less influence on black migration than expansion or contraction of white employment has on white migration. Persky and Kain speculate that this differential responsiveness may involve differences in the demographic characteristics of the two populations.

Although Okun's procedure of treating the racial composition of migration streams as exogenous while treating migration itself as endogenous is questionable, his attempt to introduce migrant characteristics into a simultaneous-equations model of migration is meaningful. As the literature on the externalities of migration so strongly suggests, not only the quantity of migration but also the characteristics of the migrants importantly determine the consequences of migration. An appropriate step in a more fully specified simultaneous-equations model is to treat migrant characteristics as endogenous in an attempt to better explain both the composition of migration streams and the impacts of out- and in-movement of persons of different characteristics.

The Theory

Following what we might call the traditional approach to the regional factor-market adjustment mechanism, let us, for the sake of simplicity, assume a two-region, two-factor economy in which relative endowments of the two factors initially differ between the regions. Further assume that each factor is homogeneous and fully employed. Let the factors be represented by K (capital) and L (labor) and assume that region H (the high-wage region) has a greater capital–labor ratio than region L (the low-wage region):

$$\frac{K_0^h}{L_0^h} > \frac{K_0^l}{L_0^l}$$

One view of the factor-price adjustment mechanism suggests that under the specified circumstances either commodity trade in the absence of factor mobility, factor mobility in the absence of commodity trade, or some combination of factor

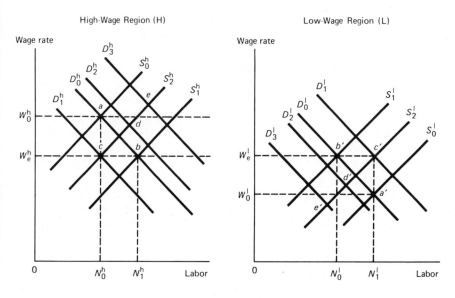

FIGURE 6.2.   Labor migration from low-wage region (L) to high-wage region (H).

mobility and commodity trade will lead to convergence of regional factor prices of comparable inputs.[1]

   If we assume that labor is a mobile factor and that in response to interregional wage differentials labor migrates from the low-wage region L to the high-wage region H, then out-migration from L will put upward pressure on wages in L while in-migration to H places downward pressure on wages in H. If psychic, information, and transportation costs are all assumed negligible, then migration will continue from L to H until wage equalization occurs. This argument is reflected in Figure 6.2 as a decrease in labor supply in L from S_0^l to S_1^l and as an increase in labor supply in H from S_0^h to S_1^h. Given respective labor demands of D_0^l and D_0^h, wage equalization occurs at $W_e^h = W_e^l$ (equilibrium points b and b', respectively).

   Because the labor–capital ratio is relatively high in L and relatively low in H the rate of return on capital tends to be relatively high in the low-wage region and relatively low in the high-wage region. If we assume that capital is also mobile and migrates in response to interregional differences in its rate of return, we would find capital migrating from H to L. Labor demand would fall in H because the decrease in capital would cause labor's marginal product schedule to shift to the left. Similarly, labor demand would rise in L because of the influx of capital.

―――――――――――――

[1]See, for example, Borts (1960), Borts and Stein (1964), Mundell (1957), and Samuelson (1948, 1953).

The above alternative is demonstrated in Figure 6.2 by demand D_1^h and supply S_2^h in the high-wage region and by demand D_1^l and supply S_2^l in the low-wage region (equilibrium points c and c', respectively). Note that these two pairs of curves are drawn so that employment levels in both regions remain unchanged relative to initial levels. Depending on the magnitudes of demand and supply elasticities and of the relative shifts of demand and supply, we could also show wage equalization at levels of employment greater or less than that initially prevailing in the respective regions. The important point to note here, however, is that the model predicts that out-migration of labor will put upward pressure on wage levels and that in-migration of labor will put downward pressure on wage levels. If capital is also free to migrate, the effects on wage levels will be reinforced, but the change in employment will be indeterminate a priori. Borts and Stein point out that if labor is mobile relative to capital, high-wage regions will experience more rapidly increasing employment than low-wage regions. Whether labor is in fact more mobile than capital is, however, an empirical question.

One objective of this study is to formulate a model that predicts that in-migration of labor will cause increased employment and that out-migration will cause decreased employment but that also predicts that the effects of migration on average wage levels are indeterminate a priori. At least two complementary approaches might be followed. The first is to assume that each region produces an export commodity and a commodity that is locally consumed. Now if in-migration causes an increase in demand for the locally produced and consumed commodity, marginal revenue will rise in this industry, and the derived demand for labor will also rise. If the industry accounts for a significant fraction of local employment, labor demand in the locality as a whole will rise, and consequently upward pressure will be exerted on both local employment and wage levels. An opposite set of consequences will prevail in the region experiencing out-migration.

This situation is depicted in Figure 6.2 by supply curve S_2^h and either demand curve D_2^h or D_3^h (equilibrium points d or e). Given an increase in labor supply to S_2^h, average wage levels in region H will fall if demand shifts to D_2^h (point d) but will rise if demand shifts to D_3^h (point e). Since the relative magnitudes of the shifts of the demand and supply curves of labor are not determinate a priori, in-migration's effect on average wage levels is indeterminate, but, clearly, in-migration causes increased employment in the region. An opposite set of occurrences (shown by S_2^l and either D_2^l or D_3^l) may prevail in the region experiencing out-migration.

It might reasonably be argued that the demand shift associated with out-migration, for example, is unlikely to be of sufficient magnitude to result in demand D_3^l. A second argument that might be made, which reinforces the previous argument, assumes that rather than being a homogeneous input, labor is heterogeneous. This assumption does in fact reflect real-world conditions. More-over, assume that the grades of labor that on the average embody the most human capital are also the most mobile.[2] Now, if the labor that migrates out of the low-wage region is relatively heavily endowed with human capital compared to that remaining behind, the marginal product schedule of the remaining workers could shift downward due to the loss of a complementary input. This conse-quence would be especially likely if the migrants were members of the entre-preneurial class. Out-migration from L might therefore be expected to result in decreased employment, but whether wage levels would rise or fall would depend on the magnitude of the resulting demand shift (to $D\frac{1}{2}$ or $D\frac{1}{3}$) relative to the supply shift (to $S\frac{1}{2}$).

The above argument suggests that the effects on sending and receiving regions need not be symmetrical because, whereas the out-migrants from L might be relatively well-endowed with human capital compared to those left behind at L, the migrants may possess less human capital than that possessed by the average resident of H. This particular possibility is probably reflective of the situation that has prevailed in rural to urban migration in the United States and other developed economies.

Finally, we might argue that even if capital were also mobile, a number of factors suggest that it might be attracted more than proportionately to the high-wage region rather than to the low-wage region. Borts and Stein (1964) argue that in-migration may induce capital accumulation. One reason for such capital accumulation to occur is that the demands of new migrants cause an increase in capital's rate of return in the locally oriented industry (which for Borts and Stein is the service industry). Moreover, certain industries are attracted to locate in regions with relatively highly skilled work forces, and if the highly skilled workers are being attracted to high-wage regions, these industries would also tend to locate in such regions. If the high-wage regions experience both a higher rate of growth of labor supply and a higher rate of capital accumulation, then we would expect employment to grow most rapidly in such regions, but whether wage levels would increase or decrease is an empirical question dependent upon the relative magnitudes of labor demand and supply changes.

Specification of the Model

The basic urban growth model estimated for the study consists of 14 equations (9 structural and 5 identities) in 14 jointly dependent (endogenous) variables. The endogenous variables include the rate of CLF out-migration

[2]That better-educated and higher-income persons tend in fact to be the most mobile has been well-documented in the migration literature. For a detailed discussion of the relevant literature, see Greenwood (1975b).

(OMR), the rate of CLF in-migration (IMR), the rate of income growth ($I\dot{N}C$), the rate of employment growth ($E\dot{M}P$), the rate of unemployment growth ($UN\dot{E}MP$), the rate of natural growth of the CLF ($N\dot{A}T$), and the rate of total CLF growth ($C\dot{L}F$). Out-migration is disaggregated to out-migration to other SMSAs ($OMTSR$) and out-migration to nonmetropolitan areas ($OMTNR$). In-migration is disaggregated to in-migration from other SMSAs ($IMFSR$) and in-migration from nonmetropolitan areas ($IMFNR$). Finally, employment growth is disaggregated into component changes in manufacturing employment ($MA\dot{N}U$), government employment ($GE\dot{M}P$), and other nonmanufacturing employment ($NMA\dot{N}U$). Specifically, the model is of the following form:

$$OMTSR = f_1(IM\hat{S}FR, \hat{I}\dot{N}C, E\hat{\dot{M}}P, UN\hat{\dot{E}}MP, INC, UNR, CLF, EDU, AGE,$$
$$D1, D2, D3, D4, e_1), \tag{6.1}$$

$$OMTNR = f_2(IM\hat{F}NR, \ldots, e_2), \tag{6.2}$$

$$IMFSR = f_3(OM\hat{T}SR, \hat{I}\dot{N}C, E\hat{\dot{M}}P, UN\hat{\dot{E}}MP, INC, UNR, CLF,$$
$$D1, D2, D3, D4, e_3), \tag{6.3}$$

$$IMFNR = f_4(OM\hat{T}NR, \ldots, e_4), \tag{6.4}$$

$$I\dot{N}C = f_5(O\hat{\dot{M}}R, I\hat{\dot{M}}R, N\hat{\dot{A}}T, UN\hat{\dot{E}}MP, INC, E\dot{D}U, NW, ARMFC,$$
$$D1, D2, D3, D4, e_5), \tag{6.5}$$

$$MA\dot{N}U = f_6(O\hat{\dot{M}}R, I\hat{\dot{M}}R, N\hat{\dot{A}}T, MANU, INC, RRET, E\dot{D}U, ARMFC,$$
$$D1, D2, D3, D4, e_6), \tag{6.6}$$

$$GE\dot{M}P = f_7(O\hat{\dot{M}}R, I\hat{\dot{M}}R, N\hat{\dot{A}}T, INC, GEMP, E\dot{D}U, ARMFC, D1, D2,$$
$$D3, D4, e_7), \tag{6.7}$$

$$NMA\dot{N}U = f_8(O\hat{\dot{M}}R, I\hat{\dot{M}}R, N\hat{\dot{A}}T, MA\hat{\dot{N}}U, NMANU, INC, ARMFC, D1,$$
$$D2, D3, D4, e_8), \tag{6.8}$$

$$UN\dot{E}MP = f_9(O\hat{\dot{M}}R, I\hat{\dot{M}}R, N\hat{\dot{A}}T, INC, UNR, NW, ARMFC, D1, D2,$$
$$D3, D4, e_9), \tag{6.9}$$

$$OMR \equiv OMTSR + OMTNR, \tag{6.10}$$

$$IMR \equiv IMFSR + IMFNR, \tag{6.11}$$

$$C\dot{L}F \equiv \frac{EMP}{CLF} \cdot E\dot{M}P + \frac{UNEMP}{CLF} \cdot UN\dot{E}MP, \tag{6.12}$$

$$E\dot{M}P \equiv \frac{MANU}{EMP} \cdot MA\dot{N}U + \frac{GEMP}{EMP} \cdot GE\dot{M}P + \frac{NMANU}{EMP} \cdot NMA\dot{N}U, \tag{6.13}$$

$$N\dot{A}T \equiv C\dot{L}F + (2 \cdot OMR) - (2 \cdot IMR) - 1. \tag{6.14}$$

Detailed definitions of each variable employed in the model, as well as data sources, are to be found in the Appendix to this chapter. All variables except the regional dummies ($D1$, $D2$, $D3$, $D4$) are expressed as logarithms. Each variable that relates to a change is defined as the ratio of the end-of-period to beginning-of-period level of the variable. Hence, these variables are defined as rates of growth.

Data characteristics that led to certain of the variable definitions employed in this study should be mentioned. Since the migration data refer to CLF movements that occurred between 1955 and 1960 (1965 and 1970), but data relating to the other endogenous variables and certain exogenous variables refer to changes that occurred between 1950 and 1960 (1960 and 1970), two options regarding variable definitions are available. The option chosen in this study is to assume that the migratory movements that occurred between 1950 and 1955, for example, were identical to those that occurred between 1955 and 1960. Thus, logical consistency requires that the migration figures all be multiplied by 2. This multiplication does not result in changes in the parameter estimates of the explanatory variables of the model.

It should be noted, however, that to the extent that CLF migration differed between 1950–1955 and 1955–1960 and between 1960–1965 and 1965–1970, an unknown degree of bias may be imparted to the results. Since during the first half of the 1950 decade the Korean War was a dominant factor in the economy, while during the second half of the decade general sluggishness characterized the economy, the volume of migration that occurred over the two 5-year periods may well have been different. Somewhat the same type of situation may have prevailed during the 1960s due to the importance of the Vietnam War during the latter half of the decade. It is unlikely, however, that the CLF migration that occurred between 1955 and 1960 (1965 and 1970) was drastically different from that that occurred between 1950 and 1955 (1960 and 1965), since migratory movements generally appear to be dominated by longer-run phenomena, though they are surely somewhat sensitive to the cyclical behavior of the economy.

The second option available was to define other endogenous variables and exogenous variables, where possible, in a fashion consistent with the migration variables. This option would require the assumption that the appropriate changes occurred at a constant average annual rate between 1950 and 1960 (1960 and 1970). The 1955 (1965) level of each variable could thus be interpolated and the 1955–1960 (1965–1970) change estimated. This alternative is no more desirable than the first, and probably less so, since it requires the assumption that the 1950–1955 (1960–1965) behavior of each variable except migration was identical to that variable's 1955–1960 (1965–1970) behavior. Given the simultaneous nature of the model, there does not appear to be good reason to suppose that migration differed over the two periods while the variables that influence and are influenced by migration behaved similarly. Moreover, since under the second option even the exogenous variables must be defined for 1955 (from 1950 and

1960 data) and for 1965 (from 1960 and 1970 data), these as well as other variables would be sensitive to the respective 1960 and 1970 levels and hence sensitive to the differential impact that migration may have had during the two 5-year periods. Although neither option is without obvious shortcomings, the former appears to be preferable to the latter.

A few words are in order concerning the identities that close the system. The identities for $C\dot{L}F$, $E\dot{M}P$, and $N\dot{A}T$ are obtained as follows. First, 1970 CLF, for example, is decomposed into its components—employment and unemployment:

$$CLF70 \equiv EMP70 + UNEMP70. \qquad (6.15)$$

This expression is then divided through by 1960 CLF to yield

$$\frac{CLF70}{CLF60} \equiv \frac{EMP70}{CLF60} + \frac{UNEMP70.}{CLF60} \qquad (6.16)$$

The two terms on the right-hand side of the identity are then multiplied, respectively, by $EMP60/EMP60$ and $UNEMP60/UNEMP60$. When the two right-hand terms are rearranged, the expression becomes

$$\frac{CLF70}{CLF60} \equiv \frac{EMP60}{CLF60} \cdot \frac{EMP70}{EMP60} + \frac{UNEMP60}{CLF60} \cdot \frac{UNEMP70.}{UNEMP60} \qquad (6.17)$$

This expression is then written as

$$C\dot{L}F \equiv \frac{EMP}{CLF} \cdot E\dot{M}P + \frac{UNEMP}{CLF} \cdot UN\dot{E}MP. \qquad (6.18)$$

Note then that each component rate of growth is weighted by the respective beginning-of-period share of civilian labor force.

A comparable procedure is followed in the derivation of the identity for the rate of employment growth ($E\dot{M}P$). Note that in this instance each component rate of growth is weighted by the respective beginning-of-period share of total employment.

The identity for the natural growth of the CLF is based on the notion that, in any given locality over any given period of time, the actual change in CLF must be equal to the difference between local labor force entrants and exits plus CLF out-migrants minus CLF in-migrants. Hence, a locality's natural change in CLF between 1950 and 1960, for example, would be given by

$$NAT \equiv CLF60 - CLF50 + 2OM - 2IM. \qquad (6.19)$$

Migration is multiplied by 2 because of the assumption that 1950–1955 migration was equal to 1955–1960 migration. In reality, even if migration over the 1950–1955 period were identical to that over the 1955–1960 period, by 1960 more of the 1950–1955 migrants would be likely to have moved elsewhere, left the labor force, or died.

For the reasons mentioned above, the adjustment factor of 2 is undoubtedly too high. The resulting estimates of natural CLF change for areas with roughly zero net migration would, however, be little affected by the adjustment factor because the adjustments on in- and out-migration would offset one another. For areas with substantial net out-migration, natural increase tends to be overestimated, while for areas with substantial net in-migration, natural increase tends to be underestimated.

The identity given by (6.14) is in terms of rates of growth. Expression (6.14) can be derived from (6.19) by dividing the latter by $CLF50$. In fact, the rate of natural increase variable utilized in this study was calculated as shown in (6.14). Since $N\dot{A}T$ is defined in terms of endogenous variables, it must be treated as endogenous.

THE OUT- AND IN-MIGRATION EQUATIONS

The model contains two types of migration variables, one relating to out-migration and the other relating to in-migration. The use of two types of migration measures is in contrast to the use of a net-migration variable, such as has been utilized by Muth (1968, 1971), for example, in his simultaneous-equations models. For certain purposes no good alternative exists to the use of a variable relating to net migration because separate measures of out- and in-migration are not available. This appears to be the reason that Muth used a measure of net migration in his studies.

The use of both gross out- and gross in-migration variables is, however, preferable to the use of a variable relating to net migration. This point is stressed by Bowman and Myers (1967) and by Sjaastad (1962). The magnitude of the influence of certain factors on out-migration is likely to be different from the magnitude of the influence of these factors on in-migration, and certain factors that are relevant to explaining out-migration are not relevant to explaining in-migration. The use of two gross migration variables allows account to be taken of differences in the determinants and consequences of out- and in-migration. The use of a net-migration concept would involve a substantial loss of information and possesses no apparent advantages that cannot also be achieved by regarding the effect of net migration as the sum of the effects of gross out- and gross in-migration.

Since both CLF and other characteristics of nonmetropolitan areas tend to be decidedly different from those of metropolitan areas, the magnitude of the influence of various factors on migration from or to SMSAs is likely to differ from the magnitude of the influence of these factors on migration from or to non-SMSA areas. Moreover, since the characteristics of CLF members who leave SMSAs are somewhat different from those of CLF members who leave non-SMSA areas, the impact on the destination of migration from the two types of origins is likely to be different. For example, for the 50 largest SMSAs in the 1960 sample, white in-migrants from other SMSAs were older, better-educated, and had higher incomes and lower unemployment rates than white in-migrants from nonmetropolitan areas.[3] Due to these considerations the out- and in-migration variables are disaggregated according to metropolitan or nonmetropolitan destination or origin, respectively.

Much research has shown that gross migration flows between regions are importantly a function of origin and destination characteristics and the distance between the localities. One might thus argue that the proper specification of the migration equations would include as dependent variables unidirectional flows such that out-migration from A is allocated as in-migration to destinations B, C, etc. Account might therefore be taken of the likelihood that A would lose more migrants if, for example, relatively attractive income or employment opportunities were to exist in nearby localities D and E. However, in the present context a number of factors prevent this type of specification. Published census migration data relating to interarea flows concern population migration and not CLF migration, which is the variable utilized in this study. Estimates of CLF migration could be made from information on population migration, but the basic consistency of the CLF migration, employment change, and unemployment change data utilized herein would be lost.

Another and more severe problem is that if such a matrix of CLF migration flows could be introduced, the data would not be closed in the sense that the matrix would account for all in- and out-migration for any given locality. For the SMSAs that make up the present data base many migrants come from and go to SMSAs not so included, and many come from and go to nonmetropolitan areas as well. Failure to close the migration system is thus a problem that would be encountered in using unidirectional migration flows between geographic areas like SMSAs. (States would be more amenable to such an analysis because the migration system would be largely self-contained.) Since, given migrant characteristics, the consequences for a locality of gaining or losing migrants are largely independent of the migrants' point of origin or destination, any associated specification problems are limited to the migration equations themselves. If either the magnitudes of the ordinary least squares R^2s or the number of significant three-stage least squares parameter estimates are used as criteria to judge the quality of their specification, the migration equations appear to be reasonable as specified.

Because the out- and in-migration concepts are somewhat, though not com-

---

[3]The mean percentages of white in-migrants from SMSAs compared to the mean percentages of white in-migrants from nonmetropolitan areas are, respectively, as follows:

1. Percentage 15 to 29 years of age: 33.63 compared to 41.57.
2. Percentage of those 25 years of age and over with 4 or more years of college: 23.16 compared to 16.30.
3. Percentage of in-migrant families (all races) with family income greater than $10,000: 24.17 compared to 14.27.
4. Unemployment rate: 4.68 compared to 5.09.

pletely, symmetrical, the following presentation is facilitated by considering both the out- and in-migration equations in the same content. The model that is employed in this study attempts to explain gross out- and gross in-migration without the explicit introduction of an individual decision function. Rather, gross out- and gross in-migration are related to a number of aggregate proxy variables. Let us next turn to a discussion of these variables.

If migration tends to be away from relatively low-income areas and toward relatively high-income areas, then the higher the beginning-of-period income level of an SMSA (INC), the smaller its expected out-migration and the larger its expected in-migration, *ceteris paribus*. Furthermore, because relatively rapid income growth (INC) may cause potential migrants to be optimistic about future income prospects, areas with rapidly rising incomes may prove desirable destinations for migrants. Since the relevant income measure for the potential migrant to consider is the present discounted value of his stream of expected future returns, both the current income level and expected future levels enter into the potential migrant's present-value calculation. Given the current income level, the greater the expected future increase in income, for which the current actual increase may be a good proxy, the poorer is the current level as a proxy for the discounted value of the stream of expected future returns.

Migrants may, therefore, be expected to move not only to areas with relatively high income levels but also to areas with relatively rapidly growing income levels because, *ceteris paribus* (including income level), the greater the expected increase in future income, the greater will be the present discounted value of the stream of expected future returns. This argument suggests that areas experiencing relatively sizeable income growth are expected to experience relatively small out-migration and relatively large in-migration, *ceteris paribus*.[4]

Several previous studies indicate that where in-migration tends to be great, so does out-migration.[5] A number of explanations have been offered for the phenomenon. Miller (1967) suggests that areas that experience much in-migration also experience out-migration because such areas possess substantial segments of their populations that are "migration prone." Since migration is selective of that portion of the population that is highly mobile, those who have moved at least once are more likely to migrate than those who have not moved at all.[6] Eldridge (1965) estimates that 17% of the 1955–1960 interstate migrants were return migrants, which suggests that a significant fraction of out-migrants is likely to be disenchanted in-migrants from an earlier period who return home.[7]

---

[4]Bowles (1970), Sjaastad (1962), and Wertheimer (1970) discuss in some detail the rationale for the use of the present-value income concept.

[5]See, for example, Eldridge (1965), Miller (1967), and Stone (1971).

[6]Eldridge (1965, p.449) estimates that for 1955–1960 interstate migration, the probability of primary migration was 6%, whereas the probability of remigration (secondary plus return) was 18%.

[7]Stone (1971) discusses other possible explanations for the high correlation between in- and out-migration.

Since a causal relationship is postulated between in- and out-migration, a further test of the hypothesis is rendered by the inclusion of the in-migration variables in the corresponding out-migration equations as well as the inclusion of the out-migration variables in the corresponding in-migration equations.

Localities with larger labor markets are likely to experience both absolutely more out- and in-migration. In the structural equations for migration, beginning-of-period CLF has been placed on the right-hand side of the equations because no strong a priori reasons suggests that the relationships between size of the urban area and migration from or to the area should be unitary elastic, which is the implicit assumption made by excluding CLF as an independent variable.[8] Hence, no specification is made of the direction of the relationships between CLF and the migration rates.

It is generally expected that the out-migration rate will be lower and the in-migration rate will be higher the greater the rate of employment growth (*EMP*) that occurs in a region, *ceteris paribus*. The growth of employment is here considered to be a proxy for the expansion of job opportunities in an area and is expected to reflect growing labor demand. (That migration to—or from—a given region may itself encourage more—less—rapid employment growth in that region will be treated in the discussion of the employment-change equations.)

Areas that are experiencing relatively rapid increase in excess labor supply (i.e., unemployment) are likely to experience relatively heavy out-migration and relatively light in-migration. Moreover, areas having higher unemployment rates (*UNR*) are also expected to experience both larger out-migration and smaller in-migration. Localities in which the pool of unemployment is increasing rapidly or in which the unemployment rate is high offer the potential migrant rather poor prospects for quick reemployment because jobs either are already difficult to find or are becoming more difficult to find. Furthermore, to the extent that the migrant must spend more time searching for work where such conditions prevail, his opportunity costs of entering these labor markets will be greater. Additionally, since the opportunity costs of migration are lower for unemployed CLF members, out-migration is expected to increase with increased rates of unemployment growth (*UNEMP*) and with increased rates of unemployment.

A number of personal characteristics are likely to exert important influences on the individual's decision to migrate.[9] Among these characteristics are age

---

[8]Note that a coefficient on CLF that is not significantly different from zero in an equation for the migration rate suggests that the relationship between absolute migration and CLF size is unitary elastic.

[9]At this point a certain lack of symmetry between the out- and in-migration equations is evident. This lack of symmetry results when an attempt is made to account for certain characteristics of the population at risk as migrants. The characteristics of the population at the origin are more relevant in a discussion of the population at risk, since this is the population from which the migrants are drawn.

and level of education. The probability that a labor-force member will migrate is likely to decrease as his age increases, since older persons have a shorter expected working life over which to realize the advantages of migrating, which makes the rate of return on migration lower for them. Moreover, as Becker (1962, 1964) points out, individuals for whom migration is profitable find it more profitable to move immediately because to postpone moving involves the loss during early years of returns that are discounted least. Job security and family ties are also likely to be more important for older persons than for younger ones, which will further discourage older persons from migrating. Out-migration is thus expected to be lower the higher the median age (*AGE*) of the SMSA, *ceteris paribus.*[10]

Employment information and job opportunities are both expected to increase with increased education. Each factor should in turn tend to increase the likelihood that an individual will migrate. Moreover, education may also reduce the importance of tradition and family ties and increase an individual's awareness of other localities, with the consequence that the forces that hold him to his present locality are weakened. Thus, *ceteris paribus,* the higher the level of education (*EDU*) of the SMSA, the greater the expected out-migration.

Four regional dummy variables are included in each of the migration equations as well as in the other structural equations of the model. The dummy variables are constructed to reflect the significance of the differential (intercept) shift for any one region (West, South, North Central, or Northeast) relative to each of the other regions.[11] If α_1, α_2, α_3, and α_4 are taken to be the coefficients of $D1$, $D2$, $D3$, and $D4$, respectively, then the regional intercepts are given as follows: West = α_1; South = $\alpha_1 + \alpha_2$; North Central = $\alpha_1 + \alpha_2 + \alpha_3$; and Northeast = $\alpha_1 + \alpha_2 + \alpha_3 + \alpha_4$. The *t*-value associated with α_2 thus gives the significance of the differential shift for the South as compared to the West, while the *t*-value associated with $\alpha_2 + \alpha_3$ (i.e., $(\alpha_2 + \alpha_3)/[\text{var}(D2 + D3)]^{1/2}$) gives the significance of the differential shift for the North Central as compared to the West. In similar fashion the significance of the differential shift for all 54 pairs of possibilities (six pairs for each of nine equations) can be obtained.

In the migration equations significant differential shifts might result from a number of factors. Regional differences in climate, cost of living, or social milieu could give rise to regional differences in the average propensity to migrate. Other factors that operate with differential impacts on the various regions

[10]For a detailed discussion of the relationship between age and migration, see Gallaway (1969).

[11]For purposes of analysis, the SMSAs have been grouped slightly differently than they would have been if strict census definitions of regions has been used. Baltimore and Washington, D.C. have been removed from the South and placed in the Northeast, and Pittsburgh has been removed from the Northeast and placed in the North Central region, which is otherwise identical to the North Central census region as previously defined.

and are not accounted for by existing variables in the equations could also give rise to significant differential shifts for various pairs of regions.

THE INCOME-GROWTH EQUATION

As suggested in the section entitled "The Theory" in this chapter, no strong a priori reason suggests that the signs associated with the out- and in-migration variables in the income growth equations should be positive, negative, or equal to zero. Migration from or to a given area influences labor demand as well as labor supply in that area. The movement of persons from one locality to another causes labor supply to increase in the recipient locality and to decrease in the sending locality. In itself such a movement may be expected to place downward pressure on wage rates and average (labor) income levels in the destination and upward pressure in the origin, if labor-demand functions are not perfectly elastic. However, if either the prices of locally produced goods and services or the marginal product of locally supplied labor is sensitive in a positive direction to in-migration and sensitive in a negative direction to out-migration, then the derived demand for labor will tend to increase in the recipient region and decline in the sending region.

Although the price level of the locality's exportable commodities may not be particularly sensitive to migration, the price level of those goods and services that are both locally produced and consumed is likely to be somewhat sensitive. This sensitivity may not be symmetrical between sending and receiving regions, since downward price rigidity may prevent price declines in sending localities. Moreover, if in-migration induces increased investment and if out-migration induces decreased investment in a locality, then labor's marginal product may be expected to increase in the receiving region and decrease in the sending region. Those adjustments that tend to result in outward shifts of the labor-demand function in the recipient region and in inward shifts in the sending region place upward pressure on wage rates and income levels in the destination and downward pressure in the origin.

There appears to be no reason to suppose that the labor demand shift associated with migration will dominate the labor supply shift, that the supply will dominate the demand shift, or that the shifts will not offset one another. The signs on the out- and in-migration variables are therefore regarded as an empirical matter and no a priori specification of the direction of the relationship between the out- and in-migration variables and income change is made.

For the same reasons that a sign is not specified on the migration variables in the income-change equation, a sign is not specified on $N\dot{A}T$. Greater natural CLF increase results in greater increased labor supply, but it results in greater labor demand as well. No strong reason suggests that such supply shifts will dominate or be dominated by such demand shifts.

Excess labor supply conditions are, other things being equal, expected to place downward pressure on wage levels. Hence, the greater the growth of excess labor supply, the smaller the expected income growth. In the income-change equation the sign on the unemployment-change variable is thus expected to be negative.

It is generally thought that a high correlation exists between education and income levels, and a positive relationship is expected between changes in these variables. Particularly if the latter relationship were alarmingly high, a problem could arise in specifying the direction of the relationship between $E\dot{D}U$ and $I\dot{N}C$. However, the simple correlation coefficients between neither pair of variables are particularly high.[12] Moreover, the lags involved in the relationship between income change and education change are likely to be greater than those between education change and income change, since many of the education effects of income growth accrue to offspring. Hence, the relationship is specified as running from education change to income change. If increased education $(E\dot{D}U)$ results in increased labor productivity, the consequence of the increased education will be increased labor demand. Given labor supply curves that are not perfectly elastic in the relevant ranges, increased labor demand will result in increased growth of wages and mean or median income levels.

Another variable included in the income-change equation is percentage of population that is nonwhite (NW). To the extent that discriminatory practices directed against nonwhites result in upward wage rigidities for them, it is to be expected that the greater the percentage of the locality's population that is nonwhite, the smaller will be the locality's income growth.

Systematic interregional differences in the quality of out- and in-migrants, or of new CLF entrants (net of migration), could lead to significant differential intercept shifts for regions. Moreover, differential (physical) capital growth and/or differential impacts of technical progress for regions could also account for interregional differences in income growth. Unfortunately, appropriate information on the stock of physical capital does not exist, and it is thus not possible to ascertain the independent influence of increased capital stock on either income or employment growth.

THE EMPLOYMENT-CHANGE EQUATIONS

The expected impacts of CLF out- and in-migration on a locality's level of employment are clear. Since in-migration results in rightward shifts of both labor supply and demand curves and out-migration results in leftward shifts of these curves, in-migration is expected to increase the locality's level of employment,

---

[12]The simple correlation coefficients between the raw values of the various pairs of variables are as follows: (a) $EDU50$ and $INC50 = 0.169$; (b) $E\dot{D}U50$–60 and $I\dot{N}C50$–$60 = 0.060$; (c) $EDU60$ and $INC60 = 0.276$; (d) $E\dot{D}U60$–70 and $I\dot{N}C60$–$70 = 0.135$.

whereas out-migration is expected to reduce the level. These are the results hypothesized in the previous section.

These effects may be regarded as the relatively direct effects of migration on employment in the sending and receiving regions. Certain indirect effects of migration on employment levels may also be of importance and may reinforce the direct effects. Borts and Stein (1964) argue that migration to a region is likely to induce investment in that region, which will in turn further increase the demand for labor, and thus given positive supply elasticities, the level of employment. The opposite consequences are likely to be felt in regions that are losing migrants. Thus, *ceteris paribus,* the greater the rate of out-migration, the smaller the expected rate of employment growth, and the greater the rate of in-migration, the greater the expected rate of employment growth.

Since the CLF can increase due to an excess of labor-force entrants over exits (net of migration), labor supply and hence employment may rise due to "natural" factors. The signs expected on the natural CLF increase variable ($N\dot{A}T$) are thus positive.

Employment change has been disaggregated to three components—change in manufacturing, change in government, and change in other nonmanufacturing employment. The distinction between change in manufacturing and change in other nonmanufacturing employment has been made so that these classifications might serve as crude proxies for change in employment in export- and in nonexport-oriented industries, respectively. The export-base theory of regional growth suggests that employment is in basically two types of industries, those that produce goods for export from the region and those that produce goods and services for local consumption. Employment in the "basic," or export-oriented industries, is taken to be a function of demand in the "rest-of-the-world," and is thus taken to be a function of factors exogenous to the given region. In turn, nonexport-oriented employment is taken to be a function of employment in the basic sector. Exogenous shifts in export demand are seen as causing changes in demand for labor in the export sector, and as these changes in labor demand are met by changes in labor supply, consequent changes in demand for labor in the nonexport sector occur. Hence, employment in the nonexport-oriented industries rises by some multiple of employment in the export-oriented industries. Although the sign on the $MA\dot{N}U$ variable in the $NMA\dot{N}U$ equation is expected to be positive, the view expressed herein is not that of the naïve export-base theory of growth, since both manufacturing and nonmanufacturing employment changes are made functions of changes in local labor endowments.

A reasonable argument can be made that the local public sector is largely endogenous to migration. Greater rates of in-migration, for example, are likely to result in greater rates of growth of demand for local public services of various types, such as education. To the extent that these new demands are met, higher in-migration rates result in greater rates of growth of local government employment. To a lesser extent, perhaps, state employment in the local area can also be regarded as endogenous to migration. However, prior to the *1970 Census* no distinction was made in the census between state and local government employment on the one hand and federal employment on the other, and hence total government employment is here treated as endogenous. In the 62 SMSAs that constitute the sample employed in this study, an average of 71% of total government employment was state and local in 1970.

In any given industry the higher the rate of return on capital, the greater the expected rate of capital accumulation. *Ceteris paribus,* the greater the rate of capital accumulation, the greater the rate of increase in labor demand and in employment. Appropriate state data do exist for manufacturing industries to allow the estimation of at least crude rates of return on fixed assets by SMSA. Hence, the following measure of the rate of return (*RRET*) in manufacturing industries was formulated: *RRET* = (value added minus payrolls)/(gross book value of depreciable and depletable assets). The expected sign on the rate of return variable is positive. This measure of the rate of return follows Griliches (1969). Value added and payroll data are SMSA specific. However, value of assets has been estimated for SMSAs from data on states. Assets for the state as a whole were distributed across SMSAs on the basis of the percentage of the state's value added contributed by the SMSA in question.

Borts and Stein assert that, if capital is immobile among regions while labor is mobile, employment in high-wage regions should grow more rapidly than in low-wage regions. Olvey (1970), on the other hand, argues that if high wages reflect a low return on investment, employment growth should tend to be higher the lower the wage.[13] Borts (1960) argues in a similar vein when he considers a one-product, two-factor, two-region economy in which capital is abundant relative to labor in one of the regions; and labor, relative to capital in the other. Wage rates are high in the former region relative to the latter, and the rate of return to capital is high in the latter relative to the former. As a consequence of such conditions, labor migrates to the high-wage region, where the rate of return on capital is low, and capital migrates to the low-wage region, where the rate of return on capital is high. Due to the inflow of capital in the low-wage region and the outflow in the high-wage region, the demand for labor grows more rapidly in the low-wage region, with the consequence that wages also grow more rapidly there. Moreover, labor supply grows less rapidly in the low-wage region and more rapidly in the high-wage region, which tends to promote further wage equalization. However, since the out- and in-migration variables should themselves pick up the effects of labor migration on employment growth, the beginning-of-period income-level variable, which serves as a proxy for the wage level, should reflect the effects of differential capital growth and have a negative

[13]The views of Borts and Stein and of Olvey are not necessarily inconsistent.

sign in the $MAN\dot{U}$ equation. This latter argument applies particularly well to labor intensive manufacturing industries in their search for cheap labor.

In each of the employment-change equations education growth and growth of armed forces personnel are expected to have positive signs. The beginning-of-period fraction of total employment accounted for by each employment category has also been included as an independent variable in the respective employment growth equations. In the case of manufacturing industries the existence of agglomeration economies could result in more rapid growth of manufacturing employment in areas in which manufacturing employment is relatively important. Such a phenomenon is likely to evidence itself over limited time periods, since, eventually, agglomeration economies are likely to be offset by diseconomies of scale.

In localities in which government employment is relatively important, such as in Washington, D.C. and in state capitals, government employment is likely to grow at disproportionately high rates during periods of relatively rapid expansion of government employment. However, as with manufacturing employment, it is unlikely that this phenomenon will hold indefinitely. Since no attempt is made in this study to distinguish which phase of growth the various sectors are in during the specific decade in question, no specification is made of the direction of the relationships between the beginning-of-period employment-share variables and the various employment growth rates.

Whereas product market conditions in a given SMSA are likely to have important consequences for that SMSA's nonexport-oriented industries, the consequences for export-oriented industries are likely to be much less strong, since only a relatively small fraction of the output of such industries will be purchased locally. The income-level variable is therefore included in the $NMAN\dot{U}$ equation to account for the local demand effects of higher income.

In addition to those factors mentioned in connection with regional differences in income change, certain other factors might give rise to regional differences in employment change. Fuchs (1962b) suggests that one such important factor during the 1955–1960 period was the rapid expansion of the aircraft industry in temperate climates. He further suggests that unionization discouraged, and the availability of space encouraged, the relocation of manufacturing industries. These latter two factors are likely to vary systematically between regions. Each of these factors would lead us to anticipate a differential shift in manufacturing employment growth in favor of the West and the South relative to the North Central region and the Northeast.

THE UNEMPLOYMENT-CHANGE EQUATION

Both Borts and Stein (1964) and Muth (1971) take the labor-demand curve for a locality to be perfectly elastic. However, the existence of unemployment (in excess of frictional) is not consistent with perfectly elastic labor demand. That the SMSAs serving as the data base had substantial unemployment over the 1950–1970 period is evident. The average rates of unemployment for the three census years, beginning with 1950, are, respectively, 4.8, 4.6, and 4.0%. Hence, unemployment-change is treated as an endogenous variable in this model. Moreover, the use of unemployment-change as an endogenous variable is consistent with the use of employment-change as endogenous, and the use of the former closes the system since it must necessarily be true that the change in CLF is made up of component changes in employment and unemployment.

Previously it was argued that, since migration affects labor demand as well as labor supply in both the sending and receiving areas, no a priori reason suggests that the impact on income levels will be in one direction or the other. A similar argument holds with respect to the influence of migration on unemployment. If the leftward (rightward) demand shift associated with out- (in-) migration were to dominate the leftward (rightward) supply shift associated with out- (in-) migration, unemployment would tend to rise (fall), given the wage rate at its initial, higher than equilibrium, level. There appears to be no more reason to suppose that this dominance will occur than to suppose that supply shift will dominate demand shift, thus causing out- (in-) migration to place downward (upward) pressure on unemployment levels.

A final possibility is that migration has no impact on unemployment. It should be recognized, however, that to the extent that the unemployed are over-represented in migration streams and to the extent that unemployed out-migrants from a locality tend to become unemployed in-migrants in some other locality, the supply shift associated with migration is likely to dominate the demand shift, such that out-migration results in decreased unemployment whereas in-migration results in increased unemployment. Moreover, to the extent that the percentage of the work force that is frictionally unemployed does not vary across SMSAs, out-migration should reduce unemployment by reducing the size of the labor force whereas in-migration increases unemployment by increasing the size of the CLF.

Natural increase of the CLF will tend to result in increased labor supply but increased labor demand as well. (The reasoning here is similar to that employed in the discussion of migration's impact on income levels.) However, since unemployment rates among the young tend to be relatively high, natural increase ($N\dot{A}T$) is expected to result in increased unemployment.

Appendix

VARIABLE DEFINITIONS AND DATA SOURCES—URBAN GROWTH MODEL

Each of the following variables except the dummy variables is expressed as a logarithm.

1. Endogenous variables

OMR = out-migration rate; that is, 2 times the number of individuals classified as civilian labor force (CLF) members in 1960 (1970) who resided in the Standard Metropolitan Statistical Area (SMSA) in question on April 1, 1955 (1965), but elsewhere on April 1, 1960 (1970), divided by the 1950 (1960) CLF of the SMSA. (U.S. Bureau of the Census (1963b), Table 6; (1973d), Table 16.)

OMTSR = out-migration rate to SMSAs; that is, 2 times the number of individuals classified as CLF members in 1960 (1970) who resided in the SMSA in question on April 1, 1955, but in a different SMSA on April 1, 1960 (1970), divided by the 1950 (1960) CLF of the SMSA. (Same as preceding.)

OMTNR = out-migration rate to nonmetropolitan areas; that is, 2 times the number of individuals classified as CLF members in 1960 (1970) who resided in the SMSA in question on April 1, 1955 (1965), but in a nonmetropolitan area on April 1, 1960 (1970), divided by the 1950 (1960) CLF of the SMSA. (Same as preceding.)

IMR = in-migration rate; that is, 2 times the number of individuals classified as CLF members in 1960 (1970) who resided in the SMSA in question on April 1, 1960 (1970), but elsewhere on April 1, 1955 (1965), divided by the 1950 (1960) CLF of the SMSA. (U.S. Bureau of the Census (1963b), Table 4; (1973d), Table 15.)

IMFSR = in-migration rate from SMSAs; that is, 2 times the number of individuals classified as CLF members in 1960 (1970) who resided in the SMSA in question on April 1, 1960 (1970), but in a different SMSA on April 1, 1955 (1965), divided by the 1950 (1960) CLF of the SMSA. (Same as preceding.)

IMFNR = in-migration rate from nonmetropolitan areas; that is, 2 times the number of individuals classified as CLF members in 1960 (1970) who resided in the SMSA in question on April 1, 1960 (1970), but in a nonmetropolitan area on April 1, 1955 (1965), divided by the 1950 (1960) CLF of the SMSA. (Same as preceding.)

INC = rate of income growth; that is, the ratio of the 1959 (1969) to the 1949 (1959) median income of persons residing in the SMSA on April 1, 1960 (1970), and on April 1, 1950 (1960), respectively. (U.S. Bureau of the Census (1973b), Table 194; (1963a), Table 133; and (1952), Table 87.)

EMP = rate of employment growth; that is, the ratio of the 1960 (1970) to the 1950 (1960) level of employment of the SMSA. (U.S. Bureau of the Census (1973b), Tables 85 and 121; (1963a), Tables 73 and 83; and (1952), Tables 35 and 43.)

MANU = rate of manufacturing-employment growth; that is, the ratio of 1960 (1970) to the 1950 (1960) level of manufacturing employment of the SMSA. (U.S. Bureau of the Census (1973b), Tables 87 and 123; (1963a), Tables 75 and 85; and (1952), Tables 35 and 43.)

GEMP = rate of government employment growth; that is, the ratio of the 1960 (1970) to the 1950 (1960) level of government employment of the SMSA. (U.S. Bureau of the Census (1973b), Table 88; (1963a), Table 74; and (1952), Table 35.)

NMANU = rate of nonmanufacturing-employment growth; that is, the ratio of the 1960 (1970) to the 1950 (1960) level of nonmanufacturing employment of the SMSA, where nonmanufacturing employment is net of government employment. (Same as those listed for *EMP* and *MANU*.)

UNEMP = rate of unemployment growth; that is, the ratio of the 1960 (1970) to the 1950 (1960) level of unemployment of the SMSA, where both levels are measured on April 1. (U.S. Bureau of the Census (1973b), Table 121; (1963a) Table 83; and (1952), Table 35.)

NAT = rate of natural increase of the CLF; that is, excess of CLF entrants over exits, measured between 1950 and 1960 (1960 and 1970) and defined as $NAT \equiv CLF + (2 \cdot OMR) - (2 \cdot IMR) - 1$.

2. Exogenous variables

EDU = rate of education growth; that is, the ratio of the 1960 (1970) to the 1950 (1960) median number of years of school completed by persons 25 years of age and over. (U.S. Bureau of the Census (1973b), Table 83; (1963a), Table 73; and (1952), Table 34.)

ARMFC = rate of change of armed forces personnel; that is, the ratio of the 1960 (1970) to the 1950 (1960) number of armed forces personnel in the SMSA. (U.S. Bureau of the Census (1973b), Table 85; (1963a), Table 73; and (1952), Table 35.)

INC = median 1949 (1959) income of persons residing in the SMSA in 1950 (1960). (See *INC*.)

EDU = median number of years of school completed by persons 25 years of age and over, 1950 (1960). (See *EDU*.)

CLF = civilian labor force of the SMSA, 1950 (1960). (See *EMP* and *UNEMP*.)

AGE = median age of the population of the SMSA, 1950 (1960). (U.S. Bureau of the Census (1963a), Table 20; and (1952), Table 53.)

UNR = rate of unemployment prevailing in the SMSA on April 1, 1950 (1960). (See *EMP* and *UNEMP*.)

NW = percentage nonwhite; that is, percentage of the SMSA's population that was nonwhite, 1950 (1960). (U.S. Bureau of the Census (1963a), Table 20; and (1952), Table 33.)

RRET = rate of return in manufacturing; that is, value added by manufacturing industries in the SMSA net of manufacturing payrolls in the SMSA, divided by an estimate of the gross book value of depreciable and depletable assets in the SMSA's manufacturing sector, 1957. (U.S. Bureau of the Census (1961d), Summary Statistics, pp. 9–26 to 9–41; (1961d), Area Statistics, individual state Table 3.)

MANU = percentage of the SMSA's 1950 (1960) employment in manufacturing. (See $M\dot{A}NU$ and $E\dot{M}P$.)

NMANU = percentage of the SMSA's 1950 (1960) employment in non-manufacturing (net of government). (See $NM\dot{A}NU$ and $E\dot{M}P$.)

GEMP = percentage of the SMSA's 1950 (1960) employment in government. (See $GE\dot{M}P$ and $E\dot{M}P$.)

D1, D2, D3, D4 = regional dummy variables; See Table 6.A1 for definitions.

3. Others

e_i = random errors.

TABLE 6.A1
Definitions of Dummy Variables

Region[a]	D1	D2	D3	D4
West	1	0	0	0
South	1	1	0	0
North Central	1	1	1	0
Northeast	1	1	1	1

[a] The SMSAs included in each region are indicated in Table 4.3 and Footnote 11 of Chapter 6.

7

Metropolitan Growth
and Migration:
Estimation of the Model

The data described in Chapter 4, as well as other data from the *1950, 1960,* and *1970 Census of Population,* have been utilized to estimate the simultaneous-equations model of urban growth and migration described in the previous chapter. The model has been estimated for two different periods 1950–1960 and 1960–1970. As indicated earlier, all data have been adjusted to correspond to the respective end-of-period SMSA boundaries.

For both the 1950–1960 and 1960–1970 period Table 7.1 reports the sample mean values of the variables of the model. The mean migration rates for each period are quite similar, except that the rate of in-migration to SMSAs from nonmetropolitan areas declined appreciably, from 9.7% to 6.3%. Mean rates of growth of income and unemployment, as well as of manufacturing and other nonmanufacturing employment, declined between 1950–1960 and 1960–1970. The rate of growth of government employment increased from 59.3 to 67.1%. The CLF of the average sample SMSA was 450,530 in 1950 (according to the 1960 SMSA definition) and 554,880 in 1960 (according to the 1970 SMSA definition).

TABLE 7.1
Sample Means[a]

Variables	1950–1960	1960–1970
OMR	15.5%	15.2%
IMR	23.5	19.1
OMTSR	10.2	10.8
OMTNR	5.3	4.4
IMFSR	13.8	12.8
IMFNR	9.7	6.3
INC	50.9	39.9
EMP	36.5	27.8
MANU	51.3	24.9
GEMP	59.3	67.1
NMANU	35.7	25.0
UNEMP	35.9	15.1
NAT	20.2	19.3
EDU	7.6	8.6
ARMFC	86.6	33.6
MANU	25.4	28.1
GEMP	9.5	12.3
NMANU	65.1	59.6
NW	10.3	10.1
UNR	4.8	4.6
RRET	63.5	63.7
CLF	450,530 persons	554,880 persons
INC	$2,183	$3,303
EDU	10.4 yrs.	11.1 yrs.
AGE	31.3 yrs.	29.8 yrs.

[a]*Source:* See Appendix to Chapter 6.

Estimation Procedures

A number of different techniques are available for estimating simultaneous-equations models. Except in instances where computer limitations prevented their use, three techniques have been employed to estimate the various models presented in this study. These techniques are ordinary least squares (OLS), two-stage least squares (2SLS), and three-stage least squares (3SLS). For estimating simultaneous-equations systems OLS is an inappropriate estimating technique because it lacks the consistency property that 2SLS and 3SLS possess. More-over, 3SLS is preferable to 2SLS because 3SLS has greater asymptotic effi-ciency when equations are overidentified, as the equations of the present model are, and when the equation disturbances have a nondiagonal covariance matrix. Consequently, in the discussion that follows, the 3SLS estimates of coefficients are presented and discussed.

Before we consider the empirical results, a final word of caution is in order. Since in simultaneous-equations models estimated by 2SLS and 3SLS the ratios of the estimated coefficients to their standard errors (i.e., t-ratios) are only approximately normal, t-ratios give only a rough indication of statistical significance.[1] In this chapter, when reference is made to a coefficient being statistically significant, significance at the 10% level or better is indicated ($t \geqslant 1.29$ for a one-tail test and $t \geqslant 1.67$ for a two-tail test). Moreover, when a coefficient takes a sign that is unanticipated on the basis of the theory presented herein, or when no sign is specified on a coefficient, a two-tail test of the null hypothesis is applied.

Cross-sectional studies of the sort presented here are sometimes plagued by the problems of heteroscadasticity due to the correlation between the scale of the observations on certain variables and the residuals. When the models of this study were estimated in linear form, heteroscadasticity was a problem of concern. Both the OLS and 3SLS estimates of the 1950–1960 relationships revealed a correlation between the absolute value of the residuals and CLF size in the equations for *IMFSR, INC, MANU, GEMP,* and *UNEMP.* Additionally, the 3SLS estimates revealed such correlations in the equations for *OMTSR* and *NMANU.* Both the OLS and 3SLS estimates of the 1960–1970 equations for *MANU, GEMP,* and *UNEMP* also suggested heteroscadasticity. However, when the data were transformed to logarithms, the correlation between CLF size and absolute values of the residuals virtually disappeared. Hence, each model presented in this study has been estimated in logarithmic form. Other methods of handling heteroscadasticity, such as weighted least squares, were not attempted.

Model Estimation

Three-stage least square estimates of the urban growth model discussed in Chapter 6 are presented in Table 7.2; these estimates are for the 1950–1960 period. Estimates for the 1960–1970 period are presented in Table 7.3. The asymptotic t-ratios associated with these estimates are presented in Tables 7.A1 and 7.A2, respectively, in the Appendix to this chapter. Not counting those of the dummy variables, 70 coefficients were estimated in the structural equations. Of these 70, 51 have signs that are not unexpected for the 1950–1960 period and 56 have such signs for the 1960–1970 period.[2] For 1950–1960, 30 of the 51 coefficients are significant at better than the 10% level, whereas for 1960–1970, 36 of the 56 meet such a significance test. Of the 19 coefficients that have unanticipated signs for 1950–1960, 5 are also significant at better than 10%, whereas 7 of the 14 coefficients that have unanticipated signs for 1960–1970 are

[1]Christ (1966), p.598.
[2]"Not unexpected" means either expected a priori or not specified.

TABLE 7.2
Three-Stage Least Squares Estimates of Urban Growth Model, 1950-1960[a]

Independent variables	Equation for								
	OMTRS	OMTNR	IMFSR	IMFNR	İNC	MÁNU	GÈMP	NMÁNU	UNÈMP
OMR (e)					-0.229*	0.420	-0.014	-0.418*	-0.764*
IMR (e)					0.182*	0.097	0.318*	0.324*	0.643*
OMTSR (e)			-0.706						
OMTNR (e)				1.032*					
IMFSR (e)	-0.221								
IMFNR (e)		0.897*							
İNC (e)	-5.814*	-3.081*	-7.967*	3.491*			-0.739		
EMP (e)	2.967*	-1.205*	6.209*	1.342*					-1.744*
MÁNU (e)									
UNÈMP (e)								0.419*	
NÁT (e)	-1.279*	0.092	-2.504*	-0.152	-0.226*	-2.159*			
INC50	-0.449	0.105	-0.226	-0.198	0.304*	0.085	-0.433	0.679	1.244
UNR50	-0.402*	0.528*	-0.886*	-0.573*	-0.029			-0.097	
CLF50	-0.027	-0.026	-0.048	0.016					-0.059
EDU50	0.685	0.350							
AGE50	-0.853*	-0.005							
MANU50						-0.095			
GEMP50							-0.196*		
NMANU50									
NW50					-0.003			-0.325*	-0.039
RRET						-0.169			
EDU					0.316*	1.202	0.633*	-0.565	
ARMFC					-0.006	0.162*	0.079*	-0.001	-0.005
D1	3.146	1.225	-1.854	-1.708	0.475	1.051	0.866*	0.295	-0.080
D2	-0.255	0.004	-0.333	0.052	0.006	-0.446*	-0.088	0.182	0.284
D3	0.006	-0.174	-0.000	0.177	0.014	-0.150	-0.092	-0.025	0.007
D4	-0.154	0.165	-0.283*	-0.228	-0.022	0.220*	0.150*	-0.037	-0.161*
OLS R^2	0.88	0.85	0.95	0.90	0.43	0.82	0.86	0.84	0.66

[a] Asterisk indicates that coefficient is significantly different from zero at the 10% level; e indicates endogenous.

TABLE 7.3
Three-Stage Least Squares Estimates of Urban Growth Model, 1960–1970[a]

Independent variables	Equation for								
	OMTSR	OMTNR	IMFSR	IMFNR	INC	MANU	GEMP	NMANU	UNEMP
OMR (e)					-0.072	-1.223*	-0.594*	-0.310*	-0.808*
IMR (e)					0.054	0.808*	0.400*	0.323*	0.196
OMTSR (e)			0.342*						
OMTNR (e)				0.716*					
IMFSR (e)	1.335*								
IMFNR (e)		1.295*							
INC (e)	11.281*	-18.903*	-1.264	17.504*			-1.203		0.052
EMP (e)	-1.619*	-1.224	3.333*	1.743*					
MANU (e)								0.039	
UNEMP (e)					0.027	2.162*	1.365*	0.579*	2.411*
NAT (e)	-2.148*	1.681*	-0.602*	-2.161*	0.179	-0.160		0.049	-0.598*
INC60	1.509*	-1.246	0.029	1.379*	-0.139*				
UNR60	-1.058*	0.619	-0.361*	-0.903*					
CLF60	0.154	0.487*	-0.021	-0.416*					
EDU60	-2.934*	-1.266*							
AGE60	-1.673*	-0.533*							
MANU60						-0.154*			
GEMP60							-0.126*		
NMANU60								-0.109*	
NW60					0.019*	-1.532			-0.066
RRET					0.008	0.211	0.051	0.099	-0.009
EDU					-0.000	-0.059	0.011	0.011	-3.148*
ARMFC						-0.132	-0.078	-0.345	-0.495*
D1	-2.191	16.626*	-2.529	-14.128*	1.404*	0.059	0.122	-0.053*	-0.011
D2	-1.867*	2.008*	-0.307	-2.182*	0.076*	-0.047	-0.169*	0.016	-0.164
D3	1.150*	-1.739*	-0.138	1.622*	-0.065*	-0.031	0.105*	0.015	
D4	-0.782*	1.328*	0.031	-1.264*	0.041*				
OLS R^2	0.86	0.72	0.92	0.77	0.67	0.66	0.72	0.88	0.76

[a] Asterisk indicates that coefficient is significantly different from zero at the 10% level; e indicates endogenous.

also significant.[3] The coefficients of multiple determination (R^2s) associated with the OLS estimates are presented as a rough indicator of goodness of fit. These R^2s are reasonably high, ranging from 0.95 (*IMFSR* equation) to 0.43 (*INC* equation) for the 1950–1960 period and from 0.92 (*IMFSR* equation) to 0.66 (*MANU* equation) for the 1960–1970 period.

THE MIGRATION EQUATIONS

During the 1950–1960 period greater rates of income growth significantly discouraged out-migration to both nonmetropolitan areas and to other metropolitan areas. During the 1960–1970 period such rates of growth discouraged out-migration to nonmetropolitan areas only. For each period greater rates of income growth encouraged in-migration from nonmetropolitan areas. Of the 16 income variables, including both rates of growth and levels, that appear in the migration equations of Tables 7.2 and 7.3, 7 have unanticipated signs; 6 have the anticipated sign and are significant. Though several earlier studies concerning the determinants of migration suggest that high income or wage levels are attractive to migrants, the evidence presented in this study lends little support to these earlier findings. Only 1 of the 8 income-level variables is both of the expected sign and is significant.

Several earlier migration studies have found incorrect signs or insignificant coefficients on an unemployment rate variable.[4] A number of explanations have been offered for these unanticipated findings. One of these explanations is that simultaneous-equations bias may be inherent in the parameter estimates of single-equation, multiple-regression models. Such bias is particularly likely when the unemployment variables are defined for the end of the period over which migration is measured. The unemployment variables utilized in this study perform reasonably well. The coefficient on *UNEMP* has the anticipated sign and is significant in four of eight instances, while the coefficient on *UNR* has the anticipated sign and is significant in five of eight instances.

Although the results of the present study are somewhat more affirmative concerning the role of unemployment in influencing migration than are the results of several previous studies, perhaps the explanations presented by Fields (1976) and by DaVanzo (1978) for the unanticipated findings regarding unemployment rates are more to the point than the argument regarding simultaneous-

[3]Coefficients that both have an unanticipated sign and are significant are as follows:
  1. For the 1950–1960 period: in the *OMTSR* equation—*EMP, UNEMP, UNR*50; in the *IMFSR* equation—*INC;* and in the *MANU* equation—*NAT*.
  2. For the 1960–1970 period: in the *OMTSR* equation—*INC, UNEMP, INC*60 *UNR*60, *EDU*60; in the *OMTNR* equation—*EDU*60; and in the *INC* equation—*NW*60.
Note that 8 of these 12 coefficients appear in the *OMTSR* equation.
[4]Gallaway, Gilbert, and Smith (1967), Lowry (1966), Nelson (1959), and Sjaastad (1960).

equations bias. Fields suggests that, in an explanation of migration, variables relating to job turnover are more relevant than unemployment rates. The most important consideration, he argues, is that the unemployment rate pertains to the entire stock of workers and jobs, including experienced workers who are secure in their jobs. Migrants are presumably more concerned about the rates at which hiring for new jobs is taking place and hence are presumably more concerned about job turnover. Fields' empirical results are much stronger in connection with job-turnover variables than with unemployment-rate variables.

In an important, more recent, work, DaVanzo has provided a more direct test of Fields' hypothesis that the migration response of the unemployed is likely to be more sensitive to the tightness of the labor market than the response of the employed. Her data, which relate to individual households, actually distinguish the employment status of the head of the household. DaVanzo (1978) concludes "that families with heads who are looking for work are more likely to move than those whose heads are not looking for work [p.507]." Furthermore, she concludes that "families whose heads are not unemployed appear insensitive to the level of the origin unemployment rate in deciding whether to migrate [p.507]." These findings are consistent with my own earlier explanation for the seeming inability of unemployment rates to explain migration (1975b, p.411).

Greater rates of employment growth obviously provide a significant inducement to in-migration. The coefficients on $E\dot{M}P$ in each in-migration equation are positive and highly significant. Moreover, greater rates of employment growth significantly discouraged out-migration to nonmetropolitan areas during the 1950s and out-migration to other SMSAs during the 1960s.

THE EMPLOYMENT EQUATIONS

The simultaneous nature of the relationship between the rate of migration and the rate of employment growth is evident in each employment equation, with the exception of that for manufacturing during the 1950s. Higher rates of out-migration tended to significantly discourage employment growth, whereas higher rates of in-migration encouraged such growth. During the 1960s greater rates of natural CLF increase had consequences qualitatively similar to those of in-migration.

During the 1950s, but not during the 1960s, higher rates of growth of manufacturing employment encouraged higher rates of growth of nonmanufacturing employment. Hence, increases in the export base of large metropolitan areas appear to be less important in stimulating nonexport-oriented employment than was once the case. This result seems reasonable in a system of cities in which manufacturing employment is losing its dominance to other forms of employment, such as services, but, based on the evidence presented in this study, the conclusion should be quite tentative. The reason for the tentative nature of the conclusion is that manufacturing employment growth as a whole need not serve as a particularly good proxy for export employment. A more detailed examination of these questions requires greater employment disaggregation than presented herein, in combination with the use of location quotients, or some similar device.

Each type of employment shows a fairly strong tendency to grow less rapidly in areas that have a relatively large share of that specific type of employment. Moreover, the signs on the coefficients of the variables for education growth and for growth of armed forces personnel are generally positive in the employment equations. The coefficient on $E\dot{D}U$ is highly significant in the 1950–1960 equation for $G\dot{E}MP$, and the coefficient on $AR\dot{M}FC$ is highly significant in the 1950–1960 equations for both $M\dot{A}NU$ and $G\dot{E}MP$.

INCOME AND UNEMPLOYMENT EQUATIONS

It was previously argued that no strong a priori reason suggests that the signs associated with the out- and in-migration variables in the income-growth equation should be either positive, negative, or equal to zero. The empirical results show that during the 1950s out-migration tended to significantly discourage income growth while in-migration tended to significantly encourage such growth. The signs on *OMR* and *IMR* are the same for the 1960s as the 1950s, but neither coefficient is significant for the later period. During each period higher rates of natural CLF increase influenced income growth in much the same fashion as higher rates of in-migration. During the 1960s metropolitan areas with larger fractions of nonwhite population experienced more rapid rates of income growth, *ceteris paribus*. This experience may have been due to legislation aimed at eliminating discrimination in employment practices. In the income equation the variable for education growth is positive for each period and highly significant for the 1950–1960 period.

Some tendency exists for unemployment to decrease in areas of out-migration and to increase in areas of in-migration. In the equation for $UN\dot{E}MP$ the coefficient on *OMR* is negative and significant for each period. The coefficient on *IMR* is positive for each period and significant for the 1950–1960 period.

DIFFERENTIAL SHIFT ANALYSIS

For the 1950–1960 relationships, Table 7.4 presents the *t*-ratios associated with the significance of the differential intercept shift for the various regions. Table 7.5 presents the same type of information for the 1960–1970 relationships. Relatively few significant shifts are evident in the 1950–1960 relationships,

TABLE 7.4
Asymptotic *t*-Ratios Associated with Significance of Differential Intercept Shifts for Regions:
1950-1960 Relationships[a]

OMTSR		OMTNR		IMFSR	
S = W	−1.461	S = W	0.019	S = W	−1.218
NC = W	−1.406	NC = W	−0.920	NC = W	−1.266
NE < W	−2.207	NE = W	−0.025	NE < W	−2.146
NC = S	0.037	NC = S	−1.142	NC = S	−0.003
NE = S	−1.055	NE = S	−0.056	NE = S	−1.656
NE = NC	−1.175	NE = NC	1.105	NE < NC	−1.783

IMFNR		INC		MANU	
S = W	0.264	S = W	0.197	S < W	−3.020
NC = W	1.156	NC = W	0.491	NC < W	−2.831
NE = W	0.008	NE = W	−0.042	NE < W	−1.794
NC = S	1.126	NC = S	0.515	NC = S	−0.950
NE = S	−0.319	NE = S	−0.982	NE = S	0.414
NE = NC	−1.557	NE = NC	−0.320	NE > NC	1.707

GEMP		NMANU		UNEMP	
S = W	−0.956	S = W	1.659	S = W	1.644
NC = W	−1.567	NC = W	1.117	NC = W	1.282
NE = W	−0.276	NE = W	1.117	NE = W	0.645
NC = S	−1.375	NC = S	−0.362	NC = S	0.063
NE = S	0.729	NE = S	−0.862	NE = S	−1.454
NE > NC	2.663	NE =NC	−0.531	NE < NC	−2.041

[a]Symbols: W = West; S = South; NC = North Central; NE = Northeast; " = " means not significantly different from ... at the 10% (two-tail) significance level (*t* = 1.67); " > " means significantly greater than ... at the 10% significance level; and " < " means significantly less than ... at the 10% significance level.

where the most notable shifts occur in the equation for the rate of growth of manufacturing employment. Other things being equal, the West experienced a higher rate of growth of manufacturing employment than any of the other regions. A number of factors may be responsible for such a shift. As pointed out earlier, Fuchs (1962a) suggests that the expansion of the aircraft industry in temperate climates, coupled with the lack of unionization and the availability of space, encouraged manufacturing-employment growth. To the extent that the expansion of markets is not reflected by the migration rate, rate of natural increase, and rate of income growth variables employed in this study, a shift in favor of West might be expected during the 1950s. The resource base may also

TABLE 7.5
Asymptotic *t*-Ratios Associated with Significance of Differential Intercept Shift for Regions: 1960–1970 Relationships[a]

OMTSR		OMTNR		IMFSR	
S < W	−3.131	S > W	2.874	S = W	−0.996
NC < W	−2.121	NC = W	0.610	NC < W	−2.267
NE < W	−2.938	NE > W	2.511	NE = W	−1.536
NC > S	2.493	NC < S	−2.915	NC = S	−0.526
NE = S	1.332	NE = S	−1.014	NE = S	−0.646
NE < NC	−2.821	NE > NC	3.598	NE = NC	0.209

IMFNR		INC		MANU	
S < W	−3.125	S > W	3.424	S = W	0.531
NC = W	−1.125	NC = W	0.525	NC = W	0.124
NE < W	−2.938	NE > W	2.118	NE = W	−0.176
NC > S	2.546	NC < S	−2.620	NC = S	−0.405
NE = S	0.866	NE = S	−0.985	NE = S	−0.684
NE < NC	−3.477	NE > NC	2.913	NE = NC	−0.436

GEMP		NMANU		UNEMP	
S = W	1.509	S < W	−1.871	S < W	−2.686
NC = W	−0.950	NC = W	−1.369	NC < W	−4.801
NE = W	1.131	NE = W	−0.744	NE < W	−5.208
NC < S	−1.698	NC = S	0.539	NC = S	−0.056
NE = S	−0.786	NE = S	1.016	NE = S	−1.308
NE > NC	2.633	NE = NC	0.823	NE = NC	−1.641

[a]Symbols: See Table 7.4.

have favored manufacturing-employment growth in the West. Without a more elegant model that that would directly test the hypotheses presented above, it is not reasonable to be any more definitive about the causes of the observed intercept shifts.

A number of significant intercept shifts are evident for the 1960–1970 period. Several of these shifts occur in the migration equations. Other things being equal, the rate of out-migration to other metropolitan areas was greater in the West and the North Central areas than in the South and the Northeast (W > NC > S = NE). Out-migration to nonmetropolitan areas was, however, greater in the South and the Northeast (S = NE > W = NC). In-migration from nonmetropolitan areas displayed just the opposite ranking, with the South and the Northeast lower than the other regions (W = NC > S = NE).

During the 1960s income grew more rapidly in the Northeast and in the South than in the North Central region and the West, *ceteris paribus*. This pattern of differential shifts is as follows: S = NE>W = NC. Moreover, unemployment tended to grow more rapidly in the West than in any of the other regions (W > S = NE = NC). One might speculate that heavy net in-migration to Western SMSAs during the 1960s might place upward pressure on unemployment in these SMSAs, as suggested by the empirical results previously presented. In turn, the greater unemployment could retard income growth. Although an experience like this might in fact have occurred in Western SMSAs, the variable for $I\dot{N}C$ is included in the equation for $UN\dot{E}MP$ and the variable for $UN\dot{E}MP$ is included in the equation for $I\dot{N}C$. Neither coefficient is significant for the 1960–1970 period, but each is negative and highly significant for the 1950–1960 period. In any case, these factors should be taken into account in the equations, and thus whatever differential shift occurs is presumably due to other factors operating differently on the various regions.

ESTIMATES BASED ON POOLED OBSERVATIONS

A number of the coefficients of the structural equations are similar for the two periods for which the growth model has been estimated, but enough are sufficiently dissimilar to encourage the inference that the 1950–1960 estimates would not yield reasonable predictions of behavior over the 1960–1970 period. As a test for structural differences between the two time periods, observations for 1950–1960 and 1960–1970 were pooled, and a dummy variable *DT*, where *DT* = 1 for 1960–1970 and *DT* = 0 for 1950–1960, was added to each of the structural equations (as well as to the first-stage equations). This procedure allows account to be taken of intercept shifts that occurred between the two periods but constrains the coefficients to be identical. Observations are insufficient to allow coefficient changes to be taken into account in a model as large as that presented here.

Table 7.6 presents the 3SLS estimates obtained on the basis of the pooled observations. During the 1960s both out-migration to other SMSAs and in-migration from other SMSAs were lower than during the 1950s, other things held constant. Moreover, government employment grew more rapidly during the later period, and unemployment grew less rapidly.

The conclusion that the 1950–1960 estimates would probably not yield particularly good predictions of behavior over the 1960–1970 period should not be especially surprising, since 10 years is a considerable period over which to attempt such predictions. The results emphasize the need for urban or regional information akin to annual data if we are to make substantial progress in the development of national models of urban growth and population redistribution.

TABLE 7.6
Three-Stage Least Squares Estimates of Model with Pooled Observations[a]

Independent variables					Equation for				
	OMTSR	OMTNR	IMFSR	IMFNR	$\dot{INC}$	$\dot{MANU}$	$\dot{GEMP}$	$\dot{NMANU}$	$\dot{UNEMP}$
OMR (e)	−0.351*				−0.252*	−0.406*	−0.123	−0.272*	−0.138
IMR (e)					0.144*	0.500*	0.355*	0.343*	0.176
OMTSR (e)			−0.813*						
OMTNR (e)				0.849*					
IMFSR (e)		1.138*							
IMFNR (e)									
$\dot{INC}$ (e)	−10.322*	−4.036*	−13.951*	1.148					
EMP (e)	3.612*	−1.661*	6.456*	2.405*			−0.053		−1.401*
$\dot{MANU}$ (e)								0.127*	
$\dot{UNEMP}$ (e)	−1.482*	0.889	−2.519*	−2.030*	−0.082*				
$\dot{NAT}$ (e)					0.457*				
INC	−1.073*	0.130	−1.053	−0.187	−0.132*	−0.671	0.013	0.250	−0.413
UNR	−0.863*	0.790*	−1.400*	−1.412*		−0.034		−0.056	−0.635*
CLF	0.052	0.129*	0.087	−0.077					
EDU	0.381	−0.200							
AGE	−0.330	0.094							
MANU						−0.183*			
GEMP							−0.168*		
NMANU								−0.250*	
NW					0.013*	−0.029			0.003
RRET					0.087	0.080	0.487*		
EDU					−0.008	0.066*	0.044*	−0.024	
ARMFC								0.013	0.051
D1	6.271*	1.536	3.967	−2.070	1.172*	0.574	0.358	0.585	−0.675
D2	−0.542*	0.278	−0.784*	−0.500*	−0.015	−0.113	−0.003	−0.012	−0.284*
D3	−0.372*	−0.337*	−0.581*	0.221	−0.005	−0.050	−0.031	−0.003	−0.122
D4	0.027	0.471*	0.014	−0.524*	0.001	0.021	0.100*	0.019	−0.054
DT	−0.441*	−0.031	−0.717*	−0.346	−0.027	−0.064	0.143*	−0.017	−0.297*

[a] Asterisk indicates that coefficient is significantly different from zero at the 10% level; e indicates endogenous.

Appendix

181

Appendix

TABLE 7.A1
Asymptotic *t*-Ratios Associated with 3SLS Estimates Presented in TABLE 7.2

	OMTSR	OMTNR	IMFSR	IMFNR	INC	MANU	GEMP	NMANU	UNEMP
						Equation for			
OMR					−3.947	0.982	−0.068	−1.894	−2.380
IMR					4.678	0.439	3.003	3.635	3.380
OMTSR			−1.633						
OMTNR				6.728					
IMFSR	−1.272								
IMFNR		8.376							
INC	−3.743	−2.073	−2.585	2.231			−0.948		−1.338
EMP	3.391	−1.759	5.551	2.285					
MANU								1.940	
UNEMP	−2.174	0.158	−3.455	−0.277	−3.805				
NAT					2.240	−2.313	−1.029	1.126	1.561
INC50	−1.255	0.256	−0.444	−0.460	−0.466	0.255		−0.520	
UNR50	−1.849	2.104	−2.918	−2.501					−0.473
CLF50	−0.669	−0.594	−0.779	0.291					
EDU50	1.241	0.770							
AGE50	−1.714	−0.014							
MANU50						−1.064			
GEMP50							−4.054		
NMANU50								−1.927	
NW50					−0.766				−1.402
RRET						−1.647			
EDU						3.165	1.128	1.321	−0.977
ARMFC					−0.809	1.768	1.985	−0.016	−0.075
D1	1.035	0.380	−0.469	−0.502	1.024	0.436	2.192	0.226	−0.141
D2	−1.461	0.019	−1.218	0.264	0.197	−3.020	−0.956	1.659	1.644
D3	0.037	−1.142	−0.003	1.126	0.515	−0.950	−1.375	−0.362	0.063
D4	−1.175	1.105	−1.783	−1.557	−0.982	1.707	2.663	−0.531	−2.041

TABLE 7.A2
Asymptotic *t*-Ratios Associated with 3SLS Estimates Presented in TABLE 7.3

	OMTSR	OMTNR	IMFSR	IMFNR	INC	MANU	GEMP	NMANU	UNEMP
						Equation for			
OMR					-1.178	-3.429	-2.091	-2.991	-3.243
IMR					1.476	5.160	3.145	5.939	1.402
OMTSR			1.963						
OMTNR				4.646					
IMFSR	4.847								
IMFNR		7.408							
INC	2.499	-3.197	-0.424	2.802		-1.398			0.030
EMP	-1.396	-1.003	6.197	1.335					
MANU								0.763	
UNEMP	-2.707	1.627	-1.518	-2.069	0.980				
NAT					1.217	2.545	3.342	2.404	4.358
INC60	2.203	-1.240	0.068	1.318	-2.468	-0.511		0.576	-6.349
UNR60	-2.170	0.929	-1.356	-1.321					
CLF60	-1.419	3.000	-0.289	-2.697					
EDU60	-3.100	-3.001							
AGE60	-3.734	-3.697							
MANU60						-1.907			
GEMP60							-1.725		
NMANU60								-1.528	
NW60					-1.953				-1.374
RRET						-1.581			
EDU					0.043	0.211	0.122	0.379	
ARMFC					-0.020	-1.223	0.539	0.934	-0.329
D1	-0.399	2.035	-0.726	1.671	3.178	-0.057	-0.313	-0.567	-4.429
D2	-3.131	2.874	-0.996	-3.125	3.424	0.531	1.509	-1.871	-2.686
D3	2.493	-2.915	-0.526	2.546	-2.620	-0.405	-1.698	0.539	-0.056
D4	-2.821	3.598	0.209	-3.477	2.913	-0.436	2.633	0.823	-1.641

8

A Model of Intrametropolitan Location of Employment, Housing, and Labor Force

In Chapter 5 a number of hypotheses were suggested regarding the factors behind the movement of population, labor force, and employment out of central cities and into their suburbs. Some have argued that the movement of the labor force to the suburbs has followed the movement of jobs to the suburbs. Others have argued that jobs have followed the labor force. Still others contend that the movement to the suburbs has been in response to the availability of new, high-quality, low-density housing. Many other explanations for the suburbanization of labor force and economic activity have been offered by urban scholars and urban policymakers.

In Chapter 5 it was pointed out that Mills (1972) has shown that urban areas whose population and income are not growing tend to become more centralized. Mills' findings thus suggest that metropolitan areas with different growth characteristics may exhibit different intraurban location patterns. The present chapter follows Mills' line of thinking in that the model of urban growth developed in Chapters 6 and 7 is linked with a model of intraurban location.

The model presented in this chapter recognizes that households might change location not only in response to changes in workplace but also in response to changes in housing supply conditions. Furthermore, it recognizes that household location decisions might in turn influence the distribution of employment and housing across metropolitan space. The study develops a simultaneous-equations model of urban growth and intraurban location that treats housing, employment, and labor force location within the same framework. In this sense the study differs markedly from a number of related studies that assume urban employment location and/or growth to be exogenously determined or that assume employment to be concentrated in the urban core. Let us turn to a more detailed discussion of the model of intrametropolitan location.

The Model of Intrametropolitan Location

For semantic purposes it is useful to discuss the intraurban location model as containing three blocks of equations—a housing block, a distribution block, and a location block. A fourth block for metropolitan-wide economic growth is implicit, but since the variables of this latter block are assumed to influence those of the other three blocks without in turn being influenced by the variables of these blocks, the relationships between the growth block and the remainder of the model are recursive. As such, the specification of the growth block does not influence the specification of the housing, distribution, and location blocks.

Metropolitan-wide growth of the housing stock is determined in the housing block, and in the distribution block this growth is distributed to either the central city or the suburban ring. Metropolitan-wide growth of employment, civilian labor force, and income are also distributed to central city or suburbs in the distribution block. In the location block the suburban relative to central city location of CLF in-migrants is determined, along with CLF movements between central city and suburbs and between suburbs and central city. Variables of the location and distribution blocks are determined simultaneously, and location decisions in turn influence metropolitan-wide growth of the housing stock.

A number of linkages are assumed to exist between metropolitan growth and the remainder of the model. Growth of CLF residents is hypothesized to induce growth of the housing stock, but growth of the housing stock is assumed not to influence growth of residents. In other words, households are assumed to select the metropolitan area of their residence on the basis of factors such as employment and earnings opportunities, locational amenities, etc. After they have determined the metropolitan area in which they desire to live, they demand housing in the locality. A second linkage is between the growth block and the location block. In-migrants to the metropolitan area must locate in either the central city or the suburban ring. Finally, metropolitan-wide growth of the CLF, of employment, and of (median) income are implicitly assumed to be determined in the growth block and then to exogenously feed into the distribution block, where the growth is distributed within the metropolitan area. The relationships between the various blocks are summarized in Figure 8.1.

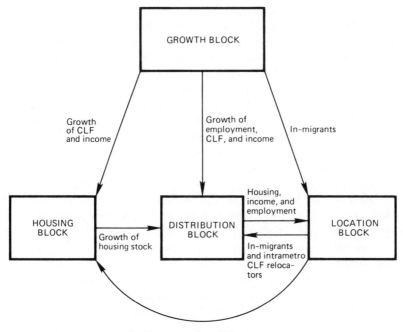

FIGURE 8.1. Diagrammatic representation of intrametropolitan location model.

THE HOUSING BLOCK

Metropolitan areas experiencing greater rates of growth of labor force residents ($\dot{R}$) should experience greater rates of growth of their housing stocks ($\dot{H}$); moreover, metropolitan areas with static population or labor force could also experience increasing housing stocks due to the demands of their residents for new housing. (Detailed definitions of the variables employed in the model are contained in the Appendix to this chapter.) If, for example, new housing is constructed in the suburbs in response to the demands of central city residents, and old central city housing does not filter out of the housing stock as rapidly as new suburban housing is constructed, then metropolitan-area housing might grow in spite of no increase occurring in the number of households demanding housing. Net intrametropolitan relocation of CLF members from central city to suburbs (*NMOV*), which is an endogenous variable of the model, is expected to proxy the demand of existing residents for new housing and hence should have a positive sign in the housing-growth equation.

In most studies that have examined the relationship between consumption of housing services and income, some value measure of housing consumption has been employed as the dependent variable.[1] Clearly, a positive relationship is expected between income and these measures of housing consumption, and many studies have empirically verified the existence of such relationships.[2] The value measures of housing consumption, of course, typically reflect some combination of the quantity and quality attributes of the housing services consumed, and several studies specifically introduce various quality characteristics as control variables. For present purposes, the development of such detailed housing equations is unnecessary, since the relationship between CLF and number of housing units is of primary concern. Moreover, Muth (1967) has argued that "it is hard to make a strong case statistically for the condition of the central city housing stock having any effect on urban population distribution at all [p. 297]."

However, the problem that is encountered when value relationships are not considered and number of housing units or its change is utilized as the dependent variable is that the sign on the income-growth variable in the housing equation becomes ambiguous. Muth has demonstrated that, since higher income households consume greater quantities of housing, population density is lower in higher income residential areas. Furthermore, he has also shown that, since higher income households have stronger preferences for newer housing, population density tends to be lower in newer areas. Hence, within any given urban spatial area or subarea, higher family income may be associated with fewer dwelling units that are larger in size and/or occupy more land. Consequently, in the equation for growth of the metropolitan housing stock, no sign is specified on the income-growth variable.

Higher vacancy rates at the beginning of the period (V_{t-10}) are expected to result in lower rates of housing growth both because more vacant housing is available to new residents and to households relocating in the metropolitan area and because in metropolitan areas characterized by high vacancy rates the supply response of builders is likely to be less vigorous. Hence, the housing block consists of a single equation of the following form[3]:

$$\dot{H} = f_1(\dot{R}, \; N\hat{M}OV, \; \dot{Y}, \; V_{t-10}, \; e_1). \qquad (8.1)$$

[1]Exceptions do exist in which some physical measure of housing consumption is utilized as a dependent variable, but this measure is typically not the number of housing units. See Muth (1965), for example.

[2]deLeeuw (1971) summarizes these results and also discusses the different measures used for housing consumption.

[3]A number of other factors, such as differences in mortgage rates, redlining practices, construction costs, and condition of the standing stock of housing are relevant in explaining interurban differences in housing starts, conversions, and demolitions, which in turn contribute to the explanation of change in the housing stock. However, for present purposes such additional detail is unnecessary. Emphasis on changes in the housing stock as related to changes in the CLF of the metropolitan area seems adequate.

THE DISTRIBUTION BLOCK

The structural equations of the distribution block are intended to explain the rates of suburban growth relative to central city growth for a number of economic activities deemed relevant to explaining residential location decisions of CLF members. Three implicit identities define the variables of the distribution block. Let us explicitly consider one such identity, that for housing. Metropolitan housing in, for example, 1970 ($H70$) must be located in either the central city ($HC70$) or the suburbs ($HS70$). Hence, we have the following accounting identity:

$$H70 \equiv HC70 + HS70. \qquad (8.2)$$

Dividing through the identity by $H60$ and multiplying the two terms on the right side respectively by $HC60/HC60$ and $HS60/HS60$, we obtain

$$\frac{H70}{H60} \equiv \frac{HC60}{HC60} \cdot \frac{HC70}{H60} + \frac{HS60}{HS60} \cdot \frac{HS70}{H60} \cdot \qquad (8.3)$$

Rearranging terms results in an expression for the rate of metropolitan housing growth as consisting of component central city and suburban rates of growth, with each component rate weighted by the respective 1960 SMSA share of central city and suburban housing:

$$\dot{H} \equiv \frac{HC60}{H60} \cdot \dot{HC} + \frac{HS60}{H60} \cdot \dot{HS} \cdot \qquad (8.4)$$

Identity (8.4) in turn yields the following identity for the rate of growth of suburban housing relative to the rate of growth of central city housing:

$$\dot{H}' \equiv \frac{\dot{HS}}{\dot{HC}} \equiv \frac{H60}{HS60} \cdot \frac{\dot{H}}{\dot{HC}} - \frac{HC60}{HS60} \qquad (8.5)$$

Henceforth the convention will be followed of priming any variable, such as $\dot{H}'$, that measures a suburban relative to a corresponding central city value. A double prime will indicate the inverse of the primed variable and hence will measure central city relative to suburban values.

Similarly, identities and corresponding behavioral equations can be formed for the rate of actual employment growth in the suburbs relative to the central city ($\dot{E}'$) and for the rate of growth of suburban CLF residents relative to the rate of growth of central city CLF residents ($\dot{R}'$).[4] With the addition of a behavioral equation for the relative rates of suburban and central city income growth ($\dot{Y}'$), the distribution block consists of the following four structural equations:

---

[4] Note that each identity contains two endogenous variables. The variables of particular interest in this study are those for suburban relative to central city rates of growth, and hence a behavioral relationship is specified for these. Variables for the inverse of central city growth relative to metropolitan-wide growth (e.g., $\dot{H}/\dot{HC}$) are thus implicitly suppressed along with the corresponding identities, and the number of equations remains equal to the number of endogenous variables.

Housing: $\dot{H}' = f_2(\hat{\dot{R}}', \hat{\dot{Y}}', V'_{t-10}, e_2).$ (8.6)

Employment: $\dot{E}' = f_3(\hat{\dot{R}}', \hat{\dot{Y}}', e_3).$ (8.7)

Labor Force: $\dot{R}' = f_4(N\hat{M}\hat{O}V, I\hat{M}', e_4).$ (8.8)

Income: $\dot{Y}' = f_5(\hat{\dot{R}}', \hat{\dot{E}}', Y'_{t-10}, e_5).$ (8.9)

Suburban relative to central city housing growth is a function of both suburban relative to central city growth of CLF residents and of suburban relative to central city income growth. The former variable is clearly expected to have a positive sign, whereas the sign on the latter is ambiguous for reasons given in the earlier discussion of the anticipated relationship between growth of metropolitan income and growth of the metropolitan housing stock. The higher the beginning-of-period suburban vacancy rates are relative to central city vacancy rates (V'_{t-10}), the lower the expected rate of growth of suburban housing relative to central city housing.

$\dot{R}'$ is expected to have a positive sign in the equation for $\dot{E}'$ because CLF growth should reflect both increased labor supply and increased product demand. The sign on $\dot{Y}'$ should also be positive, at least for the employment components that are related to nonexport demand, such as retail trade and services tend to be, because this variable also reflects product demand, given the $\dot{R}'$.

In the equation for $\dot{R}'$, net intrametropolitan relocation of CLF members from central city to suburbs ($NMOV$) and in-migration of CLF members to the suburbs relative to in-migration to the central city (IM') should clearly have positive signs. Unfortunately, out-migration data for the various metropolitan areas do not distinguish whether the migrants were residents of the central city or the suburban ring, and hence out-migration cannot be incorporated into the model in any meaningful fashion, except in the growth block.

Suburban relative to central city income growth is a function of the relative growth of CLF members. Whether $\dot{R}'$ takes a positive or a negative sign in the equation for $\dot{Y}'$ is dependent in part upon the differential characteristics of incremental CLF residents of the two areas. If residents locating in the suburbs have sufficiently higher incomes than those locating in the central city, then suburban income growth could be greater than central city income growth. The sign on $\dot{R}'$ is, however, ultimately an empirical matter that cannot be specified without some reference to the data themselves. Greater rates of suburban relative to central city income growth have frequently been attributed in large part to differential rates of employment growth. A positive sign on $\dot{E}'$ would be consistent with this hypothesis.

THE LOCATION BLOCK

In-migrants to a metropolitan area must locate in either the central city or the suburban ring. On-going residents who relocate have the same two choices. Various intraurban location models suggest that households optimize location by selecting some combination of housing and proximity to place of work. In addition to a structure, housing includes both a parcel of land and a neighborhood. Other things being equal, the typical household not already at its optimal location would prefer to move closer to its place of work so as to minimize commuting time.

The foregoing discussion suggests changes of two types that influence the relocation decisions of indigenous households and the location decisions of in-migrant households—changes in job location (X_1) and changes in housing market supply conditions (X_2). Two other types of changes are also likely to influence relocation decisions of urban households—changes in income or wealth (X_3) and life-cycle factors (X_4), such as changes in household composition. If the X's represent vectors of variables related to each type of explanatory change, change in household location (ΔL) can be expressed as a function of changes of four types:

$$\Delta L = f(X_1; X_2; X_3; X_4). \qquad (8.10)$$

In the present model change in employment $(\dot{E})$ proxies change in job location (X_1). Changes in housing supply conditions (X_2) are in part proxied by change in the housing stock $(\dot{H})$. Because the income measure $(\dot{Y})$ employed in this study is specific to place of residence, it reflects in part differential changes in neighborhood quality, such as schools, and hence proxies this important component of housing quality. Neighborhood quality is also reflected by the crime rate $(CRMC)$, by the percentage of population nonwhite (NW), and by population density (PDC), all defined at the beginning of the period. Changes in income and wealth (X_3) are taken into account by the income variable $(\dot{Y})$ itself. The incorporation of life-cycle changes (X_4) into the model is precluded by the aggregate nature of the data employed in the study.

The equations of the location block are therefore as follows:

Movement from central city to suburbs:

$$MCS = f_6(\hat{\dot{H}}', \hat{\dot{E}}', \hat{\dot{Y}}', RC_{t-10}, CRMC_{t-10}, NW''_{t-10}, PDC_{t-10}, e_6) \qquad (8.11)$$

Movement from suburbs to central city:

$$MSC = f_7(\hat{\dot{H}}'', \hat{\dot{E}}'', \hat{\dot{Y}}'', RS_{t-10}, CRMC_{t-10}, NW'_{t-10}, PDC_{t-10}, e_7). \qquad (8.12)$$

In-migration to suburbs relative to central city:

$$IM' = f_8\,(\hat{H}',\ \hat{E}',\ \hat{Y}',\ CRMC_{t-10},\ NW'''_{t-10},\ PDC_{t-10},\ e_8). \qquad (8.13)$$

Net intrametropolitan movement:

$$NMOV \equiv MCS/MSC. \qquad (8.14)$$

The signs on the variables for differential housing growth, for differential employment growth, and for differential income growth should be positive in the structural equations of the location block. Although the signs on the former two variables are straightforward, that on the latter is not. To the extent that $\dot{Y}'$ (and $\dot{Y}'''$) proxies neighborhood characteristics, it should have a positive sign. However, Muth's model of residential location suggests that, in response to an increase in income, the household's optimal location will shift toward its place of employment if its income elasticity of demand for housing is less than its income elasticity of marginal transportation costs. Hence, an increase in income could cause a household to move in either direction, depending upon its relative income elasticities. The income effects of increases in central city (suburban) income relative to suburban (central city) income are therefore not of unequivocal sign.

Neighborhood crime is a disamenity that is likely to act as a repulsive force on location decisions. In SMSAs characterized by higher central city crime rates, movement from central city to suburbs should be greater and movement from suburbs to central city should be less. In such SMSAs in-migrants are also more likely to choose suburban locations.[5]

Central city population density is likely to proxy a number of factors, including pollution, congestion, and land prices. These factors are interrelated, but they are not all related in a positive direction. It cannot unequivocally be claimed that greater central city population density should encourage the selection of a suburban residence. Central city pollution, congestion, and land prices might well discourage many households from locating there. However, if the household locates in the suburbs and commutes to work in the central city, congestion in densely populated urban areas would impose relatively heavy (commuting) time costs on the household. These costs could be sufficient, espe-

---

[5]Ideally, the crime variable should be a measure of the crime rate in the central city relative to the crime rate in the suburbs. In 1950 crime statistics are reported only for cities, not for SMSAs or for counties. Hence, suburban crime data are unavailable for 1950. In 1960, however, crime rates can be calculated for both central city and suburbs. Such computations were made for 1960, and the results were compared in the 1960–1970 relationships with those obtained using only 1960 central city crime rates. The conclusions of the study are not sensitive to this data shortcoming. As alternatives to the overall crime rate, the crimes against persons rate and the crimes against property rate were also used.

cially for some higher income households, to induce location in the central city. This argument is consistent with Muth's model of intraurban location.[6]

Percentage of population nonwhite (NW) is included to pick up the effects of racial discrimination on location patterns. To the extent that greater concentrations on nonwhite persons induce whites to seek locations with lesser minority concentrations, a higher percentage of central city nonwhite population relative to suburban nonwhite population would encourage relocation of on-going SMSA residents to the suburbs and the location of new SMSA residents in the suburbs.

Finally, beginning-of-period central city CLF (RC_{t-10}) is included in the equation for movement from central city to suburbs to normalize the flow. The larger the CLF of the central city is, the greater the expected movement to the suburbs. For the same reason, suburban CLF (RS_{t-10}) is included in the equation for movement from suburbs to central city.

The Data

Much of the data utilized in estimating the model just described has been discussed in some detail in the section entitled "The Data" in Chapter 5. That chapter also contains a descriptive discussion of the behavior of a number of the variables that are central to the model. The same 62 SMSAs that were used in the estimation of the urban growth model constitute the observation base for the estimation of the intraurban location model. As with the urban growth model, the intraurban location model has been estimated for two different time periods, 1950–1960 and 1960–1970. All data have been adjusted to correspond to end-of-period SMSA boundaries, and all data have been adjusted for central city annexations of outlying territory. The adjustment procedures are described in Chapters 4 and 5. Table 5.2 contains 1950–1960 and 1960–1970 central city and suburban sample mean values of variables of particular concern in the intraurban location model.

The Empirical Results

ESTIMATION OF THE MODEL

Excluding the growth block, the model consists of eight structural equations—(8.1), (8.6), (8.7), (8.8), (8.9), (8.11), (8.12), and (8.13)—and

---

[6]Note that suburban population density does not enter the model. The reason is that for many SMSAs in the sample the suburban area includes very sparsely populated land. The Ontario–Riverside–San Bernardino SMSA and the Phoenix SMSA are examples where the suburban ring includes virtually uninhabited desert.

one (explicit) identity (8.14) in nine jointly dependent variables. The structural equations have been estimated in logarithmic form by three-stage least squares, by two-stage least squares, and by ordinary least squares. The results obtained using each estimation technique are very similar, and only the three-stage least squares estimates are presented. Table 8.1 contains the results for the 1950–1960 period, and Table 8.2 contains those for the 1960–1970 period. (Tables 8.A1 and 8.A2 in the Appendix to this chapter present the t-ratios corresponding to Tables 8.1 and 8.2.) For each period the coefficients generally have the expected signs and are significant. Of 68 coefficients estimated for the two periods, 56 have signs that are not unexpected, and 41 of these are significant at better than the 10% level. The ordinary least squares R^2s, which are also reported in Tables 8.1 and 8.2, demonstrate a wide range of values, from a low of 0.054 (1950–1960 equation for suburban relative to central city employment growth) to a high of 0.972 (1950–1960 equation for growth of the metropolitan housing stock).

Growth of the metropolitan housing stock is highly responsive to growth of the CLF, which is not surprising. Moreover, growth of suburban relative to central city housing attracted both in-migrants and previous central city residents to the suburbs. Suburban income growth also attracted CLF members from the central city in each period, presumably in response to improvements in neighborhood amenities proxied by relative income growth. In the equation for movement from central city to suburbs, the employment variable is positive and significant for each period. In the in-migrant location equations the employment variable is marginally significant (10%) for the 1960–1970 period but is actually negative in sign for the 1950–1960 period. Moreover, the coefficients on $\dot{E}'$ are considerably smaller than those on either $\dot{H}'$ or $\dot{Y}'$. Hence, movement to the suburbs appears to have been somewhat more responsive to the availability of new suburban housing and to improvements in neighborhood amenities than to employment opportunities per se.

In those SMSAs in which the central city housing stock grew relatively rapidly compared to the suburban housing stock, CLF members tended to shift their place of residence from suburbs to central city. This tendency was evident in each period, though the coefficient on $\dot{H}''$ is not significant for the 1950–1960 period. CLF members also shifted their residence from suburbs to central city in those areas where central city income growth kept better pace with suburban income growth, though the coefficient on $\dot{Y}''$ is not statistically significant for the 1950–1960 period. Furthermore, the 1960–1970 coefficient of 7.363 on $\dot{Y}''$ is the highest coefficient estimated in the system for either period, which serves to emphasize the importance of neighborhood in household location decisions.

During the 1960s greater central city employment growth actually resulted in less relocation from suburbs to central city. Although this phenomenon is curious, given the relatively heavy weight associated with manufacturing employment in the measure of total employment utilized in the present study, the finding appears to be consistent with Steinnes' (1977) conclusion that greater

TABLE 6.1

Three-Stage Least Squares Estimates of Intraurban Location Model, 1950–1960[a]

Independent variables	Equation for							
	Housing block	Location block			Distribution block			
	$\dot{H}$	MCS	MSC	IM'	$\dot{H}'$	$\dot{E}'$	$\dot{R}'$	$\dot{Y}'$
$\dot{R}$	0.941**							
NMOV (e)	0.003						0.082*	
$\dot{Y}$	−0.382**							
V_{t-10}	−0.025**							
$\dot{H}'$ (e)		1.521**	0.521	1.378**				
$\dot{H}''$ (e)								
$\dot{E}'$ (e)		0.643**	0.054	−0.134				
$\dot{E}''$ (e)								0.019
$\dot{Y}'$ (e)		4.484**	0.366	0.333	1.186**			
$\dot{Y}''$ (e)						0.302		
$\dot{R}'$ (e)					0.448**			0.064**
IM' (e)						0.385**	0.818**	
RC_{t-10}		0.098*	0.017					
RS_{t-10}		−0.009	0.092					
$CRMC_{t-10}$			0.156**	0.120*				
NW'_{t-10}		0.171**		0.022				
NW''_{t-10}								
PDC_{t-10}		−0.378**	−0.279**	0.128**				
Y'_{t-10}					0.008			
V'_{t-10}								−0.180**
CON	0.233**	−1.085	−0.111	−0.406	0.089	0.343**	−0.333**	0.079
OLS R^2	0.972	0.734	0.325	0.664	0.340	0.054	0.359	0.241

[a] Double asterisk indicates that coefficient is significantly different from zero at the 2.5% level (i.e., $t \geq 2.00$ for a one-tail test); single asterisk indicates that coefficient is significantly different from zero at the 10% level (i.e., $t \geq 1.30$ for a one-tail test); e indicates endogenous variable. Single prime indicates suburban relative to central city value; double prime indicates central city relative to suburban value.

TABLE 8.2
Three-Stage Least Squares Estimates of Intraurban Location Model, 1960-1970[a]

Independent variables	Equation for							
	Housing block	Location block			Distribution block			
	$\dot{H}$	MCS	MSC	IM'	$\dot{H}'$	$\dot{E}'$	$\dot{R}'$	$\dot{Y}'$
$\dot{R}$	0.894**							
$NMOV\ (e)$	0.013**						0.143**	
$\dot{Y}$	-0.044							
V_{t-10}	-0.018*							
$\dot{H}'\ (e)$		2.859**		1.171**				
$\dot{H}''\ (e)$		1.369**						0.034
$\dot{E}'\ (e)$		0.729**	-0.787**	0.309*				
$\dot{E}''\ (e)$						0.281		
$\dot{Y}'\ (e)$		4.892**		-0.493	-1.407**			
$\dot{Y}''\ (e)$			7.363**					-0.002
$\dot{R}'\ (e)$					0.492**	0.353**		
$IM'\ (e)$							0.545**	
RC_{t-10}		0.205**						
RS_{t-10}			0.101*					
$CRMC_{t-10}$		-0.067	0.089	-0.011				
NW'_{t-10}			0.074					
NW''_{t-10}		-0.044		-0.088*				
PDC_{t-10}		-0.390**	-0.365**	0.053				
Y'_{t-10}					0.083*			-0.124**
V''_{t-10}					0.226**			
CON	-0.045	-3.022**	0.008	-0.201		0.264*	-0.027	0.072**
OLS R^2	0.955	0.628	0.370	0.363	0.509	0.071	0.622	0.064

[a]See footnotes on Table 8.1.

concentrations of central city manufacturing employment result in greater central city population losses. Steinnes speculates that the observed tendency for population to flee from areas characterized by heavy concentrations of manufacturing may be due to "pollution or other disamenities." Some years earlier Muth (1965) observed a tendency for the intensity of residential land use to be lower in the vicinity of manufacturing centers in South Chicago.

As a direct test of the Steinnes hypothesis that the central city manufacturing sector is encouraging population dispersal to the suburbs, variables for the relative growth of each type of employment (manufacturing, retail, service, and wholesale) were substituted for the overall (relative) rate of employment growth in the location block. The results suggest that, rather than manufacturing encouraging movement to the suburbs, it discourages the movement from the suburbs to central city. Suburban relative to central city growth of manufacturing employment is actually significant in attracting labor force members to the suburbs. The statistically significant results (t-values in parentheses) of this specification of the model are, briefly:

1. 1950–1960:
   In the equation of MCS, 0.459 (2.118) $WHOLE'$; 0.785 (2.621) RET'; and 0.232 (1.431) $MANU'$.
2. 1960–1970:
   In the equation for MCS, 0.350 (1.627) $MANU'$; in the equation for MSC, -0.298 (1.668) $MANU''$; in the equation for IM', 1.317 (1.656) SER'.

During the 1950s SMSAs with relatively high concentrations of nonwhite population in the central city compared to the suburbs experienced significantly greater CLF movements from central city to suburbs and significantly smaller movements from suburbs to central city. However, these tendencies are not evident in the results for the 1960s. Muth (1967), studying 1950 urban population distribution, finds that relative growth in the central city's black population contributed to population decentralization. Bradford and Kelejian (1973), however, after examining a similar 1960 relationship, conclude that central city racial composition did not significantly influence residential location decisions. The findings of Muth and of Bradford and Kelejian, in combination with those of the present study, may indicate a tendency for the importance of racial composition as a determinant of residential location decisions to decline over time.

Central city crime rates do not appear to be of particular importance in explaining residential relocation decisions of metropolitan CLF members. The crime rate variable is marginally significant only in the in-migrant location equation for the 1950–1960 period. Crimes against persons and crimes against property rates were also calculated and were separately substituted for the overall crime rate in the CLF location equations, but the empirical results were essentially unchanged.

During each period significantly greater rates of suburban relative to central city CLF growth were induced both by the net movement of CLF members from central city to suburbs and by the location of in-migrant CLF members in the suburbs. In turn, the location of CLF members in the suburbs encouraged growth of both suburban housing and suburban employment. SMSAs characterized by greater rates of suburban relative to central city income growth experienced greater rates of suburban relative to central city employment growth in each period, but the relationship is statistically significant for neither period.

Higher relative rates of income growth also significantly influenced the relative rates of housing growth during each period, but the direction of the relationship between the variables is positive during the 1950s and negative during the 1960s. These results do not suggest a negative income elasticity of demand for housing during the 1960s because a value measure of housing consumption has not been utilized as the dependent variable. It was previously argued that the sign on the income variable in the housing equations could be positive or negative, with the actual sign ultimately dependent upon the complex relationships between income and the quantity and quality of housing consumed. Although definitive conclusions cannot be drawn from the results presented here, it is tempting to speculate that the sign reversal is due to the increasing relative importance of housing quality in expenditures for housing services, with an important quality component being land. If more land is demanded per household in higher income suburbs, then population and dwelling unit density would tend to be lower in higher income areas, and within a given geographic area, the number of dwelling units could fall.

The results of a number of Muth's studies, as well as those of the literature on housing market segregation, suggest that the racial composition of the population be included as a determinant of the distribution of housing growth. An alternative equation that included NW'''_{t-10} was therefore estimated. The variable should have a negative sign, which would indicate that in SMSAs characterized by a high percentage of nonwhite population in the central city compared to the suburbs, growth of the central city housing stock is high relative to that of the suburban housing stock. If nonwhite households are effectively restricted to central city neighborhoods, then the relative number of dwelling units demanded there should be high compared to the suburbs. To the extent that NW'''_{t-10} proxies income distribution, the sign should also be negative since lower income households tend to demand dwelling units of lower quality, including less land. Hence, population and dwelling unit density should tend to be higher where the percentage of nonwhite population is larger. Indeed, for the 1950–1960 period NW'''_{t-10} is negative and highly significant (coefficient $= -.054$, t-ratio $= -2.422$), but for the 1960–1970 period it fails significance. These results seem consistent with those of the location block, where racial composition proves to be a significant determinant of CLF location decisions in the 1950s but not in the 1960s.

SECTOR-SPECIFIC EMPLOYMENT GROWTH

As previously indicated, data on actual central city and suburban employment change for each metropolitan area were obtained by summing over four employment sources—manufacturing, retail, service, and wholesale. Since such aggregation conceals the behavior of the various employment components, which are of interest in themselves, and since sector-specific employment, especially in manufacturing, has been the subject of previous attention by others, the employment data were disaggregated and separate regressions were run on suburban relative to central city growth of each employment type. To close the system, an identity for total (suburban relative to central city) employment change is introduced, where total employment change is the sum of the weighted component employment changes, with the weights being beginning-of-period employment shares.

Three-stage least squares estimates of the sector-specific employment equations are presented in Table 8.3.[7] (Corresponding t-ratios are presented in Table 8.A3 in the Appendix to this chapter.) The disaggregation is revealing. When $\dot{R}'$ and $\dot{Y}'$ alone are included in the relationships, the sign on $\dot{R}'$ is positive in each equation, but the coefficient is highly significant only in the equations for retail employment. The coefficient on $\dot{R}'$ is marginally significant in the 1950–1960 equation for manufacturing employment and in the 1960–1970 equation for service employment. The coefficient on $\dot{Y}'$ is highly significant only in the 1950–1960 equation for retail employment. In general, the two explanatory variables perform reasonably well only in the retail employment equations, and even then the explained variance (in the OLS estimates) is but 10%.

Table 8.3 also contains two alternative specifications of the sector-specific employment equations. In the first alternative, beginning-of-period central city population density and crime rate are included. Urban location models, such as that developed by Muth, typically suggest a negatively sloped land-price gradient as distance from the city's center increases. These models also commonly predict more intensive utilization of land and consequently increasing population density closer to the city's core. Population density should therefore serve as a reasonable proxy for central city land prices. The greater are these prices, the stronger the expected tendency for land intensive activities to opt for suburban locations, other things being equal. This tendency should be particularly evident for wholesale and especially for manufacturing activities. Of the employment sources defined in this study, service is likely to be least land-intensive and hence least affected in its location decisions by land-price considerations.

---

[7]Because three-stage least squares is a system estimation technique, alteration of one equation affects the estimates of other equations in the system. Since disaggregation of the employment equation results in no qualitative changes (i.e., sign changes) in other equations of the model and in very slight quantitative changes, estimates of the other equations are not reported a second time.

TABLE 8.3
Three-Stage Least Squares Estimates of Sector-Specific Employment Equations, 1950-1960 and 1960-1970[a]

Independent variables	Manufacturing		Retail		Services		Wholesale	
	1950–1960	1960–1970	1950–1960	1960–1970	1950–1960	1960–1970	1950–1960	1960–1970
$\dot{R}'(e)$	0.412*	0.199	0.297*	0.280**	0.110	0.235*	0.203	0.099
$\dot{Y}'(e)$	−0.385	0.494	1.683**	−0.350	0.615	0.114	−0.667	1.417
CON	0.366**	0.210	0.412**	0.495**	0.428**	0.399**	0.528**	0.656**
OLS R^2	0.045	0.005	0.098	0.105	0.017	0.057	0.043	0.002
$\dot{R}'(e)$	0.315*	0.370*	0.259**	0.371**	0.040	0.307*	0.162	0.207
$\dot{Y}'(e)$	−0.512	0.180	1.441	−0.272	0.279	0.199	0.474	0.985
PDC_{t-10}	0.101	0.152*	0.013	0.072*	0.042	0.058	0.256**	0.105*
$CRMC_{t-10}$	0.123	0.020	0.042	−0.034	0.093	−0.034	−0.029	0.037
CON	0.094	−1.097	0.539	−0.329	0.554	−0.292	−2.004	−0.125
OLS R^2	0.078	0.021	0.170	0.132	0.079	0.067	0.274	0.038
$\dot{R}'(e)$					−0.252**	−0.064	0.191	−0.326**
$\dot{Y}'(e)$					−0.633	0.379	1.134	1.201*
PDC_{t-10}					0.004	−0.015	0.232**	−0.026
$CRMC_{t-10}$					0.019	−0.005	−0.010	0.064
$MANU'(e)$					0.312**	0.004	0.164	0.332**
$RET'(e)$					0.746**	0.992**	−0.440**	1.168**
CON					0.075	0.036	−1.540	0.550
OLS R^2					0.577	0.571	0.304	0.627

[a]See footnotes to Table 8.1.

The population density variable is positive in each equation and is significant in both wholesale equations and in the 1960–1970 manufacturing equation. It is also significant in the 1960–1970 retail employment equation but fails significance in the service equations. The results suggest, then, that higher central city land prices, and whatever other factors the population density variable may reflect, have encouraged more rapid suburban manufacturing and wholesale employment growth rates. Note, however, that with the exception of the 1950–1960 wholesale employment equation, the inclusion of the population density (and crime rate) variable contributes relatively little to increasing the OLS R^2.

The location decisions of business firms as well as of households are frequently claimed to be a function of neighborhood crime rates. Previously we saw that crime rates do not appear to be a significant determinant of household location decisions, *ceteris paribus*. The results presented in Table 8.3 indicate that crime rates do not act as a significant determinant of business location decisions either. Again the crimes against property and crimes against persons rates were separately substituted for the overall crime rate, and again the empirical results were essentially unchanged by these alterations.[8]

In the final version of the employment-change equations, growth of suburban relative to central city manufacturing employment ($MA\dot{N}U'$) and growth of suburban relative to central city retail employment ($R\dot{E}T'$) are included in the equations for service and for wholesale employment. The hypothesis that underlies this formulation is that service employment, much of which includes business services, and wholesale employment are closely tied to other sources of employment growth. Since, other things being equal, closer proximity to demand sources is desirable, service and wholesale employment should grow most rapidly where manufacturing and retail employment are growing most rapidly.

The results presented in Table 8.3 indicate clearly that growth of suburban service and wholesale employment is a function of the growth of suburban manufacturing and especially suburban retail employment. Note, too, that the inclusion of $MA\dot{N}U'$ and $R\dot{E}T'$ in the service and wholesale employment equations results in an appreciable increase in the OLS R^2s.

Suburban retail employment growth induced a higher rate of central city wholesale employment growth during the 1950s but a higher rate of suburban wholesale employment growth during the 1960s. One possible explanation for this phenomenon is that substantial lags exist in the locational adjustment patterns of wholesalers. Immediately after World War II and well into the 1950s, wholesaling activities were predominantly located in the central cities. As suburban retail activities grew dramatically during the early post-World-War-War-II years, suburban retail demand may have been served largely out of central city facilities. Over time, however, the wholesale activities may have adjusted to

---

[8]The only exception is that the crimes against persons rate appears as marginally significant in the wholesale employment equation for the 1960s (coefficient = 0.098).

locations closer to major sources of demand. Adjustments to growth of suburban manufacturing appear to have been more contemporaneous.

The results obtained by disaggregating the employment data are in sharp contrast to Steinnes' (1977) recent findings that "manufacturing and services jobs are following people, while retail jobs are not [p. 78]." The findings of the present study support the conventional position of central place theory that suburban retail employment growth is a function of growth of suburban demand, which was suggested some years ago by Muth's (1961) empirical work as well as that of others.

Moreover, the evidence uncovered in this study does not strongly support the positions of Mills and of Steinnes that manufacturing activities follow people to the suburbs nor the position of Steinnes that service jobs follow people to the suburbs. Some evidence presented in Table 8.3 does, however, indicate that CLF growth was marginally significant in explaining manufacturing employment growth during each period. The hypothesis that manufacturing follows people to the suburbs is based on the notion that proximity to a skilled labor force is attractive to manufacturing establishments since local suburban demand is not seen as being sufficient to support many manufacturing activities. In this study $\dot{R}'$ directly measures quantity changes in the suburban relative to the central city labor force, and $\dot{Y}'$ should serve as a good measure of changes in the skill and educational levels of suburban relative to central city residents. The facts that in the manufacturing employment equations the coefficients are at best marginally significant and that the OLS R^2s are quite low suggest that factors other than labor force availability and skill, such as perhaps local fiscal conditions, transportation networks, and supplier location, are crucial in explaining growth of suburban manufacturing employment.

Moses and Williamson (1967) present preliminary empirical results that suggest that racial composition of the population may contribute importantly to the explanation of the location of urban manufacturing employment, with zones having higher percentages of nonwhite population being less desirable destinations for manufacturing firms. When NW'''_{t-10} is included in the sector-specific employment equations, the coefficient fails significance in each 1950–1960 equation but is positive and highly significant in the 1960–1970 equation for service employment (coefficient = 0.126) and significant at 5% in the equations for retail and wholesale employment (coefficients = 0.060 and 0.097, respectively). Hence for three of the four employment types a tendency is evident in recent years for suburban employment growth to be relatively greater where the central city contains relatively more nonwhite persons. Manufacturing employment growth does not appear to be sensitive to racial composition at the level of aggregation used in this study.[9]

[9]The following explanatory variables were utilized in these regressions: $\dot{R}'$, $\dot{Y}'$, PDC_{t-10}, $CRMC_{t-10}$, NW''_{t-10}. Results associated with variables other than NW'''_{t-10} are qualitatively identical to those reported in Panel 2 of Table 8.3 and are quantitatively very similar.

When the manufacturing and retail employment growth variables are included in the service employment equation for the 1950–1960 period, the results suggest that greater rates of suburban CLF growth actually induced greater rates of central city service employment growth, which is contrary to Steinnes' finding. The explanation could again be that lags in the locational adjustment process resulted in growing suburban consumer demands for services being satisfied out of central city offices. Furthermore, given the composition of service employment as defined in this and in Steinnes' study, a strong case can be made that this employment is a direct function of other employment types. The results presented herein tend to support this position.

Summary and Conclusions

Much controversy has existed concerning the direction of the causal relationship between the location of employment opportunities and the location of the labor force within metropolitan areas. It has been argued that suburban employment opportunities have attracted labor force members to the suburbs, that the presence of a suburban labor force has attracted employers and hence employment to the suburbs, and, recently, that central city manufacturing employment has actually encouraged flight to the suburbs. Many studies that have focused on the intraurban locations of jobs and labor force have ignored the importance of housing and of neighborhood as determinents of residential location decisions.

This study has attempted to go beyond the usual static explanation of the spatial distribution of urban housing, employment, and labor force at a point in time and, in the context of intraurban location decisions, to explain the growth of these variables over time as being jointly determined. The major findings of the study are as follows:

1. Growth of the urban labor force has encouraged urban housing growth, and urban housing growth has been concentrated primarily in the suburbs. Housing availability has attracted labor force members from the central cities to the suburbs and has encouraged in-migrant labor force members to the various metropolitan areas to locate in the suburbs.

2. During both the decade of the 1950s and that of the 1960s, central city residents and in-migrants were attracted to the suburbs more by suburban housing growth than by suburban employment growth. In turn, the locational decisions of CLF members influenced the location of both urban housing and urban employment, but housing was influenced somewhat more than employment.

3. During each decade the growth of labor force members residing in the suburbs encouraged the growth of suburban retail employment. Moreover, manufacturing and retail employment growth in the suburbs significantly influenced

the growth of suburban service and wholesale employment. Evidence uncovered in this study does not strongly support the position that manufacturing jobs are attracted to the suburbs because of the location of labor force members there.

4. During the 1960s greater rates of central city housing growth have induced labor force members to shift their residences from suburbs to central city, but central city employment growth has not attracted labor force members from the suburbs. Some evidence suggests that in SMSAs characterized by greater central city employment growth, labor force members actually opted for suburban residential locations, others things being equal.

One of the basic conclusions is that housing and neighborhood considerations have been somewhat more important than employment opportunities per se in attracting labor force members to the suburbs. This result is consistent with Muth's (1967) earlier finding that "The distribution of population in urban areas would appear to be consistent with a set of variables which can be given plausible interpretations in terms of the relative demand and supply of housing in different locations [p.296]."

Furthermore, as pointed out above, this study has demonstrated that the location of labor force members in the suburbs has in turn encouraged the growth of both the suburban housing stock and suburban employment, with the responsiveness of the housing stock being greater than that of employment. The findings regarding the housing stock are also consistent with Muth's earlier results. However, Muth also tentatively concludes that the location of urban employment is largely determined by exogenous forces.[10] The present study shows an unmistakable tendency for suburban employment growth to be a function of the growth of the suburban labor force. Certain earlier studies, such as those of Mills and of Steinnes, have concluded that suburban labor force growth has encouraged suburban growth of manufacturing employment, but the present study reveals a much stronger tendency for suburban labor force growth to encourage suburban growth of retail employment. Suburban growth of manufacturing employment appears to be largely determined by forces exogenous to the present model.

Whereas a number of the coefficients of the structural equations are similar for the two periods for which the model has been estimated, enough are sufficiently dissimilar to suggest that changes in model structure occurred between the two periods. For example, the results associated with the equation for movement from suburbs to central city differ considerably for the two decades. As a partial test for structural differences between the two time periods, observations for 1950–1960 and 1960–1970 were pooled and a dummy variable DT ($=0$ for 1950–1960; $=1$ for 1960–1970) was added to each structural equation (as well as to the first stage equations). Table 8.4 shows the three-stage least squares estimates based on the pooled observations. For four of the eight structural equations

[10]Muth (1967), p. 286.

TABLE 8.4
Three-Stage Least Squares Estimates of Intraurban Location Model, Pooled Observations[a]

Independent variables	Equation for							
	Housing block	Location block			Distribution block			
	$\dot{H}$	MCS	MSC	IM'	$\dot{H}'$	$\dot{E}'$	$\dot{R}'$	$\dot{Y}'$
$\dot{R}$	0.912**							
$NMOV$ (e)	0.006*							
$\dot{Y}$	−0.185**						0.088**	
V_{t-10}	−0.017**							
$\dot{H}'$ (e)		2.322**	0.342	1.247**				
H'' (e)								0.051**
$\dot{E}$ (e)		0.527**	−0.052	0.122				
$\dot{E}''$ (e)					0.348**	0.688		
$\dot{Y}'$ (e)		4.885**	−0.259	−0.614				
$\dot{Y}''$ (e)								
$\dot{R}'$ (e)					0.514**	0.501**	0.759**	0.015
IM' (e)								
RC_{t-10}		0.147**	0.126**					
RS_{t-10}		−0.080	0.002					
$CRMC_{t-10}$			0.059	0.041				
NW'_{t-10}		0.065*		−0.031				
NW''_{t-10}								
PDC_{t-10}		−0.415**	−0.365**	0.059*				
Y'_{t-10}					0.038			−0.142**
V'_{t-10}								
DT	−0.117**	−0.175	0.068	0.010	−0.076*	−0.094	0.189**	−0.025**
CON	0.152**	−1.863**	−1.344	−0.069	0.150**	0.252**	−0.300**	−0.025
OLS R^2	0.971	0.697	0.304	0.492	0.325	0.070	0.435	0.225

[a]Double asterisk indicates that coefficient is significantly different from zero at the 2.5% level (i.e., $t \geq 2.00$ for a one-tail test); single asterisk indicates that coefficient is significantly different from zero at the 10% level (i.e., $t \geq 1.30$ for a one-tail test); e indicates endogenous variable. Single prime indicates suburban relative to central city value; double prime indicates central city value relative to suburban value.

significant differential shifts occurred for the 1960–1970 period relative to the 1950–1960 period. The rate of growth of the metropolitan housing stock and rate of growth of the suburban relative to the central city housing stock both declined, *ceteris paribus*. The rate of suburban relative to central city income growth also declined. Finally, the rate of growth of the suburban CLF relative to the rate of growth of the central city CLF increased.

The results of this study clearly confirm the endogeneity of the growth and the intraurban location of housing, employment, and labor force. The results also seem generally reasonable in terms of magnitudes, and where differences are apparent for the two periods studied, they appear to be internally consistent. In general, the findings are consistent with the combined results of a number of Muth's studies regarding the intraurban location of economic activities.

Appendix

VARIABLE DEFINITIONS AND DATA SOURCES—INTRAMETROPOLITAN LOCATION MODEL

Each of the following variables except the dummy variable is expressed as a logarithm.

1. Endogenous variables

MCS = rate of CLF in-movement to the suburbs from the central city; that is, the number of CLF members residing in the suburbs of $SMSA_i$ in 1960 (1970) who resided in the central city of $SMSA_i$ in 1955 (1965), divided by the number of CLF members residing in the suburbs of i in 1950 (1960). (U.S. Bureau of the Census (1973d), Table 15; (1963b), Table 4.)

MSC = rate of CLF in-movement to the central city from the suburbs; that is, the number of CLF members residing in the central city of $SMSA_i$ in 1960 (1970) who resided in the suburbs of $SMSA_i$ in 1955 (1965), divided by the number of CLF members residing in the central city of i in 1950 (1960). (Same as preceding.)

$NMOV$ $\equiv MCS/MSC$

IM' = rate of CLF in-migration to the suburbs relative to the rate of CLF in-migration to the central city; that is, number of CLF members residing in the suburbs of $SMSA_i$ in 1960 (1970) who resided outside of $SMSA_i$ in 1955 (1965) divided by the number of CLF members residing in the suburbs of $SMSA_i$ in 1950 (1960) relative to the comparable measure defined for the central city. (Same as preceding.)

$\dot{R}'$ = rate of suburban CLF growth relative to the rate of central city CLF growth; that is, ratio of 1960 to 1950 (1970 to 1960) suburban CLF residents relative to the ratio of 1960 to 1950 (1970 to 1960) central city residents. (U.S. Bureau of the Census (1973b), Table 85; (1963a), Table 73; (1952), Table 36.)

$\dot{E}'$ = rate of suburban employment growth relative to the rate of central city employment growth; that is, ratio of 1960 to 1950 (1970 to 1960) suburban employment relative to the ratio of 1960 to 1950 (1970 to 1960) central city employment. (See Table 5.5.)

$\dot{E}''$ = $1/\dot{E}'$.

$M\dot{A}NU'$ = rate of suburban manufacturing employment growth relative to the rate of central city manufacturing employment growth. (See Table 5.7).

$R\dot{E}T'$ = rate of suburban retail employment growth relative to the rate of central city retail employment growth. (See Table 5.8.)

$S\dot{E}R'$ = rate of suburban service employment growth relative to the rate of central city service employment growth. (See Table 5.9.)

$WH\dot{O}LE'$ = rate of suburban wholesale employment growth relative to the rate of central city wholesale employment growth. (U.S. Bureau of the Census (1951c), Tables 102 and 103; (1956c), Tables 102 and 103; (1961c), Tables 102 and 103; (1966c), Tables 4 and 5; (1970c), Tables 4 and 5; and (1976d), Tables 2 and 4.)

$\dot{Y}'$ = rate of suburban income growth relative to the rate of central city income growth; that is, ratio of 1960 to 1950 (1970 to 1960) suburban family median income relative to the ratio of 1960 to 1950 (1970 to 1960) central city family median income. (U.S. Bureau of the Census (1973b), Table 89; (1963a), Table 76; (1952), Table 37.)

$\dot{H}$ = rate of growth of the SMSA housing stock; that is, ratio of the 1960 to the 1950 (1970 to 1960) number of housing units in the SMSA. (U.S. Bureau of the Census (1972b), Table 1; (1963d), Table 12; and (1953b), Table 1.)

$\dot{H}'$ = rate of growth of the suburban housing stock relative to the rate of growth of the central city housing stock; that is, ratio of 1960 to 1950 (1970 to 1960) suburban housing stock relative to the ratio of 1960 to 1950 (1970 to 1960) central city housing stock. (See preceding.)

$\dot{H}''$ = $1/\dot{H}'$.

2. Exogenous variables

$\dot{R}$ = rate of growth of the CLF of the SMSA; that is, ratio of 1960 to 1950 (1970 to 1960) CLF of the SMSA. (U.S. Bureau of the Census (1973b), Tables 85 and 121; (1963a), Tables 73 and 83; and (1952), Tables 35 and 43.)

$\dot{Y}$ = rate of growth of SMSA income; that is, ratio of 1960 to 1950 (1970 to 1960) SMSA family median income. (See $\dot{Y}'$.)

RC_{t-10} = number of 1950 (1960) central city CLF members. (See $\dot{R}'$.)

RS_{t-10} = number of 1950 (1960) suburban CLF members. (See $\dot{R}'$.)

NM'_{t-10} = percentage of suburban population nonwhite in 1950 (1960) relative to the percentage of central city population nonwhite in 1950 (1960). (U.S. Bureau of the Census (1952), Table 33; and (1963a), Table 20.)

NW''_{t-10} = $1/NW'_{t-10}$.

Y'_{t-10} = ratio of 1950 (1960) suburban to central city family median income. (See $\dot{Y}'$.)

V_{t-10} = percentage of SMSA housing stock unoccupied in 1950 (1960). (U.S. Bureau of the Census (1953b), Table 1; and (1963d), Table 12.)

V'_{t-10} = percentage of the suburban housing stock unoccupied in 1950 (1960) relative to the percentage of the central city housing stock unoccupied in 1950 (1960.) (See preceding.)

PDC_{t-10} = population density of the central city in 1950 (1960). (U.S. Bureau of the Census (1961e), Table 30; (1952), Table 33; and (1963a), Table 5.)

$CRMC_{t-10}$= crime rate of the central city in 1950 (1960). (U.S. Department of Justice (1951), Table 35; and (1961), Table 38.)

DT = dummy variable, where $DT = 0$ for observations on the 1950–1960 period and $DT = 1$ for observations on the 1960–1970 period.

TABLE 8.A1
Asymptotic t-Ratios Associated with 3SLS Estimates Presented in TABLE 8.1

Independent variables	Housing block $\dot{H}$	Location block			Distribution block			
		MCS	MSC	IM'	$\dot{H}'$	$\dot{E}'$	$\dot{R}'$	$\dot{Y}'$
$\dot{R}$	32.955							
NMOV	0.591						1.612	
$\dot{Y}$	−3.933							
V_{t-10}	−2.404							
$\dot{H}'$		3.877		6.486				
$\dot{H}''$			1.043					
$\dot{E}'$		2.792		−1.142				0.721
$\dot{E}''$			0.195					
$\dot{Y}'$		4.130		0.573	2.506	0.331		
$\dot{Y}''$			0.279					
$\dot{R}'$					5.429	2.486		2.371
IM'							5.724	
RC_{t-10}		1.555						
RS_{t-10}			0.215					
$CRMC_{t-10}$		−0.074	0.645	1.950				
NW'_{t-10}			2.275					
NW''_{t-10}		3.115		0.758				
PDC_{t-10}		−3.655	−2.027	2.785				
Y'_{t-10}								−3.254
V'_{t-10}					0.144			
CON	3.311	−1.016	−0.086	−0.743	1.338	2.972	−2.939	4.522

TABLE 8.A2
Asymptotic *t*-Ratio Associated with 3SLS Estimates Presented in TABLE 8.2

	Housing block	Location block			Distribution block			
Independent variables	$\dot{H}$	MCS	MSC	IM'	$\dot{H}'$	$\dot{E}'$	$\dot{R}'$	$\dot{Y}'$
$\dot{R}$	27.093							
$NMOV$	2.338						5.463	
$\dot{Y}$	−0.471							
V_{t-10}	−1.394							
$\dot{H}'$		6.503		3.776				
$\dot{H}''$			2.638					
$\dot{E}'$		2.837		1.667				0.961
$\dot{E}''$			−2.995					
$\dot{Y}'$		2.807		−0.427	−3.006	0.301		
$\dot{Y}''$			4.369					
$\dot{R}'$					7.058	2.494		−0.066
IM'							8.342	
RC_{t-10}		3.092						
RS_{t-10}			0.141					
$CRMC_{t-10}$		−0.618	0.775	−0.147				
NW'_{t-10}			1.288					
NW''_{t-10}		−0.741		−2.101				
PDC_{t-10}		−4.181	−3.812	0.850				
Y'_{t-10}								−2.433
V'_{t-10}					1.774			
CON	−0.759	−2.501	0.006	−0.277	4.217	2.735	−0.601	3.759

Equation for

TABLE 8.A3
Asymptotic t-Ratios Associated with 3SLS Estimates Presented in TABLE 8.3

| | Equation for | | | | | | | |
| | Manufacturing | | Retail | | Services | | Wholesale | |
Independent variables	1950–1960	1960–1970	1950–1960	1960–1970	1950–1960	1960–1970	1950–1960	1960–1970
$\dot{R}'$	1.931	0.772	2.350	2.057	0.710	1.476	1.198	0.490
$\dot{Y}'$	−0.303	0.293	2.242	−0.398	0.673	0.112	−0.683	1.090
CON	2.307	1.201	4.292	5.393	3.714	3.735	4.256	4.851
$\dot{R}'$	1.471	1.360	2.087	2.598	0.258	1.818	1.076	0.986
$\dot{Y}'$	−0.391	0.102	1.896	−0.300	0.298	0.187	0.519	0.734
PDC_{t-10}	1.027	1.675	0.236	1.626	0.643	1.090	3.700	1.527
$CRMC_{t-10}$	0.928	0.176	0.585	−0.591	1.058	−0.502	−0.317	0.424
CON	0.090	−1.095	0.942	−0.668	0.795	−0.495	−2.725	−0.165
$\dot{R}'$					−2.240	−0.539	1.247	−2.360
$\dot{Y}'$					−0.907	0.522	1.188	1.405
PDC_{t-10}					0.084	−0.396	3.264	−0.579
$CRMC_{t-10}$					0.273	−0.097	−0.100	1.148
$MANU'$					3.194	0.054	1.236	3.870
RET'					5.408	8.550	−2.336	8.636
CON					0.133	0.087	−1.970	1.142

9

Thoughts on the Policy Aspects of Migration and Urban Employment Growth

Long-term trends in the regional distribution of population, labor force, and employment are the results of powerful economic and social forces. Many of these same forces also reshape the intraurban distribution of economic activity. Technological change, in combination with rising incomes and desires for different life-styles, has facilitated and encouraged the Westward and Southward movements of population and employment as well as the movements of population and employment to the suburbs of the nation's major metropolitan areas. Although the federal government has played some role in these broad movements of population and employment, this role has probably been minor relative to those played by the major economic and social forces discussed in this study. Good quantitative evidence of the role of the federal government in determining the interregional and intraurban distributions of labor force and employment is not presently available, so judgments concerning this role remain largely subjective.

The present chapter has two major parts. The first develops the rationale for public intervention to deal with problems associated with the geographic distribution of population and economic activity. The second considers selected policy options to deal with problems discussed earlier in the study.

The Rationale for Public Intervention

Various regions of the country cannot reasonably be expected to experience the same rates of employment and population growth. In a market economy spatial differentials in real wage rates and in employment opportunities provide signals to workers that encourage spatial mobility. This mobility not only increases the well-being of the migrants themselves, but it also results in improved resource allocation. Migration is not only a consequence of economic growth but is also an indispensable cause of such growth.

Productive resources are, however, not perfectly adaptable to new uses that arise in the natural course of economic growth and change. Because of the lack of perfect adaptability, adjustments in the allocation of resources require time. In certain instances, without public intervention the labor adjustment process would require indefinitely long periods during which socially unacceptable hardships would be borne by the less adaptable (i.e., less mobile) persons in society. Some form of public intervention is required.

What is frequently not recognized is that any migration results in redistributions of income in both the place of origin and the place of destination as well as between the two places. In other words, in both sending and receiving areas certain individuals and groups are made better off due to the migration, while other individuals and groups are made worse off. Broadly speaking, four groups can be distinguished, though in practice the individual members of each group may not easily be identified:

1. The migrants themselves
2. The employers of the migrants
3. The consumers affected by the migrants
4. The workers affected by the migrants

Let us briefly consider how income redistribution caused by migration might affect certain of these groups.[1]

The migrants themselves are one of the groups that most clearly benefits from the migration. After presumably weighing the expected costs of their actions against the expected gains, they migrate, which makes obvious the outcome of their benefit-cost calculus. A number of factors might underlie the migration decision, such as job and earnings opportunities and place amenities. Several studies have specifically focused on the monetary returns to migration. Generally, the findings have been that the monetary returns are greater for the young than for the old, are greater for the more educated, and are greater for whites than for blacks, but are positive for all.[2] If we are going to have policy concerns about

---

[1]For a more detailed discussion of the income redistributions associated with migration, see Gerking and Greenwood (1977).

[2]R. F. Wertheimer (1970).

such groups, we probably want to base our concerns not on the fact that the groups are migrants but rather on the fact that certain of them are poor, old, unemployed, poorly housed, or whatever, despite their having gained due to migration.

What spatial employment problems resulting from interregional or intraurban mobility merit a public policy response? Much interregional and intraurban mobility is itself a consequence of spatial employment disparities, and such mobility generally tends to alleviate these disparities. We have seen, for example, that during the 1960s the direct effect of migration was to decrease unemployment in the Northeast. However, in making his decision to move the migrant takes into account only the private costs and benefits of his move. To the extent that the social costs associated with migration are not internalized by the individual, private migration decisions can result in socially nonoptimal consequences that justify public intervention. An obvious example of these social costs is the increased congestion and pollution in already crowded cities due to migration from less populated areas.

Thurow (1970) makes the following point, which emphasizes the importance of migration-induced income transfers between consumers of public goods:

> Private incomes may increase enough to more than make up for the costs of moving, but the social costs of accommodating people in a crowded urban area may exceed the net private gain. More public services must be provided, and congestion may increase. Excess capacity, and hence waste, may develop in the production of social services (schools, etc.) in areas from which people are moving, and new investment in social services may be needed in area to which they are moving [p.33].

Whether consumers of public goods benefit from the presence or absence of migrants is a complex question. In part the answer is dependent upon the number of migrants affecting any given area; in part, upon the migrants' demand for public goods; in part, upon the magnitude of the migrants' tax bill; in part, upon whether the public good is produced under conditions of rising or falling average costs; and in part, upon still other factors. What makes the answer especially difficult is that it may be different for different localities and within a locality for different public goods.

It is not difficult to conjure up a fairly realistic situation in which a public good like education or police protection is provided in a large or moderately large city under conditions of rising average cost. Since public goods are presumably priced at average cost, a migrant who consumes an average quantity of the public good and pays the average tax bill would impose a burden on the indigenous residents of the locality because they would find that their tax bills would have risen. If the migrants tend to be lower income individuals and/or to consume disproportionately much of the good, the burden on the indigenous residents would be particularly great. Even if the nominal price of the public good were unchanged after the influx of the migrants, the real price could still rise due to quality deterioration resulting from congestion.

If we were to judge on the basis of the increasing number of communities that are adopting "local growth management" policies, we might conclude that more and more localities are interested in protecting their indigenous residents from the social costs of in-migration. Local growth management policies include public acquisition of land, public improvements, environmental controls, zoning techniques, subdivision techniques, tax and fee systems, and restrictive convenants. Although these policies can be extremely effective in controlling local growth, each of them is likely to have spillover effects on neighboring communities or to have relatively heavy impact on particular groups. The next decade is likely to see a number of legal battles fought over local growth management policies that are now being implemented in communities across the country.[3]

The effects of migration need not be symmetrical in sending and receiving localities. For example, if the migrants were to come from rural communities where certain public goods are produced under conditions of decreasing cost, then the individuals left behind in these localities could also experience an increase in their tax bills. Or if the migrants had relatively high incomes, such as those who leave central cities to move to the suburbs, the burden of local taxes could fall more heavily on those left behind—perhaps on individuals who are least able to bear such increased burdens.

With reversal of the historical trend of net migration out of nonmetropolitan areas and into metropolitan areas, concern about the social costs of increased congestion, pollution, and provision of public services in large cities should be somewhat mitigated, at least relatively. More concern will now be directed at the social costs of increased population densities in nonmetropolitan areas. To the extent that in-migration to nonmetropolitan areas is motivated by the availability of natural resources, such as clean air and water, scenery, and recreational amenities, the environmental costs of migration are likely to receive added attention in years to come.

Selected Employment Policy Options

To this point the policy discussion has focused more directly on population than on employment. The reason is that in the interregional and the intraurban contexts the distinction between population policy on the one hand and employment policy on the other becomes blurred. The blurring is due to the joint dependency between population and employment growth. In many instances the

---

[3]Evans and Vestal (1977) have a detailed discussion of many of the economic and legal issues associated with local growth management policies.

best way to influence employment growth is to influence population growth. A number of papers were previously cited that suggest that the primary cause of spatial employment redistribution has been spatial redistribution of market demand resulting from population redistribution. A strategy of encouraging population growth may be particularly relevant because of the tendency for higher-income, better-educated, and younger persons to have greater migration rates and for the local employment effects of migration to be especially sensitive to persons with these characteristics.

Nevertheless, the causal relationship running from employment to population cannot be ignored. Chapter 3 of this study emphasized that to a large extent the state of the national economy determines interregional and intraurban employment growth differentials. Particularly during periods of high national unemployment and slow growth of GNP, employment growth in the Northeast and North Central regions and in the central cities of the major metropolitan areas appears to be adversely affected relative to employment growth in their counterparts. Thus, the exercise of fiscal and monetary policies to maintain full employment must stand as a cornerstone of any regional or urban employment policy.

Even during periods of full employment, however, the incidence of unemployment falls unevenly on various localities—and within localities on various population groups—and employment and earnings growth proceed at differential rates that encourage migration. At least directly, employment policy concern should be with the less mobile elements in society, who have difficulty engaging in the mainstream of economic activity.

A number of factors are responsible for lack of mobility. These factors include both personal and labor market characteristics. The goal of public policies intended to influence geographic mobility must be to alter the costs and/or benefits of migration as perceived by the less mobile segments of society. A similar goal would be applicable to situations in which the net social costs of migration exceed the net private gain. The means by which private perceptions of the benefits and costs of migration might be altered can be broadly grouped into two categories, direct and indirect. A partial list of the alternatives included under each category follows.[4]

I. Policies operating *directly* on individual incentives:
1. Subsidize moving costs
2. Subsidize housing
3. Provide public employment
4. Provide tax incentives

[4]For a discussion of policies adopted in other countries, see DeJong (1975), Hansen (1974), and Sundquist (1975).

    5. Provide manpower training programs
    6. Provide employment and other information
    7. Alter minimum wages
    8. Change welfare requirements
II. Policies operating *indirectly* on individual incentives:
    1. Encourage private sector employment growth through
       a. Investments in public infrastructure
       b. Tax or subsidy incentives to firms
       c. Government procurement policies
       d. Credit institutions
    2. Encourage planning for growth or decline
    3. Reduce local disamenities, including pollution, congestion, and crime
    4. Influence aggregate labor supply by means of immigration policy

Some degree of arbitrariness is inherent in this classification scheme. For example, Alternative II.3 could be regarded as direct and Alternative I.7 could be regarded as indirect. The distinction here is that certain policies operate immediately on the individuals involved, whereas others operate in such a way as to affect the environment in which they live and work or the markets in which they supply their labor services. Clearly, many of the policies that influence individuals or families directly also influence the environment in which they live and the markets in which they participate.

Of the above alternatives, the following can be characterized as employment policy options: I.3, I.5, I.6, I.7, II.1, II.2, and II.4. Let us consider certain of these options.

PLANNING FOR GROWTH OR DECLINE

A sound case can be made for developing local institutional planning capabilities. Planning activities should be directed not only at facilitating growth in expanding local economies but also at accommodating lagging local economies to lower levels of economic activity. One of the most important aspects of the planning process is forecasting local labor demand by detailed occupational category. This type of information should contribute to the efficiency of the migration mechanism, as well as to the functioning of the local labor market, by allowing better-informed decisions regarding the occupation and location in which an individual will render his labor services.

In many ways rapidly growing areas have the greatest need for planning assistance. The need arises from the desirability of avoiding future externalities, and avoiding such externalities should be one of the major consequences of good planning. Community planning efforts should be coordinated at the SMSA level, and SMSA and other multi-county planning efforts should be coordinated at the regional level. Two reasons exist for the desirability of coordinating planning over fairly broad geographic areas:

1. Controls placed on growth in one locality can influence the pattern of growth in neighboring localities. Planners should be cognizant of the effects of their decisions on neighboring communities and should take account of these effects in making their decisions and recommendations. The problem is analogous to attempting to "internalize the externalities" associated with a given action.

2. The importance of national and broad regional factors in determining the local economic growth experience suggests the need not only for state planning efforts but also for some coordination with multistate planning units. If, for example, regional forecasts of economic activity were essential to various local planning efforts, scale economies in developing such forecasts might be achieved if the forecasts were made by multistate units that were coordinated through a federal agency. Rather than each local or state planning office developing its own regional forecasts, a regional office might perform this service and make its forecasts available to state and local planners. In this way, the regional modeling effort could be somewhat larger than what might be sustained by any given state or locality, and the average and total cost of generating a given amount of information would decline for the locality.

TRAINING PROGRAMS

Manpower training programs have a primary objective of overcoming personal characteristics that limit employment alternatives and consequently reduce occupational and geographic mobility. Such programs have traditionally been directed at the minority and low-income population, and hence they have a high degree of geographic specificity (namely, in areas where minorities and the poor reside). Because manpower programs have not in themselves been an unqualified success, as evidenced by the high unemployment and underemployment rates of blacks, an argument can be made for instituting complementary programs that affect labor demand in areas with high concentrations of less mobile persons.

A number of market imperfections prevent local and national labor markets from functioning more efficiently. One of the most important of these is that many workers and potential workers either do not have access to information regarding job and earnings opportunities in various alternative locations and occupations, or they are unable to decipher the complex information that is available. Public intervention to provide information to potential migrants and/or occupational changers is appropriate.

For some individuals who receive manpower training, the probability of migrating out of an area rises. This tendency is not undesirable, except inasmuch as the loss of a potential complementary input affects the employment of others in the locality. Policymakers recognize that manpower programs should be coordinated with the planning process if the programs are to achieve a reasonable degree of success. Information generated through the planning process and by other means should be made available to recipients of manpower training so that they can make better-informed choices regarding whether and where to migrate and regarding the occupation in which to render their labor services. The combination of planning, training, and dissemination of information is likely to have some impact on labor mobility and on local labor markets, but a reasonable assessment of the magnitudes of the impacts is not available at this time.

IMMIGRATION POLICY

Immigration policy is an aspect of public intervention that has potentially dramatic effects on labor supply. Recently illegal aliens have come under special scrutiny because of their apparently large and growing numbers. Various reports in the popular press and by government agencies have placed the number of illegal U.S. residents at between 4 and 12 million persons. In fiscal 1975 766,600 deportable aliens were apprehended in this country, of which 89% were Mexicans. This percentage overstates the percentage of illegal Mexican aliens relative to the total number of illegal aliens, but it does indicate that Mexico is an extremely important source of illegal alien labor.[5] Available information indicates that illegal aliens tend to be young and to have a high degree of labor force attachment. Moreover, they are concentrated along the Southwestern border and in the central cities of the nation's major metropolitan areas. New York City alone is estimated to contain over 1 million illegal aliens.

Fullerton and Flaim (1976), using Bureau of Labor Statistics data, estimate that between 1980 and 1985 the expected increase in the labor force will be slightly less than 7 million. If an estimate of 250,000 incremental (permanent) illegal alien labor force members per year is made, then the incremental illegal alien labor force would be 18% of the incremental domestic labor force. Since the projected incremental male labor force is somewhat smaller than the projected incremental female labor force and since the preponderance of illegal aliens—at least Mexican aliens—tends to be male, the relative impact on the male labor force would be considerably greater. The impact on the young labor force would be very large indeed, for rather than declining absolutely as is now projected, the young labor force would probably rise. Finally, the relative im-

---

[5]The reason that Mexicans are overrepresented in apprehensions is that the U.S. and Mexico have a common border across which the Mexicans typically enter the U.S. and along which the U.S. Border Patrol can be deployed to apprehend them as, or shortly after, they enter. Mexicans are also more physically identifiable than many other nationalities that contribute importantly to the illegal alien population.

pacts on the civilian labor forces of the Southwest and West, and of the central cities of the major metropolitan areas, would also be great.[6]

Two hypotheses have been advanced regarding the employment effects of illegal alien labor. One hypothesis, referred to as the "segmentation hypothesis," states that labor markets are sufficiently segmented that illegal alien workers do not take jobs that would otherwise be taken by domestic workers. Illegal alien workers are presumed to occupy low wage jobs that would not interest domestic workers.[7] The other hypothesis, called the "replacement hypothesis," states that illegal alien workers do displace domestic workers.[8] It can easily be demonstrated that the direct effects of illegal alien labor must be to displace domestic workers, although counteracting effects occur due to the complementarity of illegal and domestic workers and due to the local demand effects of illegal workers. Since the illegal aliens generally tend to be unskilled, they compete in the labor market with low-wage domestic workers, principally blacks, Mexican Americans, and teenage workers.

The measurement of the net effects of the presence of illegal alien workers must await a detailed empirical analysis of the problem, which does not now exist. However, immigration policy directed at greatly reducing the flow of illegal alien labor into this country will have dramatic labor force effects, and many of these effects will be localized.

JOB CREATION PROGRAMS

Three aspects of policy on the demand-side of the labor market seem particularly relevant—economic development programs, public service employment, and alterations in minimum wage laws. Only the former two options will be discussed here.

The debate over inadequate aggregate demand versus structural factors as causes of unemployment has gone on for some time. The Economic Development Administration (U.S. Department of Commerce, 1976) financed a study that used National Planning Association state employment projections to estimate the number of state-specific jobs required in 1980 and in 1985 to reduce state-specific unemployment rates alternatively to 6, 5, and 4%. Suppose that we utilize these estimates, make the assumption that macroeconomic policies will reduce the unemployment rate of each state to 6% in 1985, and ask how many

---

[6]Dagodag (1975) provides fairly comprehensive information on the characteristics of illegal Mexican aliens. He shows that Mexican aliens tend strongly to be young males and to be seeking employment.

[7]E. Abrams and F. S. Abrams (1975) and Nafziger (1975), for example, support the segmentation hypothesis.

[8]Briggs (1975) is a proponent of the replacement hypothesis.

additional jobs between 1980 and 1985 would be needed in each region to reduce the region's unemployment rate to 4%. This two-percentage-point reduction would presumably have to be accomplished via structural economic policies.

The estimates indicate that the following 1980–1985 regional employment growth would be required to reduce unemployment rates from 6 to 4%: Northeast, 978,000 jobs; North Central, 1,244,000 jobs; South, 1,454,000 jobs; and West, 824,000 jobs. Nationally, 4,480,000 additional jobs would be required. If we assume an average annual cost of $10,000 per job, which is a rough estimate of the average cost of a public service job, almost $45 billion would be necessary in 1985 alone (assuming no secondary effects, which is probably unrealistic given magnitudes of this kind) to reduce the unemployment rate by two percentage points. Although a number of criticisms can be made of the employment estimates and of the technique used to derive the $45 billion figure, the expenditures required to achieve even modest increases in employment and decreases in unemployment are tremendous. A similar estimate of the cost of reducing the unemployment and underemployment rate of black males, 16–24 years of age, from 37.0% to 10% is $4.24 billion.

Since programs such as public service employment would require on-going expenditures of tremendous magnitudes, manpower programs in combination with economic development programs seem more reasonable for dealing with long-run problems of local distress. Note too that the magnitudes so far discussed are slight relative to those that would be required in the unfortunate instance that an attempt were made to reverse the major spatial employment trends discussed herein.

In a discussion paper prepared by the staff of the Economic Development Administration (U.S. Department of Commerce, 1977, p. II-4), economic development programs are defined as "the planned investment of public resources to attract private investment to specific areas and communities in order to create permanent private sector jobs and strengthen local private economies." A distinction is made between "general development programs," or programs that are parts of various federal activities that have primary objectives other than subnational economic development but nevertheless have local economic development consequences as by-products, and "economic development programs," or programs whose primary objective is local economic development. Federal economic development programs are shown to be a relatively small fraction of federal development programs—about 13%, as indicated in Table 9.1.

A sensible case is made in the EDA paper that current and likely future levels of economic development financing are sufficiently low so that, when spread across many areas and communities, the impacts in any given locality will be rather minimal. However, if economic development programs are coordinated with the more sizeable general development programs, such as those indicated in Table 9.1, significant beneficial effects may be forthcoming.

TABLE 9.1
Federal Development Assistance: Fiscal 1978 Estimates (in millions of dollars)

Department/Agency	General development Amount	General development Percentage	Economic development Amount	Economic development Percentage
HUD	3,600	12.0	550[a]	12.3
USDA	5,780	19.4	927[b]	20.8
DOC				
EDA			400	9.0
OMBE			11	.3
NOAA/OCZM	27	.1		
DOL (CETA)			1,880[c]	42.2
DOD				
Economic Adjustment			NA	
Corps of Engineers	50	.2		
DOT (FHA, UMTA)	10,500	35.2		
ARC			300	6.7
Title V Regional Comm.			100	2.2
BIA	650	2.2	150[d]	3.4
CSA	358	1.2	42[e]	.9
EPA (Sewers)	4,500	15.1		
SBA	3,100	10.4	100[f]	2.2
FAA	550	1.8		
TVA	45	.2		
GSA	12	.0		
HEW	650	2.2		
Total	29,867	100.0	4,459	100.0

[a] Assumes that 10% of the Community Development Block Grant ($4 billion) is used for economic development purposes. Also includes $150 million of Federal disaster assistance. Does not include proposed funding for the Urban Development Action Grant.

[b] Includes emergency adjustment, aid to Indian areas, and Community Facilities Loans that include activities not necessarily directed at economic development.

[c] Excludes funding for Public Services Employment in Titles II and VI. Includes only Title I, which provides funding for job training in the private sector.

[d] Includes only industrial/business development grant and loan program and Disaster Relief Programs.

[e] Includes only the Community Economic Development Program, Emergency Energy Conservation Program, and grants for State Economic Opportunity Centers.

[f] Includes only disaster relief funding and aid to minority/disadvantaged small businessmen.

Employment considerations are only one factor of importance in determining the intrametropolitan location decisions of labor force members. Housing services and neighborhood amenities are at least as important and, in many instances, probably considerably more important. In future years rising gasoline prices could alter this situation by significantly increasing the out-of-pocket costs of commuting. In any case, central city economic development programs are in themselves not the answer to central city problems. This situation suggests the appropriateness of central city funding strategies that include not only economic development projects but also housing and transportation projects and projects to improve the quality of neighborhood life. Such funding strategies should be designed for some reasonable, but finite, period of time, say 10 to 20 years.

Harrison (1974b) and others have made strong cases for ghetto or for central city economic development programs that would have as a target group the immobile or at least the less mobile central city minorities. Such programs would seem to have the greatest probability of success if they were coordinated with general development programs, as recommended by the Economic Development Administration. The employment impacts of these kinds of Federal programs cannot easily be forecasted because the impacts differ greatly by specific type of program. Moreover, much uncertainty exists regarding the average cost of job creation through economic development programs. If the average cost were $10,000 per (permanent) job, then approximately 446,000 permanent jobs could be created via economic development programs, given the estimated Fiscal 1978 expenditures. Such an average cost is obviously unrealistically low, for if $10,000 were a reasonable estimate, Congress would have learned long ago that economic development programs are simply too good to pass up as a means of relieving unemployment.

It was previously pointed out that the decline of the manufacturing sector in the central cities of the major metropolitan areas of the Northeast and North Central regions has contributed appreciably to central city problems. Some temptation may therefore exist to conclude that central city economic development programs should be oriented toward manufacturing employment. However, if Steinnes is correct that people are moving away from manufacturing employment, the encouragement of manufacturing employment growth in central cities could be partially self-defeating.

Certain of the policy alternatives mentioned above are more relevant in influencing the migration decisions of low-income persons than of persons with higher incomes. Policies that operate directly on individual incentives are typically, but not exclusively, of this type, whereas policies that operate indirectly on incentives are generally relevant in influencing the migration decisions of a broad spectrum of society. Subsidized moving costs, subsidized housing, public employment, manpower programs, and changes in welfare requirements are all likely to have their greatest impacts on the low-income population. The availability of tax incentives and of information would presumably be of some importance to all potential migrants, regardless of income level. Similarly, economic development programs, planning programs, and reductions in local disamenities should benefit both low- and high-income persons. The labor supply effects of more restrictive enforcement of immigration laws would be most beneficial for workers in occupations with lower wages, but in a broader sense much of society would be affected, either positively or negatively, by more restrictive enforcement.

One rationale for economic development programs, in spite of their not directly influencing the low-income and disadvantaged populations, has been that such programs have "trickle down" effects on the target populations. Chinitz (1971) makes the case for economic development programs by arguing that the "welfare of an individual . . . depends on the environment in which he lives as well as his own attributes, assets, and skills [p.25]." An additional related advantage of utilizing economic development programs and other programs that yield potential benefits to a broad spectrum of society, in combination with programs that have more direct impact on the disadvantaged population, is that population composition should be more "normal" in the various localities if the programs appeal to a wide variety of persons.

Localized programs that tend to benefit only the disadvantaged population can encourage the undesirable side-effect of attracting such persons to concentrate in specific localities, such as in the central cities of the major metropolitan areas. Such concentrations of low-income persons can spur higher-income persons to leave in order to avoid the local income redistributive effects of various local programs, with the consequence that the local public sector is placed under considerable strain. Hence, a balanced policy approach seems essential. This balance must be struck not only within the framework of employment policy but also between employment and other forms of policy.

Policymakers should be careful to recognize that the past 10 years have been highly unusual for the American economy. This study has documented a number of factors that have encouraged differentially sizeable numbers of families and individuals to relocate. These relocation decisions have profoundly influenced the types of problems confronted by various localities. Although many of the same problems will remain, the emphasis is likely to change, and policymakers should be in a position to anticipate these changes.

References

Abrams, E., and F. S. Abrams. (1975). "Immigration Policy—Who Gets In and Why?" *The Public Interest*, 3-29.

Allaman, P. M., and D. L. Birch. (1975). "Components of Employment Change for States by Industry Group, 1970-1972." Working Paper No. 5, Joint Center for Urban Studies of the Massachusetts Institute of Technology and Harvard University.

Alonso, W. (1978). "The Current Halt in the Metropolitan Phenomenon." In C. L. Leven (ed), *The Mature Metropolis*. Lexington: Lexington Books.

Beale, C. F. (1977). "The Recent Shift of the United States Population to Nonmetropolitan Areas, 1970-75." *International Regional Science Review* 2, 113-122.

Becker, G. S. (1962). "Investment in Human Capital: A Theoretical Analysis." *Journal of Political Economy* 70, Supplement, 9-49.

Becker, G. S. (1964). *Human Capital*. New York: National Bureau of Economic Research; distributed by Columbia University Press.

Berry, B. J. L. (1977). "Transformation of the Nation's Urban System: Small City Growth as a Zero-Sum Game." Policy Note P77-1, Harvard University.

Berry, B. J. L., and D. C. Dahmann. (1977). "Population Redistribution in the United States in the 1970s." Washington, D.C.: National Academy of Sciences.

Birch, D. L. (1970). *The Economic Future of City and Suburb*. CED Supplementary Paper No. 30. New York: Committee for Economic Development.

Blanco, C. (1962). *The Determinants of Regional Factor Mobility*. The Hague: Drukkerij Pasmans.

Blanco, C. (1963). "The Determinants of Interstate Population Movements." *Journal of Regional Science* 5, 77-84.

Blanco, C. (1964). "Prospective Unemployment and Interstate Population Movements." *Review of Economics and Statistics* 46, 221-222.

Borts, G. H. (1960). "The Equalization of Returns and Regional Economic Growth." *American Economic Review* 50, 319-347.

Borts, G. H., and J. L. Stein. (1964). *Economic Growth in a Free Market*. New York: Columbia University Press.

Bowen, W. G., and T. A. Finegan. (1969). *The Economics of Labor Force Participation*. Princeton: Princeton University Press.

Bowles, S. (1970). "Migration as Investment: Empirical Tests of the Human Investment Approach to Geographical Mobility." *Review of Economics and Statistics* 52, 356-362.

Bowman, M. J., and R. G. Myers. (1967). "Schooling, Experience, and Gains and Losses in Human Capital through Migration." *Journal of the American Statistical Association* 62, 875-898.

Bradford, D. F., and H. H. Kelejian. (1973). "An Econometric Model of Flight to the Suburbs." *Journal of Political Economy* 81, 566-589.

Briggs, V. M., Jr. (1975). "Illegal Aliens: The Need for a More Restrictive Border Policy." *Social Science Quarterly* 56, 477-484.

Brown, H. J. (1975). "Changes in Workplace and Residential Locations." *Journal of the American Institute of Planners* 41, 32-39.

Burrows, J. C., C. E. Metcalf, and J. B. Kaler. (1971). *Industrial Location in the United States*. Lexington: Heath Lexington Books.

Chalmers, J. A., and M. J. Greenwood. (1977). "Thoughts on the Rural to Urban Migration Turnaround." *International Regional Science Review* 2, 167-170.

Chinitz, B. (1971). "National Policy for Regional Development." In J. F. Kain and J. R. Meyer (eds.), *Essays in Regional Economics*. Cambridge: Harvard University Press, 21-39.

Christ, C. F. (1966). *Econometric Models and Methods*. New York: John Wiley and Sons, Inc.

Cohen, B. I. (1971). "Trends in Negro Employment within Large Metropolitan Areas." *Public Policy* 19, 611-622.

Cohen, B. I., and R. G. Noll. (1968). "Employment Trends in Central Cities." Social Science Discussion Paper 69-1, California Institute of Technology.

Dagodag, T. W. (1975). "Source Regions and Composition of Illegal Mexican Immigration to California." *International Migration Review* 9, 499-511.

DaVanzo, J. (1978). "Does Unemployment Affect Migration? Evidence from Micro Data." *Review of Economics and Statistics* 60, 504-514.

DeJong, G. F. (1975). "Population Redistribution Policies: Alternatives from the Netherlands, Great Britain, and Israel." *Social Science Quarterly* 56, 262-273.

deLeeuw, F. (1971). "The Demand for Housing: A Review of Cross-Section Evidence." *Review of Economics and Statistics* 53, 1-10.

Eldridge, H. T. (1965). "Primary, Secondary, and Return Migration to the United States; 1955-60." *Demography* 2, 444-455.

Evans, V. J., and B. Vestal. (1977). "Local Growth Management: A Demographic Perspective." *North Carolina Law Review* 55, 421-460.

Fields, G. S. (1976). "Labor Force Migration, Unemployment and Job Turnover." *Review of Economics and Statistics* 58, 407-415.

Fields, G. S. (1979). "Place-to-Place Migration: Some New Evidence." *Review of Economics and Statistics* 61, 21-32.

Fuchs, V. R. (1962a). *Changes in the Location of Manufacturing in the United States Since 1929*. New Haven: Yale University Press.

Fuchs, V. R. (1962b). "Statistical Explanations of the Relative Shift of Manufacturing among Regions of the United States." *Papers and Proceedings of the Regional Science Association* 8, 106-126.

Fullerton, H. N., Jr., and P. O. Flaim. (1976). "New Labor Force Projections to 1990." *Monthly Labor Review* 99, 3–13.

Gallaway, L. E., (1969). "Age and Labor Mobility Patterns." *Southern Economic Journal* 36, 171–180.

Gallaway, L. E., R. F. Gilbert, and P. E. Smith. (1967). "The Economics of Labor Mobility: An Empirical Analysis." *Western Economic Journal* 5, 211–223.

Gerking, S. D., and M. J. Greenwood. (1977). "Illegal Aliens in the United States: Who Enjoys the Benefits and Who Bears the Costs?" Presented at the NIH-INS Belmont Conference on Illegal Aliens, Belmont, Maryland.

Goldstein, G. S., and L. N. Moses. (1973). "A Survey of Urban Economics." *Journal of Economic Literature* 11, 471–515.

Graves, P. E. (1979). "A Life-Cycle Empirical Analysis of Migration and Climate, by Race." *Journal of Urban Economics* 6, 135–147.

Graves, P. E., and P. D. Linneman. (1979). "Household Migration: Theoretical and Empirical Results." *Journal of Urban Economics* 6, 383–404.

Greenwood, M. J. (1973). "Urban Economic Growth and Migration: Their Interaction." *Environment and Planning* 5, 91–112.

Greenwood, M. J. (1975a). "A Simultaneous-Equations Model of Urban Growth and Migration." *Journal of the American Statistical Association* 70, 797–810.

Greenwood, M. J. (1975b). "Research on Internal Migration in the United States: A Survey." *Journal of Economic Literature* 13, 397–433.

Greenwood, M. J. (1976). "A Simultaneous-Equations Model of White and Nonwhite Migration and Urban Change." *Economic Inquiry* 14, 1–15.

Greenwood, M. J. (1980a). "Metropolitan Growth and the Intrametropolitan Location of Employment, Housing, and Labor Force." *Review of Economics and Statistics* 62, 491–501.

Greenwood, M. J. (1980b). "Population Redistribution and Employment Policy." In B. J. L. Berry and L. P. Silverman (eds.), *Population Redistribution and Public Policy*. Washington, D.C.: National Academy of Sciences, 114–168.

Greenwood, M. J. and D. Sweetland. (1972). "The Determinants of Migration between Standard Metropolitan Statistical Areas." *Demography* 9, 665–681.

Griliches, V. (1969). "Capital-Skill Complementarity." *Review of Economics and Statistics* 51, 465–470.

Hansen, N. M. (ed.). (1974). *Public Policy and Regional Economic Development*. Cambridge: Ballinger Publishing Company.

Harrison, B. (1974a). "Discrimination in Space: Suburbanization and Black Unemployment in Cities." In G. M. vonFurstenburg, B. Harrison, and A. R. Horowitz (eds.), *Patterns of Racial Discrimination*. Vol. 1, *Housing*. Lexington Books.

Harrison, B. (1974b). *Urban Economic Development*. Washington, D.C.: The Urban Institute.

Kain, J. F. (1962). "The Journey-to-Work as A Determinant of Residential Location." *Papers and Proceedings of the Regional Science Association* 9, 137–160.

Kain, J. F. (1968a). "Housing Segregation, Negro Employment, and Metropolitan Decentralization." *Quarterly Journal of Economics* 82, 175–197.

Kain, J. F. (1968b). "The Distribution and Movement of Jobs and Industry." In J. Wilson (ed.), *The Metropolitan Enigma*. Cambridge: Harvard University Press.

Kain, J. F., and J. J. Persky. (1971). "The North's Stake in Southern Rural Poverty." In J. F. Kain and J. R. Meyer (eds.), *Essays in Regional Economics*. Cambridge: Harvard University Press.

Kuznets, S. (1964). "Introduction: Population Redistribution, Migration, and Economic Growth." In *Population Redistribution and Economic Growth: United States, 1870–1950*. Vol. III by H. T. Eldridge and D. S. Thomas, *Demographic Analysis and Interrelations*. Philadelphia: The American Philosophical Association.

Kuznets, S. (1965). *Economic Growth and Structure*. New York: Norton.

Lansing, J. B., and E. Mueller. (1967). *The Geographic Mobility of Labor*. Ann Arbor: Survey Research Center, Institute for Social Research, University of Michigan.

Lansing, J. B., and J. N. Morgan. (1967). "The Effect of Geographical Mobility on Income." *Journal of Human Resources* 2, 449–460.

Liu, B. C. (1975). "Differential Net Migration Rates and the Quality of Life." *Review of Economics and Statistics* 57, 329–337.

Lowry, I. S. (1966). *Migration and Metropolitan Growth: Two Analytical Models*. San Francisco: Chandler Publishing Company.

Mazek, W. F., and J. Chang. (1972). "The Chicken or Egg Fowl-Up in Migration: Comment." *Southern Economic Journal* 39, 133–139.

McCarthy, K. F., and P. A. Morrison. (1977). "The Changing Demographic and Economic Structure of Nonmetropolitan Areas in the United States." *International Regional Science Review* 2, 123–142.

Meyer, J. R., J. F. Kain, and M. Wohl. (1965). *The Urban Transportation Problem*. Cambridge: Harvard University Press.

Miller, A. R. (1967). "The Migration of Employed Persons to and from Metropolitan Areas of the United States." *Journal of the American Statistical Association* 62, 1418–1432.

Mills, E. S. (1970). "Urban Density Functions." *Urban Studies* 7, 5–20.

Mills, E. S. (1972). *Studies in the Structure of the Urban Economy*. Baltimore: The Johns Hopkins Press.

Mincer, J. (1978). "Family Migration Decisions." *Journal of Political Economy* 86, 749–773.

Mooney, J. D., (1969). "Housing Segregation, Negro Employment and Metropolitan Decentralization: An Alternative Perspective." *Quarterly Journal of Economics* 83, 299–311.

Moses, L., and H. F. Williamson, Jr. (1967). "The Location of Economic Activity in Cities." *American Economic Review Proceedings* 57, 211–222.

Mundell, R. A. (1957). "International Trade and Factor Mobility." *American Economic Review* 47, 321–335.

Muth, R. F. (1961). "The Spatial Structure of the Urban Housing Market." *Papers and Proceedings of the Regional Science Association* 7, 207–220.

Muth, R. F. (1965). "The Variation of Population Density and Its Components in South Chicago." *Papers and Proceedings of the Regional Science Association* 15, 173–183.

Muth, R. F. (1967). "The Distribution of Population within Urban Areas." In R. Ferber (ed.), *Determinants of Investment Behavior*. New York: Columbia University Press, 271–380.

Muth, R. F. (1968). "Differential Growth Among Large U.S. Cities." In J. R. Quirk and A. M. Zarley (eds.), *Papers in Quantitative Economics*. Lawrence: The University Press of Kansas, 311–355.

Muth, R. F. (1969). *Cities and Housing*. Chicago: University of Chicago Press.

Muth, R. F. (1971). "Migration: Chicken or Egg." *Southern Economic Journal* 37, 295–306.

Myrdal, G. (1957). *Rich Lands and Poor*. New York: Harper and Row, Publishers.

Nafziger, J. A. R. (1975). "Undocumented Aliens." Paper presented at the Regional Meeting of the International Association of Law (Mimeographed).

Nelson, P. (1959). "Migration, Real Income and Information." *Journal of Regional Science* 1, 43–74.

Noll, R. (1970). "Metropolitan Employment and Population Distribution and the Conditions of the Urban Poor." In J. P. Crecine (ed.), *Financing the Metropolis*. Beverly Hills: Sage Publications, 481–509.

North, D. (1974). *Immigrants and the American Labor Movement*. Manpower Research Monograph No. 31, U.S. Department of Labor.

North, D., and A. LeBel. (1978). *Manpower and Immigration Policies in the United States.* Report prepared for the National Commission for Manpower Policy.

Okun, B. (1968). "Interstate Population Migration and State Income Inequality: A Simultaneous Equation Approach." *Economic Development and Cultural Change* 16, 297-313.

Olvey, L. D. (1970). "Regional Growth and Inter-Regional Migration—Their Pattern of Interaction." Unpublished Ph.D. dissertation, Harvard University.

Olvey, L. D. (1972). "Regional Growth and Inter-regional Migration—Their Pattern of Interaction." *Review of Regional Studies* 2, 139-163.

Persky, J. J., and J. F. Kain. (1970). "Migration, Employment, and Race in the Deep South." *Southern Economic Journal* 36, 268-276.

Raimon, R. L. (1962). "Interstate Migration and Wage Theory." *Review of Economics and Statistics* 44, 428-438.

Renshaw, V. (1974). "Using Gross Migration Data Compiled from the Social Security Sample File." *Demography* 11, 143-148.

Samuelson, P. A. (1948). "International Trade and the Equalization of Factor Prices." *Economic Journal* 58, 163-184.

Samuelson, P. A. (1953). "Prices of Factors and Goods in General Equilibrium." *Review of Economic Studies* 21, 1-20.

Siegel, J. (1975). "Intrametropolitan Migration: A Simultaneous Model of Employment and Residential Location of White and Black Households." *Journal of Urban Economics* 2, 29-47.

Sjaastad, L. A. (1960). "The Relationship Between Migration and Income in the United States." *Papers and Proceedings of the Regional Science Association* 6, 37-64.

Sjaastad, L. A. (1962). "The Costs and Returns of Human Migration." *Journal of Political Economy* 70, Supplement, 80-93.

Steinnes, D. N. (1977). "Causality and Intraurban Location." *Journal of Urban Economics* 4, 69-79.

Steinnes, D. N., and W. D. Fisher. (1974). "An Econometric Model of Intraurban Location." *Journal of Regional Science* 14, 65-80.

Stone, L. O. (1971). "On the Correlation Between Metropolitan Area In- and Out-Migration by Occupation." *Journal of the American Statistical Association* 66, 693-701.

Sundquist, J. L. (1975). *Dispersing Population: What America Can Learn from Europe.* Washington, D.C.: The Brookings Institution.

Thompson, W. R., and J. M. Mattila. (1959). *An Econometric Model of Postwar State Industrial Development.* Detroit: Wayne State University Press.

Thurow, L. C. (1970). *Investment in Human Capital.* Belmont, Calif.: Wadsworth.

U.S. Bureau of the Census. (1950). *Census of Manufactures: 1947.* Vol. III, *Statistics by States.* Washington, D.C.: U.S. Government Printing Office.

U.S. Bureau of the Census. (1951a). *Census of Business: 1948.* Vol. III, *Retail Trade-Area Statistics.* Washington, D.C.: U.S. Government Printing Office.

U.S. Bureau of the Census, (1951b). *Census of Business: 1948.* Vol. VII, *Service Trade-Area Statistics.* Washington, D.C.: U.S. Government Printing Office.

U.S. Bureau of the Census. (1951c). *Census of Business: 1948.* Vol. V, *Wholesale Trade-Area Statistics.* Washington, D.C.: U.S. Government Printing Office.

U.S. Bureau of the Census. (1952). *Census of Population: 1950.* Vol. II, *Characteristics of the Population.* Parts 2-52. Washington, D.C.: U.S. Government Printing Office.

U.S. Bureau of the Census. (1953a). *Census of Population: 1950.* Vol. II, *Characteristics of the Population.* Part 1, United States Summary. Washington, D.C.: U.S. Government Printing Office.

U.S. Bureau of the Census. (1953b). *U.S. Census of Housing: 1950.* Vol. I, *General Characteristics,* Parts 2–6. Washington, D.C.: U.S. Government Printing Office.

U.S. Bureau of the Census. (1956a). *Census of Business: 1954.* Vol. II, *Retail Trade-Area Statistics.* Washington, D.C.: U.S. Government Printing Office.

U.S. Bureau of the Census. (1956b). *Census of Business: 1954.* Vol. VI, *Selected Service Trade-Area Statistics.* Washington, D.C.: U.S. Government Printing Office.

U.S. Bureau of the Census. (1956c). *Census of Business: 1954.* Vol. IV, *Wholesale Trade-Area Statistics.* Washington, D.C.: U.S. Government Printing Office.

U.S. Bureau of the Census. (1957). *Census of Manufactures: 1954.* Vol. III, *Area Statistics.* Washington, D.C.: U.S. Government Printing Office.

U.S. Bureau of the Census. (1961a) *Census of Business: 1958.* Vol. II, *Retail Trade-Area Statistics.* Washington, D.C.: U.S. Government Printing Office.

U.S. Bureau of the Census. (1961b). *Census of Business: 1958.* Vol. VI, *Selected Services-Area Statistics.* Washington, D.C.: U.S. Government Printing Office.

U.S. Bureau of the Census. (1961c). *Census of Business: 1958.* Vol. IV, *Wholesale Trade-Area Statistics.* Washington, D.C.: U.S. Government Printing Office.

U.S. Bureau of the Census. (1961d). *Census of Manufactures: 1958.* Vol. III, *Area Statistics.* Washington, D.C.: U.S. Government Printing Office.

U.S. Bureau of the Census. (1961e). *U.S. Census of Population: 1960.* Part A, *Number of Inhabitants.* Washington, D.C.: U.S. Government Printing Office.

U.S. Bureau of the Census. (1963a). *Census of Population: 1960.* Vol. I, *Characteristics of the Population.* Parts 2–52. Washington, D.C.: U.S. Government Printing Office.

U.S. Bureau of the Census. (1963b). *Census of Population: 1960.* Subject Reports, *Mobility for Metropolitan Areas.* Washington,D.C.: U.S. Government Printing Office.

U.S. Bureau of Census. (1963c). *Current Population Reports,* Series P-20, No. 122. "Marital Status and Family Status: March 1962." Washington, D.C.: U. S. Government Printing Office.

U.S. Bureau of the Census. (1963d). *U.S. Census of Housing: 1960.* Vol. I, *States and Small Areas,* Parts 2–8. Washington, D.C.: U.S. Government Printing Office.

U.S. Bureau of the Census. (1964). *Census of Population: 1960.* Vol, I, *Characteristics of the Population.* Part 1, United States Summary. Washington, D.C.: U.S. Government Printing Office.

U.S. Bureau of the Census. (1966a). *Census of Business: 1963.* Vol. 2, *Retail Trade-Area Statistics.* Washington, D.C.: U.S. Government Printing Office.

U.S. Bureau of Census. (1966b). *Census of Business: 1963,* Vol. 7, *Selected Services-Area Statistics.* Washington, D.C.: U.S. Government Printing Office.

U.S. Bureau of the Census. (1966c). *Census of Business: 1963.* Vol. 5, *Wholesale Trade-Area Statistics.* Washington, D.C.: U.S. Government Printing Office.

U.S. Bureau of the Census. (1966d). *Census of Manufactures: 1963.* Vol. III, *Area Statistics.* Washington, D.C.: U.S. Government Printing Office.

U.S. Bureau of the Census. (1966e). *Current Population Reports,* Series P-20, No. 150. "Mobility of the Population of the United States: March 1964 to March 1965." Washington, D.C.: U.S. Government Printing Office.

U.S. Bureau of the Census. (1966f). *Current Population Reports,* Series P-20, No. 156. "Mobility of the Population of the United States: March 1965 to March 1966." Washington, D.C.: U.S. Government Printing Office.

U.S. Bureau of the Census. (1966g). *Current Population Reports,* Series P-20, No. 154. "Reasons for Moving: March 1962 to March 1963." Washington, D.C.: U.S. Government Printing Office.

U.S. Bureau of the Census. (1967). *Current Population Reports,* Series P-20, No. 162. "School Enrollment: October 1965." Washington, D.C.: U.S. Government Printing Office.

U.S. Bureau of the Census. (1970a). *Census of Business: 1967.* Vol II, *Retail Trade-Area Statistics.* Washington, D.C.: U.S. Government Printing Office.

U.S. Bureau of the Census. (1970b). *Census of Business: 1967.* Vol. V, *Selected Services-Area Statistics.* Washington, D.C.: U.S. Government Printing Office.

U.S. Bureau of the Census. (1970c). *Census of Business: 1967.* Vol IV, *Wholesale Trade-Area Statistics.* Washington, D.C.: U.S. Government Printing Office.

U.S. Bureau of the Census. (1971a). *Census of Manufactures: 1967.* Vol III, *Area Statistics.* Washington, D.C.: U.S. Government Printing Office.

U.S. Bureau of the Census. (1971b). *Current Population Reports,* Series P-20, No. 212. "Marital Status and Family Status: March 1970." Washington, D.C.: U.S. Government Printing Office.

U.S. Bureau of the Census. (1972a). *Census of Population: 1970.* Vol. I, *Characteristics of the Population.* Part A, *Number of Inhabitants.* Section 1, *United States, Alabama-Mississippi.* Washington, D.C.: U.S. Government Printing Office.

U.S. Bureau of the Census. (1972b). *U.S. Census of Housing: 1970.* Vol. I, *Characteristics for States, Cities, and Counties,* Parts 2–51. Washington, D.C.: U.S. Government Printing Office.

U.S. Bureau of the Census. (1973a). *Census of Population: 1970.* Vol. 1, *Characteristics of the Population.* Part 1, United States Summary. Washington, D.C.: U.S. Government Printing Office.

U.S. Bureau of the Census. (1973b). *Census of Population: 1970.* Vol. 1, *Characteristics of the Population.* Parts 2–52. Washington, D.C.: U.S. Government Printing Office.

U.S. Bureau of the Census. (1973c). *Census of Population: 1970.* Subject Reports, *Lifetime and Recent Migration.* Washington, D.C.: U.S. Government Printing Office.

U.S. Bureau of the Census. (1973d). *Census of Population: 1970.* Subject Reports, *Mobility for Metropolitan Areas.* Washington, D.C.: U.S. Government Printing Office.

U.S. Bureau of the Census. (1973e). *Census of Population: 1970.* Subject Reports, *Mobility for States and the Nation.* Washington, D.C.: U.S. Government Printing Office.

U.S. Bureau of the Census. (1975a). *Current Population Reports,* Series P-20, No. 287. "Marital Status and Living Arrangements, March 1975." Washington, D.C.: U.S. Government Printing Office.

U.S. Bureau of the Census. (1975b). *Current Population Reports,* Series P-20, No. 285. "Mobility of the Population of the United States: March 1970 to March 1975." Washington, D.C.: U.S. Government Printing Office.

U.S. Bureau of the Census. (1976a). *Census of Manufactures: 1972.* Vol. III, *Area Statistics.* Washington, D.C.: U.S. Government Printing Office.

U.S. Bureau of the Census. (1976b). *Census of Retail Trade: 1972.* Vol. II, *Area Statistics.* Washington, D.C.: U.S. Government Printing Office.

U.S. Bureau of the Census. (1976c). *Census of Selected Service Industries: 1972.* Vol. II, *Area Statistics.* Washington, D.C.: U.S. Government Printing Office.

U.S. Bureau of the Census. (1976d). *Census of Wholesale Trade: 1972.* Vol. II, *Area Statistics.* Washington, D.C.: U.S. Government Printing Office.

U.S. Bureau of the Census. (1976e). *Current Population Reports,* Series P-20, No. 301. "Fertility of American Women, June 1975." Washington, D.C.: U.S. Government Printing Office.

U.S. Bureau of the Census. (1976f). *Current Population Reports,* Series P-20, No. 303. "School Enrollment-Social and Economic Characteristics of Students: October 1975." Washington, D.C.: U.S. Government Printing Office.

U.S. Bureau of the Census. (1977). *Current Population Reports,* Series P-20, No. 305. "Geographical Mobility: March 1975 to March 1976.'' Washington, D.C.: U.S. Government Printing Office.

U.S. Bureau of the Census. (1978a). *Current Population Reports,* Series P-20, No. 331. ''Geographical Mobility: March 1975 to March 1978.'' Washington, D.C.: U.S. Government Printing Office.

U.S. Bureau of the Census. (1978b). *Current Population Reports,* Series P-20, No. 323. ''Marital Status and Living Arrangements: March 1977.'' Washington, D.C.: U.S. Government Printing Office.

U.S. Bureau of the Census. (1978c). *Current Population Reports,* Special Studies P-23, No. 70. ''Perspectives on American Fertility,'' by M. J. Moore and M. O'Connell. Washington, D.C.: U.S. Government Printing Office.

U.S. Bureau of the Census. (1978d). *Current Population Reports,* Special Studies P-23, No. 75. ''Social and Economic Characteristics of the Metropolitan and Nonmetropolitan Population: 1977 and 1970.'' Washington, D.C.: U.S. Government Printing Office.

U.S. Department of Commerce, Economic Development Administration. (1976). *Estimated Employment Expansion Required for Full Employment, 1976, 1980, and 1985—by State.* Washington, D.C.: U.S. Government Printing Office.

U.S. Department of Commerce. Economic Development Administration Staff. (1977). ''The Development of a Subnational Economic Development Policy.'' Mimeographed.

U.S. Department of Justice. (1951). *Uniform Crime Reports for the United States: 1950.* Washington, D.C.: U.S. Government Printing Office.

U.S. Department of Justice. (1961). *Uniform Crime Reports for the United States: 1960.* Washington, D.C.: U.S. Government Printing Office.

U.S. Department of Labor. (1976). *Employment and Training Report of the President.* Washington, D.C.: U.S. Government Printing Office.

U.S. Department of Labor. (1977). *Employment and Training Report of the President.* Washington, D.C.: U.S. Government Printing Office.

U.S. Department of Labor, Bureau of Labor Statistics. (1977). *Employment and Earnings, States and Areas, 1939–1975.* Washington, D.C.: U.S. Government Printing Office.

U.S. Department of Labor. (1978). *Employment and Training Report of the President.* Washington, D.C.: U.S. Government Printing Office.

U.S. Department of Labor, Bureau of Labor Statistics. (1979). *Handbook of Labor Statistics 1978.* Washington, D.C.: U.S. Government Printing Office.

Vaughan, R.J. (1977). *The Urban Impacts of Federal Policies.* Vol. 2, *Economic Development.* Report R-2028-KF/RC. Santa Monica: The Rand Corporation.

Vernez, G., R. Vaughan, B. Burright, and S. Coleman. (1977). *Regional Cycles and Employment Effects of Public Works Investments.* Report R-2052-EDA. Santa Monica: The Rand Corporation.

Vernon, R. (1966). ''The Changing Economic Function of the Central City.'' In J. Q. Wilson (ed.), *Urban Renewal: The Record and Controversy.* Cambridge: M.I.T. Press.

Wertheimer, R. F., III. (1970). *The Monetary Rewards of Migration Within the U.S.* Washington, D.C.: The Urban Institute

Wheat, L. F. (1973). *Regional Growth and Industrial Location.* Lexington: Lexington Books.

Subject Index